HIGH AND DRY

IN THE BVI

AMUSING AUTOBIOGRAPHY OF AN EXPAT
BRITISH VIRGIN ISLANDS
1970-72

LALLY BROWN

CONTENTS

VIRGIN ISLANDS

Anegada

Virgin Gorda

British Virgin Islands

Guana

Peter Island

Tortola

CARIBBEAN SEA

Jost Van Dyke

St John

St Thomas

U.S. Virgin Islands

St Croix

INTRODUCTION

Have you ever stopped in your tracks and said to yourself *"There must be more to life than this?"*

Well I did, and I remember with vivid clarity the time, the place, the exact moment almost half a century ago.

It was a wet, windy, miserable March day in 1970 and I had slipped out of the office to join my husband for lunch. Battling the weather, we struggled into town to grab a bite to eat before returning to our respective offices.

The pavement was narrow, the crowds pushy, the noise deafening and the fumes of passing traffic nauseating. Suddenly, out of the soggy pack of hurrying bodies a familiar face appeared in front of us, an old friend from the past. He paused, shouted a greeting and in the space of the two short minutes that followed he changed my life. Really, absolutely, completely, changed my life.

Brian told us he had just returned from India and was hoping to leave for Africa shortly.

"No, nothing was planned" he shrugged happily, his life just seemed to unfold in front of him offering exciting opportunities for him to grab.

"I just go with the flow" he grinned *"Somehow it always works out. Life is for living, and it's good!"*

He was the quintessential free spirit. He was happy and fulfilled. On that wet and dismal day he seemed to glow with joy. It was at that moment I had my epiphany.

I was inspired. There must be, I decided, more to life than this. Miserable weather, boring job, nine to five, short of money. I wanted the taste of excitement, adventure, joy, fun, just like Brian.

I decided then and there things must change. The time had come for me to become the author of my own destiny. My husband looked at me, and I knew he felt exactly the same.

That night we went home and before the enthusiasm had cooled we applied to VSO (Voluntary Services Overseas) the organization that accepts volunteers and places them wherever needed around the globe. We were a married couple willing to go anywhere and do anything.

The initial reaction to our application was very positive. VSO studied our qualifications, rapidly gave their approval, and decided to send us to Jamaica. My husband, a recently qualified Chartered Structural Engineer, was exactly the sort of professional they needed. I would teach shorthand and typing at a high school.

It was, we both agreed, almost too good to be true. We were excited and the anticipation of new horizons energized our waking hours for several weeks. Until the day, that is, we were due to have our smallpox vaccinations.

I was, it transpired, a bit of a problem! The medical team studied me, conferred, and after some minutes returned to solemnly inform me it would be inadvisable for me to have the smallpox vaccination due to a history of childhood eczema. I would be exposing myself, they told me in serious doom-laden tones, to the potential of a very nasty reaction too terrible to contemplate. It was with deep regret, they said, that because of this, VSO were therefore unable to accept us as volunteers.

Abruptly our dreams of a new life in Jamaica as VSO's had dissolved into thin air. It was a cruel blow.

Bitterly disappointed with the termination of our VSO application we were absolutely determined to go overseas, if necessary by ourselves. On a crazy impulse we decided to sell our home and buy two round trip tickets to the West Indies hoping to find work somewhere in the Caribbean.

"You're both insane!" muttered our friends. But we were stubbornly adamant. We wanted to toss our lives into the air and see what happened.

We found a berth on a Fyffes banana boat sailing from Southampton to Trinidad the following January, and looked forward to an expensive and sensational experience. We reasoned that if all else failed we would have had the holiday of a lifetime and could return to England and start our lives over again, but this time on our terms.

This was when the universe stepped in and took over. Two short weeks before we were due to depart an advert appeared in the Thursday *Daily Telegraph*. A short four-liner seeking an Associate Partner and a Draughtsman for the West Indies office of a British Civil and Structural Engineering company.

My husband replied immediately explaining that we were already booked to leave for the West Indies. He stopped just short of begging for the job. A telegram the following day invited us both for an informal interview. We could not believe our luck.

The interview was conducted at the home of the company boss and if the sight of a large mansion at the end of a long gravel drive was meant to intimidate, then it succeeded. My humble background had not prepared me for this, but I was more than capable of faking self-confidence. Sherry and sandwiches had been provided and as we juggled the buffet bits we were introduced to the family. The dog took a particular liking to me, and as my attention strayed he leaned forward and gulped down the sherry in my glass. No-one else appeared to notice, so when I was offered a refill I nodded dumbly, thinking it prudent to pretend I had downed the sherry myself. The dog showed his appreciation at my discretion by dribbling happily, nestling his head in my lap, and going to sleep.

It was the strangest interview ever conducted. We were inspected, observed and assessed by the whole family, but we must have passed the collective test because then and there my husband was offered the position of Associate Partner of the Company's office on Tortola, British Virgin Islands.

It was a dream come true. An eighteen month contract with a very attractive salary on an idyllic paradise island in the Caribbean as the Associate Partner (at the tender age of twenty-five) of a well-respected Company. Miracles do happen.

Photographs were produced showing the island and the apartment where we would be living. Advice and information was verbally pumped into my brain at a rapid rate. Most of it refused to be retained, but for some reason I recalled with great clarity the daughter's advice, *"One really must go to Harrods for one's bikini!"* Harrods? Me?

The following fourteen days were a blur. Where we had planned and packed for a few weeks, we now needed to re-plan and re-pack for almost two years. I did not go to Harrods for my bikini, BHS being my store of choice for clothes. In the end one small red trunk carried all we felt we needed. Sheets, wellies, transformer (to convert my UK electrics into the BVI equivalent), cutlery set, a few books and of course the mandatory bikini, a BHS January bargain! However, when we finally unpacked the trunk on Tortola, several weeks later, we did find some strange items neither of us would admit to packing. The football sock (singular) and the bowl of plastic fruit for instance.

During those frantic last few days we tried to find out more about Tortola and the British Virgin Islands. We scoured the local libraries and badgered the travel agents, but all we could find was the following sentence in an encyclopedia.

'British Virgin Islands - large number of islets and rocks in the West Indies. The largest island is Tortola, being twelve miles long and three miles wide. Population approximately 10,000. Capital, Road Town on Tortola.'

Armed with this sparse information we explored the atlas with a magnifying glass, but only discovered a cluster of pinheads labelled *US Virgin Islands* which we assumed must be somewhere close.

They appeared to be at the top of a crescent of islands in the Caribbean that began to the right of Puerto Rico and stretched south to stop just short of Venezuela. The other names down the chain were more familiar, Antigua, Martinique, Grenada, Barbados and Trinidad and evoked images of tropical sun-soaked, palm-fringed beaches, old colonialism and cricket.

We were absolutely delighted. From then on our dreams were filled with happy visions of living on a little slice of paradise. We simply couldn't wait to leave behind the smelly exhaust fumes and the grey pressures of the UK. We were very keen but, as we were soon to discover, very green.

CHAPTER 1

'SS CAMITO' AND PRINCESS ALICE

I lay on the floor bruised and bewildered, gasping for breath. My poor body was being hammered black and blue by the bare boards of the cabin floor rising and falling beneath me. The inky blackness around me vibrated with thunderous noise.

The fall must have stunned me and for a moment I was confused and dizzy and the muddled jigsaw pieces in my brain refused to function.

I was struggling to make sense of it all, when above the din I heard my husband's voice coming faintly from somewhere above me. I could hear him groping for the light switch and in a moment the claustrophobic little cabin was bright with light. And suddenly it all came flooding back to me. Why I was here, why we were both here. The whole stupid ridiculous adventure, and I groaned out loud.

We were passengers on the Fyffes Line *SS Camito,* a flat-bottomed banana boat with no stabilizers and we were heading towards Port of Spain in Trinidad and currently passing through the Bay of Biscay in Storm Force winds.

My husband slid clumsily from the upper bunk and hauled me to my feet, and we clung to each other, swaying unsteadily as the ship rolled wildly from side to side, plunging into the heaving waves. We were in a Force 10 gale and it was 2.00 a.m. We had sold our beautiful house and we were heading for a job on some unknown island. Last but by no means least, I wouldn't see my lovely family for more than two years. The cruel combination hit me and suddenly I was blubbering weakly.

My husband was less than sympathetic. Gripping my arm as we rocked backwards and forwards he ignored my histrionics. He shouted in my ear, reminding me of the Captain's advice earlier that evening.

"Spread your lifejacket under your mattress and wedge your bottom in the hole of the jacket. It's the only way to stay anchored in your bunk when the weather's like this."

The Captain had added, with what I had taken as a humorous afterthought *"it's also handy if should you need it in an emergency!"* The Captain also said that this old ship would roll on wet grass.

In our ignorance it had seemed to us a boat trip to Trinidad was a very romantic way to discover the Caribbean. To arrive slowly and sedately on board a ship, we thought, was far more appropriate than a fast and debilitating twelve hour flight from Heathrow. It also avoided farewell family tears since only passengers were allowed into the dock at Southampton.

We had planned our strategy carefully. The itinerary included a relaxing cruise on Fyffes *SS Camito* disembarking, we believed, refreshed, tanned, and tropicalized in Trinidad. This was to be followed by a four week holiday wandering at whim around Trinidad and Tobago, then leisurely island-hopping up the Lesser Antilles to arrive on Tortola in the British Virgin Islands sometime late February, ready and eager for my husband's new responsibilities as the fresh-faced Associate Partner of a prestigious British Consulting Engineers.

Fyffes Line had two cargo ships travelling backwards and forwards between Southampton and the Caribbean which also took passengers. They were the *SS Camito* and her sister ship *SS Golfito*. They were about as far removed from luxurious ocean liners as hot dogs are from haute cuisine. They provided a basic, single-class, nautical experience for the intrepid voyager in search of something a little different to the usual clinical Cunard cruise. Of course there was a downside to this travel choice, no stabilizers being top of the list.

The morning after my ignominious fall found the ship still battling heavy seas. Dressing for breakfast was a slow, frustrating and occasionally painful experience. My husband struggled as he attempted to put on his socks. He had no sooner lined up his foot ready to stuff it quickly into the neck of his sock, than a roll to port tipped him off balance. He tried to put his socks on standing up, he tried to put them on sitting down, and in desperation he even tried to put them on lying down flat in his bunk. But in the end he decided not to bother at all and slipped into his deck shoes barefoot.

My biggest problem proved to be getting into my knickers. Balancing on one leg was quite impossible. I stood, I sat, I lay down, I crouched, but all with no success. Frustration gave way to giggles and we finally lurched out of the cabin weak with laughter.

Fortunately the dining room was on C deck, the same deck as our cabin. It was the lowest of the three decks down in the bowels of the boat. This meant we didn't have to negotiate any stairs. The corridor was narrow and long and we zig-zagged our way to breakfast, bouncing off the walls as the ship rolled hard to port, and then unrolled herself upright. The motion of the ship was wild and nauseating.

On her previous voyage, as *SS Camito* crossed the stormy Atlantic from Bermuda to Southampton, one passenger had required stitches in a head wound and much of the furniture was smashed, damaged, or simply washed overboard. Banana boat cruising was certainly not an option for the faint-hearted.

Unfortunately the dining room, right up in the bow, took the hardest hammering from the angry waves so it was not surprising to discover that on this particular morning the dining room was almost empty. The waiters outnumbered the handful of brave passengers as they weaved uncertainly between tables, grasping the tops for support. The empty chairs were sliding backwards and forwards noisily on the short length of chain that anchored them to the deck. All around were signs and sounds of chaos. Broken china, cutlery sliding off the table onto the floor, bread rolls jumping from their baskets. We could see at a glance that breakfast was going to be a challenge.

For some reason not altogether clear to us we had been honored by an invitation to join a select group at the Chief Engineer's table. But only Willy, holding grimly to the table with one hand and trying to catch a flying bread roll with the other, was in his place. We assumed the Chief Engineer himself was in the engine room valiantly battling against the elements and heroically driving the ship, or something equally vital to our safety.

The two other absent guests who had been invited to join this intimate little group at the Chief Engineer's table were Connie from Bermuda (middle-aged, quiet, shy, a widow travelling alone) and Hilda (also middle-aged, also travelling alone, and also widowed). Connie was reportedly lying in her bunk groaning and trying not to throw up and Hilda had sent a pitiful message to say she would not leave her cabin until the weather improved and incidentally she intended to fly home.

"What's the point in paying £20 a day for a heaving cabin and four days of nausea?" She declared miserably.

Willy, a large, round, amiable barrister from Birmingham, was feeling very sorry for himself. We tried to keep straight sympathetic faces as Willy described in graphic and comic detail how he was thrown from his bunk three times in the night, tipped on his head, somersaulted over his chair, and sent sprawling across his cabin by the storm. Poor Willy showed us the bruises to prove it. Apparently I was not the only one to end up on the cabin floor.

Breakfast was more of a challenge than we had anticipated. We gripped the table with one hand and chased the toast with the other. My husband seated himself beside the column which passed up through our table to the ceiling above and wrapped one arm round it, anchoring himself firmly and rising and falling in unison with the motion of the ship. A cunning technique which enabled him to successfully drink half a cup of coffee while most of mine went into my lap.

The majority of the ninety passengers very sensibly remained holed-up in their cabins or were queuing outside the doctor's for anti-nausea injections, pills having proved useless.

The young Baroness, one of the VIP's travelling with us, had not been seen for two days and we were getting quite concerned. She had told us in Southampton that she didn't travel well at the best of times and felt sea-sick even when becalmed. She had planned to travel with her husband the Baron but at the last moment he was unable to join the ship and (prudently in our opinion) had elected to fly to Trinidad later.

As the bow of the *SS Camito* rose high on a wave, paused for a shuddering second and then crashed down, down, down, with a mighty hull-shaking bang, my husband realized that the contents of his stomach were rapidly heading upwards and he rushed, zig-zagging, back to our cabin. Willy and I struggled gallantly on while around us the few intrepid diners who had braved breakfast followed my poor husband in a hurried exit.

Soon there remained just us two, and one petite but resolute old lady. An endearing and charming soul, this white-haired lady in her soft lilac dress. Her frail appearance contradicted her obvious extraordinary resilience for despite the weather she had not yet missed a single meal. This was Princess Alice of Athlone, granddaughter of Queen Victoria. She was a frequent passenger on the *SS Camito* but now travelling on board for the last time. At eighty-eight this was her final visit to Trinidad in her capacity as Chancellor of the University of the West Indies. There was no sign of her companion, another one suffering from nausea no doubt.

The Captain cancelled the Sunday religious service and also the planned life-boat drill. He said the conditions were too rough. It seemed to me that given the conditions, the service and the drill would have been even more appropriate than usual. But he explained that the chairs in the lounge needed to be unhooked from their securing chains and lined up neatly for the service, and with the present plunging of the ship this could prove very dangerous, with the congregation sliding and tumbling all over the place. Already one poor passenger had been catapulted across the lounge as the chain snapped and the chair he was sitting on broke free.

We were told that the winds had briefly touched Force 11 and the crews quarters had been severely flooded. No wonder we were all being thrown from our bunks.

My poor husband was feeling very delicate and looked an unpleasant green colour, so leaving him in our cabin to suffer alone I staggered along to the lounge to browse through the books on the shelves. To my astonishment and delight I discovered an old book on the history of the West Indies, with some information on the Virgin Islands, and despite the wildly uncomfortable motion of the ship I spent an absorbing hour soaking up the past.

Christopher Columbus dropped anchor in the BVI on his celebrated voyage of discovery in the 15th century. He paused just long enough to claim the islands for Queen Isabella, calling them the Virgin Islands, and to give some of them individual Spanish names, before setting sail westwards again. He must have stepped ashore briefly because he called one of the islands (an otherwise insignificant twenty one square mile green ridged bump) after the prolific, timid, small brown turtle-dove he found there. And thus was labeled for all time the island of Tor-tolla, or Tortola, soon to be our new home.

According to the book there were very few visitors during the two hundred years that followed, and the islands (including Tortola) remained uninhabited and relatively ignored. Sir Francis Drake passed through in 1585 and gave his name to the strip of sea which formed a channel between Tortola and Peter Island, another of the Virgin Islands. Ten years later he returned, this time in the company of Sir John Hawkins. Then almost a hundred years elapsed before Dutch buccaneers decided Tortola was an excellent base for their illegal trade, and settled themselves so successfully and comfortably that they built a Fort, until the English came back and threw them out in 1672.

The first English settlers on Tortola were described as planters but seem to have enjoyed a lifestyle not very dissimilar to the Dutch buccaneers they replaced, and in 1717 a visitor, describing his impressions of Tortola, said bluntly *'Rum, pirates and sugar!'* However the Quakers, described as *'a quiet peaceable folk'* escaping religious persecution in England, arrived shortly afterwards and a short period of prosperity and stability followed.

Until slowly, as a result of droughts, hurricanes, and sickness, Tortola and the other British Virgin Islands deteriorated and slipped gently into slumbering anonymity. Unlike the neighbouring American Virgin Islands which steadily grew into the now prosperous and popular duty-free tourist destination frequented by cruise ships.

CHAPTER 2

SOUTHAMPTON TO TRINIDAD

The weather began to improve and our fellow passengers emerged timidly from their cabins.

Our floating community consisted primarily of elderly people. Having recovered from the Bay of Biscay experience they didn't seem to mind the loud, drumming, background noise of the engines, or the rotating bath-tub special effects of the ship, and Fyffes had thoughtfully provided some agreeable compensations, like the attentive crew (at least one handsome young mariner to every passenger) and a delicious menu, such as pheasant and roast duckling.

My husband and I were the youngest couple on board and were initially assumed to be honeymooners and were consequently nicknamed *The Happy Couple*. About half way down the time-line between us and the plucky geriatrics were two other couples. Angie and John with toddler Gavin, then Ali and Anna with their two girls and adorable seven month old baby Olaf, chubby and polished as an autumn conker.

Angie was a beautiful, elegant and intelligent Trinidadian married to John, an English agriculturalist with a passion for pigs. They had just bought a ninety-acre dilapidated cocoa plantation on Tobago and were on their way to see it, to assess how much effort it would take to get the plantation running profitably again. Initially they intended to live in the large and draughty old drying shed on the estate, but they had wonderful plans for building a beautiful home.

Ali was a Trinidadian returning home with his young family after a ten year absence. Anna, his gentle German wife, was a tender mother, quiet, long suffering and very sweet. Ali liked nothing better than a long and complicated debate on political issues, the more controversial the better, and preferably over a large glass of syrupy, yellow Advocaat. He would argue and talk with anyone prepared to give him the time and attention.

Ali was returning to Trinidad to start a new political magazine. He had spent much of his ten year absence from Trinidad in England, with his politically active Trinidadian friend, Michael Abdul Malik, whom he referred to simply as *Michael X*.

Ali's main topic of conversation was the state of Trinidadian politics, and the trial of several black soldiers taking place in Port of Spain. In February 1970 there had been an uprising in the army and thirteen Army officers were subsequently arrested and were now being tried for treason. The case was proving to be a political time-bomb and the Prime Minister, Eric Williams, had recently declared a State of Emergency. His Government was concerned that the emotions released as the trial progressed could cause an outbreak of racial violence.

We heard that a group of activists known as the Black Power Movement were busy pasting up posters in Trinidad demanding *Free Our Black Soldiers* and advocating special weeks of organized disturbance. It might be a week where sympathizers refused to pay electricity bills, or gas bills, or a week when no-one bought clothes just food. Apparently this latter suggestion resulted in the further advice of *'if you have no money, take the food and pay later'*. As a consequence gangs of youths walked into shops and just helped themselves to the goods.

The trial, according to Ali, had been deliberately prolonged by the defendants. They would arrive at the Town Hall where the trial was being conducted and complain of headaches, chest pains or something similar and the day's hearing would have to be postponed. The verdict was expected shortly and no-one seemed quite sure what would happen in volatile Port of Spain when the sentence was finally passed.

Ali and his family were unusual passengers. The norm included an Honorable, a Judge, a Barrister, a Mayor, and several wealthy widows. One of the widows was delighted to learn that my husband and I were going to live on Tortola. Her nephew had started his own accountancy company on island ten years ago and *"Absolutely loves the place"* she gushed enthusiastically.

She told us that the islands were very much off the beaten track but they had great appeal to financiers since the tax laws were very favorable to investors. Because of the proximity of the US Virgin Islands the currency in the BVI is the US dollar, but since the island remains a British Dependent Territory the dollar/sterling exchange mechanism was a simple process, quite an incentive for the financiers.

The BVI had not developed in the same explosive way as the neighboring American Virgin Islands, but apparently there had been a flurry of construction activity on Tortola over the last few months, inspired by the reclamation of an area called Wickham's Cay, in Road Harbour beside the capital of Road Town.

A building boom was sparked off in 1967 when the islands were granted a new Constitution. A Tortolian Chief Minister was appointed and there was an air of optimism about the Territory's future. An airport was built by the Royal Engineers and investors began to arrive to inspect the islands' potential. Money began to flow and speculators moved in leasing, buying and building, in anticipation of a profitable future.

A British business group leased part of the island of Anegada and also began the reclamation on Tortola of Wickhams Cay. The work began with massive dredging of the sea bed and hundreds and thousands of tons of sand were dragged up and deposited alongside the rocky shore of Road Town. Slowly a large flat plate of land grew out of the sea and it was intended that this reclaimed land would be developed by new businesses attracted to the island. However there had been a great deal of bad feeling locally about the exploitation of the Cay and a Commission of Enquiry was appointed in 1969 to investigate the original terms of the lease.

The result, a damning report, had just been released, and as a consequence the British Government had agreed to provide a loan of $5.8 million to the BVI Government to buy back the interests of the Wickham's Cay Company, putting the investment firmly back in the hands of the Tortolians.

So now there was a large, flat, piece of real estate waiting for development. The Grand Plan over the coming years anticipated new banks, stores, restaurants and tourist shops sprawling over Wickham's Cay to make Road Town an exciting business and tourist attraction. It heralded the beginning of a New Age in the history of the islands and the construction companies were arriving in droves hoping for a profitable piece of the pie. My husband, as resident representative of a British Consulting Engineers, was expected to pick up the connection between the business client and the construction companies. He would be the solo performer in a suite of offices in Road Town, connected by the umbilical cord of a Cable and Wireless Telex system to his Head Office in England. As Associate Partner for the company my husband was expected to find the work, negotiate a fee, and finally design, draw and supervise the construction of each successful commission.

Personally, I was more interested in knowing about the living conditions on Tortola. Sensible questions like *'What is my apartment like?' 'Can I drink the water?' 'Can I buy fresh food?' 'How much do things cost?'* and *'What's the weather really like?'* But no-one managed to answer these to my satisfaction.

Until we arrived on Tortola we were still on holiday and when the ship stopped pitching we began to enjoy the bracing sea air, the pleasant company and the delicious food. The weather improved considerably with air and sea temperatures both 70°F.

The ship's routine was soporific and easy to adjust to. Coffee delivered to the cabin on waking, followed by a leisurely breakfast, a short stroll round the deck, an hour in the sun on a nice new deck chair (the old ones were all washed overboard in the violent storms of the last voyage) and interesting conversations with fellow passengers. Lunch, followed by afternoon nap, then cucumber sandwiches for tea in the lounge, another leisurely stroll and deck chair slumber, then the treat of the day, dinner in the evening, followed by some form of entertainment.

It soon began to seem the most sensible decision we'd ever made, and not an absurd and foolish adventure after all.

Our evening entertainment on board was rather limited, no cabaret or floor show on this cruise. We passed the time playing Monopoly together, watching films, or having 'horse races'. The horse racing proved very popular. The lounge was cleared of chairs which were unhooked and lined up around the sides and a huge canvas track was unfolded and spread on the floor. The cloth was printed with large numbered squares and the six horses (big wooden carvings) were moved up the squares on the throw of a dice. One dice giving the number of the appropriate horse and the second dice the number of moves the horse should make.

John, Angie, my husband and myself found ourselves sitting next to Princess Alice and her companion for the horse racing evening. And being the courteous gentleman that he is, John volunteered to place Princess Alice's bets for her, and his offer was graciously accepted.

The Captain asked Angie and I to throw the dice for the first race and the evening was off to an exciting start. The punters, ranged around the room, became just as loud and unruly as any racing crowd at a genuine event. My husband and I were quite unlucky all evening but Princess Alice managed to win several times, and so did John and Angie. Princess Alice sat quietly smiling and talking in low tones to her companion in German. Apparently she was under the mistaken impression that my husband was travelling to Trinidad to take up a post as Lecturer at the University of the West Indies. It seemed a shame to disillusion her but we felt in all honesty we should explain that we were not a honeymoon couple, nor were we on our way to work at the University. Fortunately the clarification appeared to make no difference to her and she continued to smile benignly upon us.

The last horse racing event was the auctioning of the six individual horses to the highest bidder. The money was pooled, to be given to the winner, and the Baroness (who had emerged from her self-imposed cabin confinement) and I were handed the dice for the final race. It had all the excitement and tension of the real Grand National and the lounge reverberated to cheers and howls as the dice were thrown and the horses moved along the canvas track. The jubilant winner was the Judge who scooped the £51 pot, with the last horse limping home the one owned by the Baroness.

The lounge was also used to show the films. We had two on the voyage. *The Most Dangerous Man in the World* with Gregory Peck, and *Carry on Loving*. *Carry on Loving* was put on in place of the Whist Drive because not enough passengers attended to make a decent game. An enormous white canvas screen was strung up at one end of the lounge which swung through an angle of 45° as the ship rolled from side to side. We found ourselves swaying with the swing and straining to catch the dialogue over the noises of the ship's engine. We must have been an amusing sight. Fortunately most of us had seen both films before and could follow the general sense quite easily, so when the fuses blew and the sound broke down (which happened with surprising regularity) it was only a minor inconvenience. Our pleasure being in the camaraderie of our fellow passengers.

Once the balmy southern seas were upon us we had our full complement at the Chief Engineer's table for meals. The Chief Engineer joined us as often as possible but he was not a naturally gregarious man and hosting his table was a task he did with obvious trepidation. He was much more at home in white overalls in the engine room. He invited Connie, my husband and myself down into the ship's womb and showed us round his domain with a passionate enthusiasm.

We found it quite an alarming experience. The cat-walk high above the engines was made up of a metal grating about two feet wide. The surface was oily and slippery. Inching our way along we had to avoid touching the lagged hot water pipes that ran parallel to the cat-walk. The noise of the engines was almost unbearable and the Chief Engineer had to shout at the top of his voice and gesticulate to make himself understood above the din. Steam seemed to be everywhere and large pieces of ironmongery were whirling up and down and round and round in continuous motion.

My husband gazed in fascination at a clinometer that was registering a 30° swing as the ship rolled gently in what seemed to us a very placid ocean. It was a great relief to emerge from the guts of the ship but we nevertheless expressed our grateful thanks for the tour. Willy and Hilda had been wise to refuse the invitation.

Connie could not relax on the voyage. Although she was born and raised in Bermuda her two sons were US citizens and she constantly worried about her nineteen year old son who had just received his *'number'* for Vietnam. Although he was still at college he was considered eligible for service with the American

Armed Forces in Vietnam. His number was 186. The authorities anticipated that only numbers to 140 would be called-up this year, but Connie was anxious *"I can only pray he will just miss being called up"* she said.

The *SS Camito* had been instructed to arrive at a pre-arranged time in Port of Spain so that Princess Alice could be met immediately on arrival. We hoped to pull alongside the dock at precisely 7.00 p.m. on Saturday, 23rd January, when the Governor General would be waiting with his official car to whisk Her Royal Highness away. But according to the Captain we had to slow down a little since we were going far too fast and were in danger of arriving in Trinidad too early. In one day we managed to cover 425 miles making up for the distance we had lost during the dreadful storm.

We had some very tearful good-byes to say as the *SS Camito* slipped into Port of Spain. It was dusk as the ship tied up to the dock and on the grey apron below a black limousine waited to collect Princess Alice and her companion, with the Governor-General of Trinidad standing beside the open rear door.

It was a quiet welcome for her and as Princess Alice walked slowly down the steep gang plank a few of us on board lined the ship's rail and clapped and waved. She waved back as she stepped into the car and slid away into the gathering darkness of the tropical night.

As soon as the Immigration procedures had been completed it was our turn to disembark. Hilda gave me a tiny musical key-ring with an engraving of Mount Fuji on the front. Willy exchanged addresses and almost crushed me in his final embrace. Connie couldn't speak but huge tears rolled down her cheeks as we hugged. And even the Chief Engineer came running down the wharf in his greasy white overalls to shake hands and say farewell.

Feeling somewhat sad, lonely and abandoned, my husband and I disappeared into the darkness of Port of Spain, capital of Trinidad, to continue our adventure.

CHAPTER 3

PORT OF SPAIN AND MOUNT ST BENEDICT

The Guest House where we were staying was an inconspicuous little building, squeezed onto a tiny plot down a Port of Spain side street and partly obscured by lush foliage pressing in on all sides. It was off the Savannah and a short walk from the luxurious and prestigious Queen's Park Hotel, quite the contrast.

Mr. Stone, the owner, was somewhat taciturn by nature and must have thought he had a very strange pair of visitors. We had found details of his Guest House back in England while idly thumbing through the advertisement pages of *The Friend*, a Quaker magazine.

Our room was one of several built around a small courtyard in the back garden. A huge cage of budgerigars hung from the lime tree in the centre.

Mr. Stone normally hosted travelling salesmen passing through Port of Spain for one or two brief nights, they were familiar with the Caribbean and Trinidad and slid through almost unnoticed. But he had drawn the short straw with my husband and me.

However he was very patient with us. He was a portly man, aged about fifty-five, who ran a construction company as well as the Guest House. I'm sure I did not mishear when he told us he had fifteen children, but he then added that their ages ranged between nine and twenty. I puzzled the mathematics of this information which implied he must have had several pairs of twins, or triplets even, or perhaps (the more likely explanation said my husband) numerous wives and mistresses.

The Guest House was just a basic, clean, wholesome concrete square room and the daily rate included a basic, clean, wholesome breakfast at 8.30 a.m. prompt. Weak tea with a slice of lime, cereal, eggs (runny boiled, hard boiled, scrambled), toast and marmalade.

A big West Indian matriarch with a belly laugh that rocked the room commanded the kitchen, trundling in and out like a tank. She was not Mr. Stone's wife. Mrs. Stone was small, gentle and humble. She pottered quietly along, almost invisible, in the wake of her husband.

A short passage connected the dining area to the back door which opened onto our courtyard, and off this passage was the small kitchen and next to the small kitchen was a room which we supposed must be Mr. Stone's bedroom. The door was usually open and as we padded backwards and forwards during the day Mr. Stone could be frequently glimpsed swinging lazily in a huge green canvas hammock which was stretched from wall to wall in the bare, white-painted concrete block room, the dome of his stomach stretching his vest as it rose and fell with his snores.

It was a very sensible idea to have a siesta in Trinidad and if we were not so keen to see and experience everything during our short stay, we would also have been horizontal for the afternoon. The temperature was 85°F and humid. By mid-afternoon the sky turned grey and clouded over producing several short but very heavy bursts of rain. The rain helped to clean the streets and water the luxurious tropical flowers, it also replenished the cisterns.

One particular night at the Guest House remains etched into my memory. It was a dark, warm, velvety tropical evening and fortunately no other guests were around to witness my scantily clad embarrassment as I crouched in my nightie beneath the budgerigar cage beside the large lime tree in the courtyard.

The most enormous spider had just invaded our room. It thumped across the ceiling wearing what sounded like heavy army boots. When I turned on the light to investigate I discovered to my horror that this black furry giant was squatting directly over my head, glaring down at me with hostile eyes, blinking with the sudden light. I took one quick look before leaping out of bed and escaping out into the courtyard.

My husband was drowsy with sleep and slower to react and I could see him, through the open doorway, sitting on the bed dumbly gazing up at the intruder. It was enormous, ginormous, elephantine. To my terrified eye it was the size of a generous dinner plate.

We had already discovered that tropical insects in Trinidad were giant-sized and bold. Cockroaches, although not pleasant, I could accept. They were larger than I had ever seen, up to 5cm of hard shiny, bullet shaped body. Distasteful creatures, especially when found inside my suitcase, but at least they had the courtesy to scurry away when the light went on. But this spider was a fearless whopper in a league of his own.

The spider stared down at my husband as he groped for his shoe, took aim and threw it at the intruder. The monster was unmoved. A book followed the shoe, equally unsuccessful. The spider looked angry, not frightened, and it thudded menacingly across the ceiling to glower down at my husband.

Then, in a sudden movement, it turned abruptly and sprinted across the ceiling towards the door, paused for a split second, then with a mighty death-defying leap it launched itself into the courtyard, flying through the air and landing beside me, a mere inch from my bare feet.

To my credit I didn't scream, or faint, or even freeze to the spot. Fueled by adrenaline and terror I shot across the courtyard, dived into the room, slammed the door hard shut behind me and collapsed quivering onto the bed.

In order to allow air to circulate through the room (no air-conditioning here, not even a fan) the window in the bathroom was covered with a simple, course wire mesh. This meant that all sorts and sizes of Trinidadian nightlife could wander in unannounced. We had a visit from a moth with a wingspan the size of a light plane. It objected when the light was switched on and panicked, flapping and dive-bombing the bed in confusion. The moth took a long time to evict and was poked, pushed, lured, and bullied before it at last found the open door and vanished into the dark night.

As a city, and the capital of Trinidad and Tobago, Port of Spain struck us as a puzzling contradiction. Dusty streets with refuse on the pavements, pot-holed roads, mangy brown island dogs scavenging through rubbish, dilapidated shacks with rusty corrugated iron roofs, dark caves of shops with smelly interiors, a congestion of noisy old trucks and cars throbbing and honking along the main streets. But then, around and interspersed with this sandy grey decay and neglect were the most beautiful large houses painted bright and happy colours with manicured gardens alive with red poinsettias, purple bougainvillea and saucer-sized hibiscus flowers. Old colonial houses with attractive and unusual ornate fretwork decorating the entrances and the ridges of the roofs.

The town centre had a few new department stores, but we found the best places to shop were on the outskirts of town, in the St. James' area for carvings and jewelry, and the small boutiques run from private houses for unique, reasonably priced clothes, offering a personalized service with free alterations if necessary.

One of the most relaxing places to visit in Port of Spain was the Botanical Gardens. They were an absolute delight and a haven of peace and tranquility. We were exploring the Botanical Gardens (having been dropped off by Mr. Stone in his ancient car) when we met Michael, a young calypso singer practicing for the title of Calypso King in the Carnival. The Carnival, or Jump-up, was on February 22nd and 23rd and would be the first one since Prime Minister Eric Williams declared a State of Emergency in Trinidad last year.

Everyone was looking forward to it, though no-one seemed quite sure what was going to happen, whether the Carnival would be a happy and enjoyable occasion and a great success, or whether it would be used as an excuse to create trouble and racial disharmony.

The defence had just summed up in the trial of the soldiers and the case was about to wind up after three months. Michael X (Ali's friend) had arrived in Trinidad, having been refused permission to go to Jamaica. He was very popular with a reputation as a black activist in England, although he had officially resigned from the Black Power Movement. He was asking to speak to the Prime Minister to discuss the poor treatment of Trinidadians in England.

The Carnival, what is likely to happen, and the reaction of the Trinidadians to the judgment in the trial of the black soldiers, seemed to be the main topics of conversation in Port of Spain. Mr. Stone told us he was closing his Guest House for the critical week and sending his children *'out of town to the country'*. Several people advised us to leave Port of Spain before the 20th February, so we decided to spend two weeks out of town ourselves at Mayaro beach, south Trinidad, and then fly to the island of Tobago to enjoy a smaller but quieter Carnival over there with our friends Angie and John from the *Camito*.

We had been seeing quite a lot of Angie and John. They had rented a small apartment for a few days before travelling across to their newly acquired plantation on Tobago. We also bumped into several old ship-mates from the *Camito* and spent many happy hours over rum punches reminiscing about the voyage. Most of them were staying at the Hilton, or the Queen's Park Hotel and it was rather nice for us to taste a little luxury with them before we ambled back to our basic B&B at Mr. Stone's.

Port of Spain was full of interesting people. We found ourselves sharing the shelter of a large tree on the Savannah during a particularly heavy downpour with a young medical student from Westminster Hospital in London. He was in Trinidad for three months researching the subject of asthma for his thesis, with particular reference to allergies. He said that Barbados had one of the highest proportions of asthmatics to population in the world and approximately five asthmatics were taken into hospital each week. After the rain had stopped we shared a *'jelly'* nut together before going our separate ways.

A 'jelly nut' was a good and effective thirst quencher. These young green coconuts were sold from trucks parked beside the Savannah. The man selected a nut from his heap in the back of the truck, tapped it knowingly with his machete and declared it a *'jelly'*. He would strike it four times with his machete to open a small hole in the top. The water from the nut was bland, clear and tasted refreshingly good. The man then swiped the top off the nut and cut a small wedge from the shell, which was used as a spoon to scoop out the inside wobbly jelly walls of flesh. So the green nut was a cheap drink and food combined.

To slake our thirst we also tried roadside Snow Cones, but these were a bit too sweet and sickly. They were crushed ice, flavoured with fruity syrup and covered with Nestle condensed milk. We ended up very sticky!

Another taste we tried but never intend to repeat was the tree oyster. John and Angie persuaded us to try them but advised us to choose a mild sauce. The little oysters were collected from the roots of the mangrove swamps and dipped into a fiery red sauce before being popped whole into the mouth.

We had been out to the Caroni Swamp where these little delicacies were collected. We had gone to watch the beautiful Scarlet Ibis birds returning at sunset to roost in the trees of the swamp, an extraordinary sight and a memorable excursion through the swamps which took us over four hours in a small motorized punt.

Since an evening meal wasn't provided by the Guest House we preferred to eat at one of the many little Chinese restaurants tucked away down the side streets of Port of Spain. Our favourite was the *'Kapok'*, recommended to us by a group of young white Trinidadians who shared their picnic with us in the Botanical Gardens. The red flock wallpaper, paper lanterns, attentive service, scrupulous hygiene, friendly waiters and delicious food had us going back again and again. The memory of *'Sweet and Pungent'* Lobster, Kapok style, will tingle my taste buds forever!

Generally we relied on our own two feet to get us around the town but trips further afield required a taxi. There were more taxis than private cars in Trinidad. The official taxis had the prefix 'H' on the number plate but there were literally hundreds of 'pirate' taxis, hired by the driver for the day at a cost of about $10 (Trinidad and Tobago dollars).

Since he did not own car, the taxi driver had no pride in the vehicle and drove it hard and fast, hand on the horn, foot on the accelerator. His aim was to get you to your destination as fast as possible so that he could collect another lucrative fare. The taxi drivers were a chatty and happy bunch of people, and the fare was variable and open to negotiation. All we had to say was *"We're staying at Mr. Stone's"* and the fare was instantly reduced by 50%.

The pirate taxis ran up and down the bus routes gathering paying passengers and stopping anywhere along the route to drop or collect. They were very cheap, very frequent and very fast. A twitch of an eyebrow in the direction of a cruising cab and it would squeal to a halt beside the pavement, bundle you in with the other passengers and roar off again.

We negotiated with one of the taxi drivers to take us the sixty miles to Mayaro for the equivalent of £6. He confided that he had only ever been to Mayaro twice in his life before and it was something of an adventure for him.

The agent for Fyffes in Trinidad was Mr. Deans at Huggins Ltd. We spent a great deal of time in Mr. Deans' office while he refunded, changed, organized, and documented us. The young, clean, Mr. Deans, as smooth as milk chocolate, was very efficient and extremely charming. He bargained for hotel rooms on Tobago (reducing the quoted price from $90 down to $46). He cabled Fyffes in England to arrange a ticket refund on the return half of our 'cruise'. He re-wrote our flights so many times (working out the most advantageous mileage routes) we had a huge wad of stapled tickets to carry around with us. During our stay in Port of Spain Mr. Deans became a good and close friend and we had a very emotional farewell with a great deal of vigorous hand-shaking when we finally collected our tickets from his office.

But before we left Port of Spain for the beach at Mayaro we wanted to visit the Mount St. Benedict Monastery, seven miles out of the capital. Mr. Deans told us that for just over £2 we could hire a scooter for the day, and since we had both owned scooters in our youth we organized a hire so that we could visit the Monastery.

We puttered out of town, successfully found the hill leading to the Monastery, but then realized the road to the top was just too steep for the little scooter. We abandoned it at the Scarlet Ibis Hotel at the bottom of the hill and in the blistering heat of late morning we set off on foot to climb the hill.

As we toiled upwards we could see the Monastery above us, but it didn't seem to be getting any closer. We were wondering what we had let ourselves in for when to our great relief a car stopped alongside and the driver offered us a lift. We had been rescued by Father Kelvin Felix who taught at the Seminary. Apparently a young white couple on foot in Trinidad is a rare sight, and to find them crawling sweatily up the steep hill to the Monastery, he laughingly informed us, was rarer still! We were an object of intense curiosity.

Father Felix was wonderful. He gave us a guided tour of the Monastery complex before leaving us at the Rest House to enjoy a lunch of bread and cheese. He had recently returned from Bradford, a city I knew well, where he had been conducting a sociological survey of the Yorkshire people. We roared with laughter. Strange but true he insisted. Father Felix asked us to call in to the Seminary to say goodbye before we left.

When it was time for us to leave we were adopted by another Good Samaritan who drove us to the Seminary to say farewell to Father Felix. Our Good Samaritan was the Father in charge of Irish Priests in Trinidad and he was on his way to visit an Irish Priest *'in the* country'.

"Would you like to come along?" he enquired cheerfully.

And that is how we found ourselves in another car and on our way to San Fernando, some forty miles away. The Father chattered gaily and continuously as we sped along back roads lined with sugar cane fields and cocoa plantations. He kept up an amazing running commentary on the countryside, the people, the problems, and the life of Trinidad.

The sugar cane fields were ready for harvesting, some had already been set on fire and were already blazing, thick smoke rising up into the afternoon air and clouding the sun. The Trinidadians were unusual in that they set fire to the cane. The lower leaves and undergrowth burned, leaving the cane and top leaves for harvesting. They argued that this method, not adopted by any other country, got rid of any snakes hiding in the fields. But by using the burning method to harvest the cane some of the sugar was lost, and the cane had to be cut, bundled and carried to the factory as quickly as possible. In Cuba the crop was cut by hand by machete.

The Irish Priest we visited was a positive joy, full of anecdotes and stories that had us laughing until tears ran down our cheeks. He didn't get many visitors and he fussed around us, delighted to have our company. He pressed us to share with him his treasured Christmas cake.

The cherished gift was made in Ireland by his sister before being parcelled out to him. It took weeks to arrive, maturing nicely as it passed through the postal system. Once arrived the cake was carefully preserved from marauding sugar ants by a complex system of bowls filled with water which acted as a protective moat around the precious tin.

The cake was his pride and joy. Each tiny morsel slowly chewed for full appreciation, each sultana, currant and raisin carefully rolled around in the mouth for total enjoyment. Normally the Priest managed to make his Christmas cake last an astonishing twelve months, to finish just in time for the delivery of the next one. But three generous slices for three unexpected guests threatened to make an excessive breach in the whole, and we were reluctant to accept. He would have none of it and spoiled us completely with a pot of English tea to accompany the lavish slice of delicious Irish fruit cake.

As we chatted we asked what he did for amusement in such an isolated area and he showed us the model airplanes he made, and he confessed he went into Port of Spain once a week to *"regain my sanity"*.

CHAPTER 4

MAYARO BEACH AND OIL EXPLORATION

Mayaro Beach, Trinidad, was the stunning reality of our wildest dreams. Imagine eighteen uninterrupted miles of clean, bright, beautiful, deserted beach with the Atlantic Ocean dribbling and caressing the warm grains of sand on one side, and the other guarded by tall coconut palms, trunks as stiff as soldiers, with the rustling fronds chasing their own shadows. We were both in heaven.

We were staying at the rather grandly named Atlantic Beach Hotel. It was in fact an old, run-down, comfortably casual, very basic beach hotel. Set in total isolation with nine miles of nothing to the left and nine miles of nothing to the right. It was very modest, totally humble and suited us perfectly.

Three people looked after six guests. The *'Boss-lady'*, William and Momma with the part-time help of Mary and Neptune. We guests were called 'de family'. The little hotel was so far off the beaten track that few people came to stay, and those that did were not the usual type of tourist.

When we arrived at the Atlantic Beach Hotel, having driven for miles and miles along an arrow straight and dusty road which would have been monotonous but for the impressive avenue of tall palms on either side, William was standing outside waiting for us standing stiffly to attention. Before we had time to step from the taxi he coughed loudly, and speaking in very deliberate and correct English he said, and I quote:

"Mr. Deans had communicated as a matter of urgency by telephone from Port of Spain and was very keenly desirous of speaking to you".

This was the first and last time William used what he called his 'dignified' way of talking to us, next time he spoke he had thankfully lapsed back into his natural and musical Trinidadian way of speaking.

As instructed we immediately phoned Mr. Deans to discover that Huggins Ltd. had been *'the object of a robbery'* the previous night and our Travellers Cheques, used to pay for our flights, and our old but still valid BOAC tickets, had been stolen. Mr. Deans warned us that the tickets could still be used and we may have trouble when we arrived at Piarco airport for our onward flight to Tobago. Duly warned of potential problems we brushed the matter aside and settled down to enjoy our stay at Mayaro.

Our companions at the hotel were four working Americans on a seismic survey exploration for off-shore oil. They disappeared each morning in a small boat, brimming with expensive electronic equipment, and came back just in time for pre-dinner drinks in the evening. With absolutely no entertainment at the hotel all we could do to amuse ourselves was to exchange life stories, and we indulged endlessly.

It was hard to know whether Larry's stories were fact or fiction but they made very entertaining listening. Larry had a formidable paunch and looked much older than his 32 years, but it was hardly surprising when you heard the details of his action packed life.

It seemed Larry's father was an oil man who spent much of his time overseas, and as a consequence he decided to send thirteen year old Larry to Military School in the States so that he *'could get a good education'*. After finishing school Larry was offered a commission which, to everyone's astonishment, he refused. He decided instead to become an explosives expert and at twenty-two was sent out to Vietnam, leaving behind a wife and child. He was attached to the Green Berets and his job was to place explosives at night. He was parachuted into a valley which should have been clear, but was in fact surrounded by 11,000 Vietcong. Larry told us that 1,500 US troops, all young American boys, went in, but only 300 survived the appalling slaughter that followed. Larry himself was missing for forty-seven days and reported believed dead.

Sometime later Larry was posted to Egypt and when the Israeli Five-Day War commenced his landrover was strafed by Israeli aircraft and his passport was confiscated.

Not surprisingly his first marriage failed but he had remarried and told us he planned to retire in three years' time, at 35!

At Mayaro it was wonderful to hear the soothing sound of the surf all the time, and to step from our room straight on to the beach, and it was absolutely marvellous to have nothing to do and all day to do it in. During the early hours of the morning the beach at Mayaro became a road and occasional cars would pass outside our room hurtling along on their way to somewhere up the coast.

Coconut 'pirates' in beat-up trucks also used the early morning beach to poach a load of green nuts from the gently swaying palms. This was an offence, and taken very seriously indeed by the authorities.

West Indians and Trinidadians in particular, loved to talk. It was a wonderful way to pass the time and they were always very interested in us and why we were here, where were we going, what were we doing. They particularly wanted to know about England and seemed to have a real longing to *'go der one day'*.

The postman came to the hotel once a week, but only if he had something to deliver. The life-guard rode by on his horse or his bicycle once a day and would stop for a chat about British politics and Edward Heath or Harold Wilson. Neptune the odd-job man talked of his wish to go to England while he tried, yet again, to fix our hot water supply. William, leaning on the bar, spoke proudly and with great affection about the *'tree'* times he had met the Queen of England's sister Princess *'MaH-grit'* who had visited Mayaro. Our days were filled with idle gossip, sunbathing, and strolls along the beach, followed by evenings of Momma's Creole cooking splashed down with rum punches, or gin and coconut water. Life was very quiet and very peaceful.

As general factotum William was absolutely indispensable. He performed the functions of barman, waiter, receptionist, telephonist, and baggage man with a wonderfully laid-back manner. His 'uniform' of choice was a too tight T-shirt stretched across his large pot belly, and very baggy shorts which hung awkwardly below his huge gut. He scuffed amiably along in his weathered flip-flops, the ideal footwear for sand, sea or stone floor.

William's most fascinating feature and his obvious pride and joy was his hair. Bald on top he had somehow managed to encourage luxuriant black hair to grow above his ears and round the back of his head. This black hair was so long it had been teased into ringlets which fell over his ears and down his neck. The wind at Atlantic Beach was quite strong, coming as it did directly off the sea, and it would blow William's ringlets into curls so that they stood away from the side of his head, like a sweep's brush. When he thought no-one was watching he licked the palms of his hands and gently smoothed the ringlets back into place.

Momma was queen of the kitchen and when she was happy (most of the time) she sang away in a bright falsetto, but when she was under stress (about half an hour before each meal) she uttered deep rumbling moans of *"Oh ...d...e....a...h"* over and over again. Momma was like an animated chocolate blancmange and when she laughed she wobbled and rippled all the way down to her woollen football socks. Momma explained to us, in confidence, that she wore woollen football socks (knee-length ones rolled down to her ankles) to keep her feet, pushed into a pair of battered old 'mules', warm. We understood completely, the dining area of the hotel was open on three sides to the elements and it could be very breezy by late evening.

We would visit Momma in her kitchen and she would try to explain what was in the mysterious dishes she prepared for us. Her meals were an exploration into the unknown and never conformed to a menu. And they were never ready when Momma expected them to be. Dinner could be served any time between 7.00 p.m. and 8.30 p.m. However we quickly discovered it was wise to arrive in anticipation of dinner at 6.30 p.m. just in case, since the clock which ticked away behind William's head in the bar was sluggish and could be anything up to half an hour behind our watches and Momma would not tolerate us being even a minute late.

But it was no hardship, we passed the time by drinking William's rum and chatting between ourselves, and it did mean that when dinner was finally presented we were all ravenously hungry and alcoholically relaxed, and eager to eat, and appreciative of whatever Momma put in front of us regardless of quality or quantity.

Our first lunch at the hotel was an unnamed dark green soup, imagine seaweed in stagnant water with a taste to match. The main dish was chicken, maize and cocoa mashed into a paste and served with evil smelling rice, accompanied by some flat battered things. The flat battered things were quite tasty, but it took us time to begin to appreciate Momma's culinary experiments. After the experience of that first lunch we elected to have Momma make us sandwiches, and these proved to be fun and unusual. One day we had three layers of bread filled with lettuce, cabbage, mayonnaise and diced fish, a strange combination to our British palates but an interesting alternative to good old traditional cheese and pickle!

An evening meal could be fried plantains (a vegetable new to us which resembled a large green banana), salad, shrimps and macaroni, all mixed up together in a large bowl. We learned by bitter personal experience to avoid the coffee Momma made since it acted like a very powerful laxative.

It was during an evening of bar-talk with William, while waiting for Momma to emerge from the kitchen with dinner, that he told us about himself. He referred often to his *'de-ah ode lay-di'* followed always by the phrase *'gawd ris she so-la'*. This was his mother who had passed away four years previously *'gawd ris she so-la'*. His dear old lady, he told us, would not approve of many of the things he now did since she passed away *'gawd ris she so-la'*. When he came up from the country to the busy capital Port of Spain ten years ago, he was about forty at the time, his dear old lady was quite sure it would be the ruin of him and he would be led away from the straight and narrow in that big iniquitous city. She would have approved his return to the country and his job at Atlantic Beach.

William had adopted an unusual work ethic, which he strongly recommended us to follow. He said he never did anything, ever *'until dah Spi-rit move meh'*. But William was restless, he dreamed of England and his fantasy was to set up a little business. He worshipped the Royal Family and called each by their Christian name. He was particularly devoted to *'MaH-grit'* and never tired of telling anyone who cared to listen of the three times he had met her.

One day, while the rest of the oil team disappeared out to sea on their daily offshore exploration, we were given a conducted tour of the nearby Texaco oil field by Karl, and we were introduced to our first oil well and a heliport. The heliport was far more exciting than the oil well, which was capped off and could have easily been missed amongst the undergrowth if Karl hadn't known its precise location. Gone are my fantasies of oil gushing skywards. All I saw was a two inch diameter pipe buried in the ground protected by a manhole cover.

When the team returned that day they had bad news for Karl. The weather had not been good and the sea was a little rough. Although two of the team had expressed concern about the conditions they decided to go out in the boat as usual. Time was of the essence. The conditions worsened and some of the equipment broke loose and was smashed. Larry alone lost £4,000 worth of scientific recording equipment. They were all very depressed that night and phoned the States for replacement parts which were flown in the following day. An expert on sonar equipment also arrived. The 'expert' had recently returned from Scotland where he was using his equipment to hunt for the legendary Loch Ness Monster. He told us he had discovered a number of huge underwater caves which *"looked very promising"* and he was now developing new equipment so that he could rush back to Loch Ness to carry on with his search for Nessy.

As the day of our departure drew closer William became more and more maudlin and depressed. We had become, he said, part of the family. With hugs and floods of tears on both sides the time came to say goodbye to our Atlantic Beach family and we headed for Piarco airport. We were on our way to the little island of Tobago and Keg was our driver. The journey through the sun-kissed palms along the straight grey highway took an hour and a half, and Keg kept up a running commentary all the way. He had just returned from a two week stay in New Orleans and the experience had left him stunned. As far as Keg was concerned there was no other place on earth as wonderful as New Orleans.

CHAPTER 5

TOBAGO AND MARDI GRAS

A motley group of six people lounged around bundles of baggage on the tarmac beside the tiny Tobago shuttle hut, and we sidled over to join them. The two tired Japanese in uniform turned out to be the pilot and co-pilot, and when they picked up our suitcases and headed off across the tarmac we presumed we should follow.

As a result we found ourselves crammed onto the 3.00 p.m. Trinidad to Tobago flight, squeezed in behind the pilot and beside Country and Western singer *Mad Jack* who insisted on wearing his ten gallon hat.

Surprisingly, the extrovert *Mad Jack* proved to be a nervous passenger and he tried to combat his anxiety with incessant and loud chatter. He calmed his nerves by engaging the pilot in conversation, and the pilot politely twisted round in his seat to reply while the little plane raced down the runway at colossal speed. I closed my eyes and gripped the seat. But all was well, twenty minutes later the little plane arrived on Tobago, wobbling and bouncing down the runway, and *Mad Jack* and I heaved huge audible sighs of relief and my new best buddy *Mad Jack* gave me an enormous bear hug and invited us to visit him in Spring Valley.

Tobago airport was small and informal and as we crossed the tarmac two officials watched us come through the barrier and one of them handed my husband a note. It was from our *SS Camito* friends John and Angie who had apparently been down to the airport three times already to meet Trinidad flights in the hope of finding us on board one of them.

They had just rushed off to collect a 'conch souse' for supper and the note said they would return soon to collect us if we would wait. A conch souse, we discovered later, was the meat from a creature that looked like a large sea snail marinated and stewed into a sort of soup. It was Angie's idea of a heavenly meal.

Mr. Deans had recommended we stay at the Della Mira Guest House on the outskirts of Scarborough, Tobago's main town and harbour, and we arrived just in time for a candlelit dinner. Under the flickering flame the meat resembled a large sausage, but closer inspection revealed it was fish rolled into sausage shape and covered with a dark brown breadcrumb mixture. The first tentative taste revealed a coarse and strong fish with a flavour alien to us. The Manager, who hovered smilingly beside our table, explained that we were eating dolphin, a delicacy he had prepared himself especially for our pleasure. We had, it seemed, been greatly honored!

Tobago seemed to us very quiet, very beautiful, and the epitome of our image of the Caribbean. Green bushy hillsides, narrow winding roads, steep drops to white crescent beaches. It was once very rich, with sugar and cotton plantations owned by British colonists and worked with slave labour imported from Africa.

During a long and troubled history the island was regularly invaded by rival countries, captured and recaptured, with ownership passing from British, to Dutch, to Swedish, back to Britain, over to France, and then Britain again. Even the American colonists considered Tobago worth raiding and made an abortive attempt to conquer it in 1778 but were driven off by the British. Henry Morgan, the buccaneer, took advantage of all this squabbling over ownership and used Tobago as a base.

The history of Tobago was reflected in the names left behind, Dutch Fort, French Fort, Bloody Bay, Pirate's Bay, Fort King George, and Fort James. The memories lingered on. The relative prosperity of Tobago halted abruptly in 1884 when the British Company who controlled the island's sugar economy declared itself bankrupt. The land was bought by the local peasants and returned to survival farming, and Tobago was made a ward of her larger and less depressed neighbour Trinidad.

Tourism was now the main industry, with wealthy Americans encouraged to holiday.

John was trying to get his recently purchased cocoa plantation back into business. John, Angie and baby Gavin were camping out in the old cocoa shed, a long bare storehouse with two smaller rooms, one acting as temporary kitchen, the other as walk-in wardrobe.

The cocoa shed was perched high on a ridge above two valleys which sloped away and down to the cocoa trees along the valley floor. The small cocoa trees were shaded by tall and elegant Immortelle trees and huge stands of bamboo forty to sixty feet high were dotted along the winding path to the valley bottom, rubbing and creaking their stems together in the gentle afternoon breeze.

A walk down the path to explore the plantation required one member to be armed with a machete. Not just to clear the way but to use as a weapon against snakes. John was still trying to discover the extent of his land and made little sorties into his wilderness as often as he could. We helped him to cut a path through nine feet high grass, swinging the machete from side to side and wondering what animal might suddenly appear.

We decided to have an evening out and went along to the Tobago *'Panorama and Ole Mas'*. Panorama was the competition to choose the best Steel or Pan Band.

Seven bands were competing for this coveted title, each one sponsored by a large company with local interests, like Texaco. The smallest band had twenty-eight players and each player had one, two, four, five or even six drums to play. The largest band contained 150 musicians and we worked out that if they averaged four drums each that gave a staggering total of six hundred pans, all made from oil drums, all lovingly painted, or polished and tuned to the exact pitch required. The narrow four inch drums produced a very high pitch and the complete full size oil drum resonated with a deep base tone.

The most popular piece of pan music was *'Mas in Madison Square'* and to hear it played by a talented pan band of fifty or more musicians, under a star-studded velvet tropical night with fireflies darting overhead, was quite simply a sensational, unforgettable experience.

A field on the outskirts of town had been picked for the entertainment and partitioned off with bamboo poles and palm fronds. Lesser mortals (including ourselves) scrambled for the wooden benches in front of the huge makeshift stage and I found myself on the front row sandwiched between Neil (a large good-natured Canadian tourist staying with us at our Guest House) and a lively, cheeky ten-year old Tobagan lad who dreamed of being a pan player himself one day. Behind us were tiered stands and to either side the bleaches. Hundreds had turned out for the occasion and the local police were trying in vain to control the heaving, happy masses.

The judges took their role very seriously. Apparently it was not just the quality of the playing, or the presentation of the band that was watched and noted, but the band was timed from the moment the first member stepped onto the stage with his drum to the moment the last drum was removed. On average this took fifteen minutes and required an amazing amount of team coordination.

As the first band prepared to play a hush fell over the crowd, and as the first note was struck a roar of approval went up and the night took off. Few people could remain seated, the music demanded a physical response, and soon hundreds of gyrating, wriggling and bouncing bodies filled the aisles. What a night. What an experience!

After all the bands had played the judges sat back for a rest and for the next two hours we watched the pageant of *Ole Mas*. It is hard to describe *Ole Mas*. It was a little like a charade where players dressed up and acted out some past event with an attempt to mock or laugh at it. The players carried explanatory cards so that the audience could appreciate the joke, and as a consequence there was a tremendous amount of audience participation.

It has to be said that some of the puns performed bordered on the obscene, but the crowd loved it. The humour was definitely West Indian and some of it escaped us, but the yells of delight and screams of encouragement from friends in the audience created an electric atmosphere and we simply basked in the pleasure of the evening.

At the end of *Ole Mas* the judges gave their verdict on the winning band. They were all so good it was a pity to have to select just one. As we finally parted, my little Tobagan friend threw his arms around me and begged me to marry him. I was rescued by Neil and my husband who together tactfully unglued the little lad's passionate embrace.

One day the quintessence of an English colonial public school gentleman checked into the Guest House. He was staying a brief forty-eight hours, and he had hired a car. He bounded up to us, introduced himself *"Call me Bunty"* and said he intended to explore Speyside and wanted company. We soon found that Bunty was delightful in small doses but debilitating in excess.

However it was impossible to refuse his persuasive charms. His chubby pink face bubbled from behind his huge sandy handlebar moustache, and his blue eyes twinkled appealingly. It would have been churlish to refuse his invitation.

Bunty proved to be manic behind the wheel. As we travelled at breakneck speed along the unknown south coast road of Tobago it became very clear that Bunty had more enthusiasm than expertise when it came to driving. The road was narrow and twisting, rising and falling sharply with precipice like drops on either side. Not a drive for the nervous or unskilled.

The rules of the road were the same in Tobago as in England, but apparently seldom practised. A local driver much preferred the centre of the road, swerving aside at the last moment in a dangerous game of 'chicken'. Bunty was not familiar with this form of driving. This, coupled with the fact that his reflexes had slowed down with the tropical heat and the car was strange to him, combined to create a volatile cocktail and we had several close encounters with oncoming vehicles as Bunty wrestled with the wheel.

Nevertheless the scenery, when I could manage to tear my eyes away from the road, did appear very beautiful. Rocky inlets, little islands out to sea, small sandy but inaccessible bays along the coast. And at Speyside, out across the sparkling sea, we stopped to admire Little Tobago, called locally Bird of Paradise Island.

Sadly, since Hurricane Flora devastated the island in 1963, there were only about five Birds of Paradise left on this uninhabited nature reserve. At Speyside we happened to meet Mr. Lau and his wife, owners of the Paradise Inn. Mr. Lau was small and charming, a kindly gentleman, and he invited us on a tour of his property and proudly showed us the deer, ducks, land turtles and macaw he was rearing which he hoped to release later into the wild. He told us his aim was to devote his life to nature conservation. We spent a very pleasant afternoon in his company listening to anecdotes about his life and meeting his friends. It was a most unexpected and much appreciated act of friendship by Mr. Lau.

Bunty thought our Speyside trip was so successful he wanted to repeat it the following morning. A quick exploration of the north of the island before he flew off, he pleaded. But sadly, as Bunty was talking to us, he was overtaken by a sudden and quite violent bout of that well-known traveller indisposition known variously as Montezuma's Revenge, Delhi Belly, or Travellers' Tummy. He dashed off to his room in dismay and we never saw Bunty again, he simply disappeared.

We decided to join fellow guest Neil for an excursion to Pigeon Point and Buccoo Reef. Pigeon Point was reputed to be the most beautiful beach on the most beautiful island in the Caribbean and we were keen to discover for ourselves the reality of this claim. We found a taxi and collected Neil from outside the little travel agent office in Scarborough. He was clutching a bag full of fresh grapefruit, a hand of bananas and several oranges, our lunch he explained triumphantly.

There was a barrier across the road at Pigeon Point. The land above high water mark is owned by a private club who charged a fee for entry. We left the taxi beside the gate and walked down to the beach and then along the shore. Not just to avoid paying the levy but more in protest that anyone should seek to 'own' these beautiful places.

It has to be said that we were very disappointed with Pigeon Point. It was, we all agreed, far too commercialized and without the natural wild beauty of Mayaro or Buccoo Bay, and so we left in search of our boatman. Neil had arranged with the beautifully named 'Christmas' to take us in his speedboat out to the reef. We sat on the sand and waited, but Christmas never came.

Ivory ambled by and volunteered to take us out, but loyalty to Christmas made us shake our heads. We watched the shoals of small fish as they flashed silver in and out of the sparkling shallows. We saw a long lean predator slide into their midst and then leap four feet into the air as, with a thrash and splash, he attacked the quicksilver fry. And still Christmas did not come. Another young man came up to us and we agreed to go with him.

His speedboat was fast and bone-shaking and in no time at all we found ourselves bobbing directly above Buccoo Reef. We slipped on our snorkel and masks, and I put on a pair of plastic shoes (just in case my feet caught the coral) and we dipped over the side, sliding into a fantasy world of silence, colour and incredible beauty. It was a magic kingdom of colourful coral, curious fish, crystal clear water and peace.

There were orange fish, yellow fish, pretty striped black and blue fish, as much interested in us as we were in them, hundreds and hundreds of graceful, vivid, charming, large and little fish. We spent a bewitching hour floating amongst these delightful creatures and looking at the stunning coral formations and other treasures of the sea. Buccoo Reef certainly made up for the disappointment of Pigeon Point.

The highlight of the Trinidad and Tobago year was the two-day Mardi Gras Carnival. We were asked if we would march with the Band entered by the Della Mira Club in the Carnival. The Band banner read *'What the Tourist means to us $$'* and it was huge, so large it stretched across the street. Since Neil, my husband and I were the only white guests (and tourists) staying at the Guest House it seemed appropriate to join in, and we were very flattered.

The fun started on the Sunday night with lots of music, noise and dancing, and at 5.00 a.m. Monday morning the Band, with us holding the lead banner, were to take to the road and with all the supporters following we would march, sing, dance and swing our way through town, down to the judging area. Once round the judging arena and then back through town to the hotel, bouncing, jumping and gyrating all the way, strength permitting.

Monday afternoon was the official *Ole Mas* when crowds gathered in the street for the *jump-up* with the pan bands. Tuesday was the Mardi Gras pageant, the parade which everyone loved and which had been prepared for since Mardi Gras the previous year. The costumes were always a dazzle of colour and extravagance portraying themes such as *'Africa Then and Now'*. Tobago had six themes this year.

How some of the performers managed to wear their heavy and ornate costumes let alone dance in them defied understanding, but this was a time for fun, for showing off, for total unadulterated pleasure. In Port of Spain a participating Band could have as many performers as it wanted, and they could run to over five thousand, an awesome responsibility for the committee that coordinated the team.

By midnight on Sunday the Hotel Night Club was bulging at the seams with 1200 happy, laughing West Indians, and us, the three white tourists! We decided to snatch a couple of hours sleep before the 4.00 a.m. call to march and fell out of bed at 3.00 a.m. having been woken by the din coming from the Club on one side and the Community Centre on the other. We put on our Black Label Rum T-shirts which said *'Carnival - La Tropicale'* across the bosom and weaved our bleary way into the Club looking for Neil.

We found Suzy, one of the waitresses, and as we were talking to her at the door there was the sound of breaking glass. In an instant the crowd panicked. They stampeded like cattle and were pushing and shoving each other in terror towards the exit door.

Our immediate thought was that the Club had caught fire. The dried palm fronds of the roof would have blazed like an inferno and we grabbed Suzy by the wrist and ran. But the path was blocked with pushing, struggling bodies. We scrambled over the wall dividing the Hotel garden from the Club and dived into the deep ditch below, sprawling on top of each other in our confusion. And as we lay there, panting in relief, we heard someone shouting above the noise of the exodus. It was a false alarm.

Apparently two men in the Club had been quarreling over a women they both fancied, and one had stepped backwards to take a swing at the other, accidentally knocking over a beer bottle which rolled off the table and smashed on the floor. Another bottle followed and rolled off the wobbling table, then a third. The sound of breaking glass panicked the packed crowd who thought a fight had broken out, and everyone scrambled to get out of the way. The two men concerned also thought a fight had begun, and they were as keen as everyone else to rush out of the Club.

Since my husband and Neil had been appointed to hold the bamboo poles with the banner, I was assigned three escorts to look after me. They were instructed to stay close and make sure that I was not trampled, abused, or lost and that I did not collapse from exhaustion, and they took their responsibilities very seriously indeed.

It was a sensational night. My escort of Suzy, Inez and Mervyn stayed close to me and the night was filled with fun, laughter and good humour. There was no trouble, not even a hint of an offence. Mervyn normally worked as Club Doorman and he made the perfect bodyguard.

We shuffled and stamped, arms linked, singing and swinging, all through the early hours of the morning and arrived at the judging arena pouring sweat and blissfully happy having taken three hours to cover the distance from the Hotel. We finally crawled back to the hotel, having earned great admiration for our stamina to discover that we had come a noble second in the judging of the Bands. The seven hundred members of the band attributed their success to their 'white brothers' and Neil, my husband and myself became the heroes of the hour.

My husband and Neil were allowed to collapse with a well-earned drink, but I spent the next few hours dancing with what seemed to me to be the whole Band, one after the other. They were immensely polite and charming. Each dancer approached my husband, requested permission to ask me to dance, graciously escorted me into the scrum and graciously escorted me out again after the 'number', restoring me to my husband and thanking him warmly for allowing me 'out' as they so charmingly put it.

I was immensely flattered. A packed night club on Tobago and my dance partners proved to be the most charming, chivalrous and courteous of gentlemen. If, by chance, I was approached directly because my husband had momentarily disappeared, my prospective partner rushed off in search of permission before returning breathless to sweep me into the last few bars of the dance.

Tuesday 23rd February was the big day. Greasy Tuesday or Mardi Gras, and to any West Indian, the most exciting day of the year. Promptly at noon the three of us put on our Carnival T-shirts and headed to downtown Scarborough to watch the parade and join in the fun. The temperature was a wilting 89°F and the air very still. Our white faces were very conspicuous in the crowds filling the street and we kept being stopped by happy Tobagans who wanted to know if we were having a good time, or who remembered us from the march and wanted to chat, or dancing partners and friends from the Club who just wanted to say hello and pump hands, punch tums or slap shoulders in good-humoured greeting.

It was a slow, jolly stroll through the jostling, laughing West Indians, and when the marching parade came into view the atmosphere turned electric. The costumes of the slowly moving, dancing groups were stunning in their fantasy. The brilliant colours of feathers, cloth and card shimmered in the hot afternoon. The music was hypnotic and wild. The crowd went crazy with enthusiasm, running alongside, clapping applause and shouting encouragement. It was a scene of pure joy.

Maybe Port of Spain had a bigger carnival, maybe Rio and New Orleans were more professional, but the sheer good fun and friendliness of the Tobago Carnival and the happy hospitality of the people would be very hard to beat. To us the costumes were sensational, the music magic and the spirit, stamina and genuine sweetness of the people astonishing.

But that was our last day on Tobago and the following day we left for the British Virgin Islands and Tortola. It was the end of our carefree holiday with its wonderful introduction into Caribbean life and the beginning of a new future for us.

CHAPTER 6

ISLAND HOPPING TO THE BRITISH VIRGIN ISLANDS

We crept out of the hotel at 6.45 a.m. leaving a final note for Neil and feeling very depressed. On the way to the airport our taxi passed an overturned car in the river, the unhappy consequence of one reveller's Mardi Gras.

Even at that early hour the airport was packed. Tired travellers suffering from hangovers trying to get off Tobago the day after Carnival. The scene was disorganized and chaotic.

We managed to check in, had our luggage weighed, and then sat back to wait amongst the confusion of loud voices and harassed people for the 8.00 a.m. flight to Tortola. It was flying up from Trinidad and moments before it was due to arrive at Tobago we were informed that it had left Piarco Airport with only three seats spare. Our 'confirmed' flight was suddenly 'unconfirmed' and we were stranded, feeling frustrated and furious, on the tarmac with two dear old American lady tourists and no way out of Tobago.

We should have got the message and taken the hint. We should have turned around and gone back to the hotel and left the airline to sort out the problem. We should have shrugged in resignation and adopted the lovely West Indian attitude of *'no sweat man - take it easy'*. But the airline could not guarantee a place on tomorrow's flight either, at the moment, they said, it was full. They could, however, get seats for us on the flight departing in one week's time. The interpretation of the airline initials BWIA (*But Will It Arrive*) took on an ominous significance.

Not only were we now rather short on money but we wondered how the company would react to a cable sent to Tortola saying *"Sorry, delayed one week, see you soon"*.

Not very happily, we reasoned, and not a good start to a new job. We needed to show some initiative, but after a week of hectic partying our brains were not functioning quite as crisply as we would have liked. To add to the airport confusion the plane which serviced the hop between Trinidad and Tobago had broken down and the airline was trying to cram forty-eight extra passengers into two small Beechcraft already overflowing. The annoyed passengers milling around the airport were turning hostile.

Working on the premise that 'God helps those who help themselves' we helped ourselves to the airline timetable and discovered there were two planes leaving Trinidad for Antigua.

The Caribbean island of Antigua had a good flight link with Tortola in the British Virgin Islands and the US Virgin Islands. We thought that if we could get that far north we might stand a chance of making Tortola within the week. We grabbed the phone from a harassed clerk who tried unsuccessfully to snatch it back, and contacted the Scarborough Travel Agent.

"Any flights to Trinidad?" We bellowed. He phoned us back an hour later saying that all flights were fully booked with tremendous waiting lists, and warned us we could be stuck for days.

It was afternoon and the crowds were growing by the minute, nasty and intimidating. The last straw came when a very depressed official confidentially informed us that one of the stand-in beachcomber planes had *"just packed up"*, presumably through overwork.

We begged him to add our names to the next flight out to Trinidad and he was too exhausted to refuse. The next flight turned out to be the BWIA plane which had broken down earlier. No one seemed quite sure whether it had been repaired or not, and as they threw the baggage into the hold the engines reluctantly spluttered into life, belching clouds of black smoke and coughing ominously. We were fairly convinced that she was still very sick and boarded her with some trepidation, visualizing an ignominious and watery end somewhere between Tobago and Trinidad. But the old plane arrived safely and looking at the time we calculated that we had been trapped at Tobago Airport for ten hours.

However, our troubles were far from over, as we soon discovered. Piarco was as crowded, and as angry, and as hot, as Tobago, just on a much larger scale. The snake of people in front of the BWIA desk was vicious and volatile. My husband saw at a glance that it was every man for himself. He pushed purposefully to the front of the queue and vaulted the desk. Behind the desk the door marked *BWIA Personnel Only No Entry* was firmly closed. My husband thrust it open and stepped inside. I waited, and waited, hovering anxiously outside, watching the angry snake of passengers grow longer by the minute.

My husband told me afterwards that as the door swung open he discovered he was standing in the heart of the BWIA organization. Frenzied pilots, exhausted ground staff, hot hostesses and sweaty secretaries were attempting to organize the Carnival crowds out of Trinidad.

There was pandemonium, with staff attempting to sort out the mess of too many passengers, too few flights and planes breaking down. The staff were hysterical and the noise deafening. But a pilot spotted my husband and came across, and he took pity on us, and unbelievably managed to book us on the 7.00 a.m. Antigua flight for the following morning.

A secretary passed the phone across and my husband made overnight reservations at the Airport Hotel, and a car was soon speeding on its way to collect us. The pilot suggested it might be prudent if my husband left the office by the back door, so that he would not have to run the gauntlet of the lynching mob surrounding the BWIA airport desk outside. So he crossed to the Customs Shed, jumped the baggage conveyor belt and waltzed, grinning, back to waiting me.

Easygoing Albert was at the hotel. Big, black laid-back Albert, and he greeted us like long lost family with bear hugs and back-slapping and loud deep rumbling guffaws. He had been staying with us at the Della Mira on Tobago and he too had missed his flight. Not jettisoned like us. His taxi, he explained, had been *"Too slow"*, adding, *"About 150 miles an hour too slow, I was an hour late"* and he roared with infectious laughter.

Albert was booked on the same Antigua flight the following morning. With fingers crossed we returned to the airport and successfully boarded. It was such a relief to be in the air escaping the post-Carnival chaos, but we still had to somehow get from Antigua to Tortola.

Albert got off the plane at Antigua just to say goodbye and give us a final hug. We thought for a minute that the plane would take off without him, but the pilot patiently waited while the emotional parting took place. And then we went into the relaxed terminal of Antigua and once more started looking for a flight 'up-islands' towards Tortola.

We began at one end of the terminal, BWIA, and worked our way along the desks of Air France, Pan Am, BOAC, LIAT, two small unpronounceable airlines, Carib Air and a private Charter Company (much too expensive). Then we began to comb the cargo airlines. The LIAT official added us to his waiting list on a plane due out in six hours, but sneaking a look at his list I counted at least twelve other names ahead of ours. And even though he promised to put us on the top, could we really believe him?

The only other alternative was a Carib Airlines flight leaving for St. Croix, US Virgin Islands with a connection to St. Thomas. St. Croix and St. Thomas were a mere hop from Tortola, so we decided to climb on board and head north, and half an hour later we were coming in to land at St. Croix.

This was American soil. This was not the relaxed, easy-going, West Indian good-humoured Immigration and Customs we had come to expect. A ferocious uniformed woman barked orders and verbally whipped the trembling passengers into submissive shuffling lines. This dragon in her blue uniform would have been more comfortable as a prison warder, and certainly more fulfilled. She guarded the gate to the desk official who silently glanced at passports, checked his vast tome of undesirables and finally slowly, almost reluctantly, stamped our passports and nodded us on towards the Customs Shed.

We were supposed to have been passing from one plane to another, the Immigration and Customs a mere brief formality as we crossed the tarmac. But there was absolute pandemonium in the Customs Shed. The place was in an uproar. The US Customs were valiantly trying to check in-transit baggage first but the St. Croix population, returning from wild excesses of Carnival, would have none of it. Boxes, baskets, carrier bags, plastic bags, suitcases, brown paper parcels tied with knotty string, were all hurled and heaped in confusion over the floor and desks, and US Customs were endeavouring to methodically, carefully, and thoroughly check each and every one.

A large, hot, vociferous West Indian lady with a woolly hat pulled firmly on her head was holding a plastic bag of something indeterminate. The Customs Official produced a sharp bladed knife, held the bag aloft, and slit it quickly and carefully from top to bottom. With a wail the woman watched as her green herb spilled out, it was _not_ marijuana she screamed in anguish, it was '_erbal tea_!

Everything in every suitcase and every bag was turned over, poked, sniffed, and examined. The US Customs appeared to be searching for drugs and we realized we could be there for hours. The noise in the tin shed was almost unendurable. All we had was my small insignificant hand baggage, the rest had been passed across from plane to plane. An official caught sight of us and moved slowly in our direction. We realized with enormous relief it was useful to be conspicuously white in a black crowd.

My small suitcase was bulging with badly packed clothes which were peeking out around the sides. The official glanced down and was about to make me open it, when he suddenly changed his mind and quickly waved us through. We pushed our way through the heaving mass of bodies and dived for the exit and ran across the scorching tarmac to the waiting plane.

It seemed that no sooner had we taken off than we landed again. This time at St. Thomas, and how much more civilized than St. Croix. The airport was large, with a roomy entrance lobby and all the airline desks ranged in an orderly fashion along the sides. Our cases were first off the conveyor belt and we took this as a good omen. Now all we had to do was to find a flight across from St. Thomas to Tortola. We were almost at our destination and a wave of excitement gave us some much needed energy.

St. Thomas airport felt friendly and hopeful. My husband began to work his way down the airline desks and struck lucky at once. Prinair had a flight leaving for Beef Island, Tortola in half an hour. We were told it might be full but if we called back in a few minutes they would let us know. The next desk was even more promising, a small independent company that ferried passengers back and forth to Beef Island in six seater planes. They had a flight leaving in an hour, with plenty of room for us and our mountain of baggage. They suggested we leave our luggage with them and go upstairs to Sparky's Airport Restaurant for a burger before take-off. Things were looking good and we began to smile again.

"Have a nice day" they said. Nice place, nice people. We fell in love with St Thomas.

Hank, the pilot, came looking for us. Lean and tanned this American would have been pioneering in the Wild West if he had been born a generation earlier. The other two passengers were a little boy coming for the ride (brought in order to balance our luggage in the nose) and a Tortolian lad returning home after a shopping spree.

We followed Hank as he loped onto the tarmac. We rounded a bend beside the sheds and came face to face with a tiny little plane. Hank wrenched open the door, walked round to the nose to check that our baggage was loaded, and told me to step on the wing, lower my head and climb inside.

I struggled past the pilot's seat and squeezed into the back.

"Is this a big mistake?" I whispered to my husband.

"Where's your sense of adventure?" he whispered back as he struggled in beside me. The little boy sat dutifully in the squat seat at the back as our luggage 'counterbalance' and the young teenager took the co-pilot's seat and began to play with the controls.

The door refused to shut and Hank nonchalantly explained that once we were airborne the force of the wind would keep it closed. In the meantime (after he had flicked his cigarette butt out of the door) he thoughtfully used his foot to wedge the door slightly open so that we could *"Enjoy some fresh air"*.

The little plane trundled down the runway then suddenly, with a little shudder, we were up and away, out of the airport and flying low over the shimmering sea. In the enchantment of the scene unfolding below I lost all sense of fear.

The bright sunshine sparkled off the calm Caribbean and warmed the green humps and hills of dozens of small islands, ageless and serene. The bare words of description in the book on board the *SS Camito* simply had not prepared me for the beautiful reality of the Virgin Islands. No wonder Columbus had named them after St. Ursula and her 11,000 virgins. As we left St. Thomas behind, the island of St. John rose up on our right. Apart from a small cluster of houses around a sandy palm fringed bay it looked peacefully uninhabited and still virginal.

St. John was *"Still the US Virgins"* shouted Hank over the noise of the engine *"Rockefeller likes to keep it as natural as possible. A retreat for US Presidents"* he added with a laugh, *"and Jimmy Carter, Georgia's Governor, treats it like his second home."*

Then Hank pointed to our left. Unseen by us another island had appeared, a long, green, sleeping dragon whose sharp spine stretched along its back from West to East as a steep impressive ridge. It slumbered in the sun, dozing in the bright blue of the shallows, warm and welcoming.

"That's Tortola" said Hank simply, and dipped the little plane down for a closer look.

We were looking at the island Christopher Columbus had named Tor-tolla, the Turtle Dove. If paradise exists it must surely be like this we thought. The teenager took over the controls while Hank kept up a running commentary on the unfolding Tortola. We hugged the shore and headed towards the airport on Beef Island, travelling the whole length of Tortola.

Beef Island was a small lump of rock attached to the East End of Tortola by a short narrow bridge, rather grandly named Queen Elizabeth Bridge. Beef Island worked extremely well as the airport since it allowed the runway to be extended by building out across the rocky shallows of the sea.

It took only a few minutes to fly the whole length of Tortola, from West End to East End following the white ribbon of coast road as it meandered around the sandy bays.

Where were the houses? Where were the people? Then we saw Road Town, the capital of the British Virgin Islands. It nestled beside the bite of a tiny harbour, a single main street flanked on either side by a hotchpotch of small buildings with red and blue corrugated iron roofs, and alongside a huge, flat, white plate of reclaimed land jutting out into the sea.

"Wickhams Cay, the new development area" Hank explained.

The south side of the island had a few small settlements tucked into the bays, and the hillside was dotted with an occasional house. The strip along the top of the island, known as the ridge, was much the same as it must have been for hundreds of years, a rough track along the top which petered out to nothing on either side. The north side of the island, with the exception of the crescent of Cane Garden Bay, looked rugged and untouched.

This promised to be a land of four-wheel drive expeditions, deserted beaches, and crystal clean seas full of undiscovered wonders. A good place to spend the next two years, and a world away from England, exhaust fumes and grey days.

CHAPTER 7

SETTLING IN TO SLANEY

To our delight our apartment at Slaney proved to be much nicer than anticipated. Box-like and basic it was true, but clean and cheerful, with a small balcony and a magnificent view of the Caribbean as it swept through the Sir Francis Drake Channel below.

The company representative responsible for Caribbean operations had flown out from England and was waiting for us. We had not met before and our first impression of him left much to be desired. A stocky, sandy-haired pint-sized little man, plump and rosy. His similarity to a little pink pig was so pronounced we instantly nicknamed him, perhaps rather unkindly, *Porky*.

Designed by nature for the cold northern hemisphere, poor Porky was not equipped to tolerate the tropical sun. Incapable of tanning like the rest of us, he glowed a rather startling crimson, which only reinforced his similarity to a sweaty hot pig. A friend on Tortola, searching for an apt description unkindly likened him to a moist, over-ripe tomato on legs. Why he was given the Caribbean as his company 'patch' was a mystery to us.

Unfortunately when Porky came to the BVI he was obliged to stay with us in our apartment. Fortunately he was an infrequent visitor, only flying out once or twice a year when his wife and Head Office wanted to get rid of him for a few days. But he was, without exception, always irritating and obnoxious.

When we arrived I was thrilled to discover that my apartment had a washing machine. A washing machine on Tortola was considered a very valuable asset. But without any reference to me two days after our arrival Porky sold it to a friend of his for a paltry

$100. This, according to my incredulous neighbours, was an inexcusable offence. It took all my will-power not to seem peevish in his presence, but it was hard not to be mean to a man who had sold your washing machine.

Porky was neither sensitive nor considerate. Sadly for us he proved to have a sneaky and manipulative nature and we took an instant dislike to each other. He threw us in at the deep end. We had arrived on Tortola at 5.00 p.m. travel-stained and travel-stunned from our island-hopping flight marathon, and at 8.30 a.m. the following morning Porky was banging on our bedroom door. We were summoned into the company offices on Main Street, Road Town.

I went along out of politeness and spousal support only to discover Porky expected me to do some *'urgent'* typing for him. My fatigued and disorientated husband was instructed to look through a proposed new development for Wickhams Cay which had just been brought in by the nephew of the lady we had met on *SS Camito*. It was, apparently, quite a coup for the company to be involved in this potential contract and Porky was not about to let the grass grow under his trotters. He wanted my husband to impress the client.

That first frantic morning Porky asked if I would be prepared to work at the office, for my husband, as Secretary, Receptionist, and Bookkeeper. Jet-lagged and still functioning in zombie-mode, it seemed to me like a good idea at the time, the extra money would be useful, and I heard myself agreeing. Employed on a part-time basis for US$200 per month (approximately £80). Porky tried to convince me I would not need to apply for a Work Permit, but I knew this was wrong and I insisted the company apply for the proper permissions from the authorities.

A few days after our arrival, with our suitcases still unpacked and lining the hall, Porky went one step too far. He committed the cardinal sin, even worse than selling my beloved washing machine. I should explain that I am not at my best early in the morning, I have to be approached with caution and energized slowly and sympathetically. My husband knows this and sensibly avoids any conversation or contact until well after my second cup of coffee. Porky, not being blessed with sensitivity, was blissfully unaware of my condition. Half-way through my breakfast orange juice I became conscious that Porky was scribbling something, not on the table cloth as I had supposed, but on a piece of paper. He pushed it towards me, opened his mouth and showed his teeth in what he presumably considered to be a charmingly boyish grin.

"A dinner party" I heard him say *"for later this week. These are the guests"*.

I tried to focus on his list. About twenty people at a guess. No-one had mentioned, when my husband accepted the job, that our terms of reference included my services as secretary, hostess and provider of social functions. I was caught unawares. I had never catered for more than three people in my whole life. The thought of cooking for guests, important guests at that, absolutely terrified me. Dinner parties were definitely alien territory to a humble country bumpkin like me. I was horrified, panicky, and dumb with alarm. Did he really expect me to cook and hostess a dinner party? *Me?* No! Surely not!

"Nothing special, just a few steaks" he continued disarmingly.

My vision blurred, and the image of burned shoe leather floated before my eyes. I gazed blankly at his list. He took my silence as a positive sign and babbled on oblivious to my discomfort.

"You can take the day off from the office to organize the party" he added magnanimously.

I was in shock. I couldn't believe my ears. I blinked, turned red, blue then white. Shock turned to anger. I didn't know what to say. I hedged for time. I tentatively pointed out that I had no crockery and no cutlery. Porky sensed my negativity and became visibly irritated by my less than enthusiastic response. He was abrupt.

"The guests" he said, could *"bring their own plates and things!"*

I laughed, borderline hysteria, hastily leapt from the table, dived into the bedroom, closed the door and had a silent scream. After I had recovered my composure I offered Porky a compromise. I suggested that if he wanted to entertain he could take us and our guests out to a restaurant, like everyone else, where we could all enjoy a good meal, paid for out of the company entertainment budget.

Sadly Porky neither understood nor sympathized and got his revenge by inviting a select company of personal friends to an extravagant hotel dinner, on office expenses of course, while deliberately leaving us at home.

Our office was located on Main Street, halfway between Barclays Bank and O'Neal's department store, opposite the Anglican Church and HM Prison, above a small but modern furniture store. Originally designed as an apartment it was smarter than we had expected. A flight of steps at the front of the store rose up beside an old mango tree and onto a narrow balcony to the office entrance. There was a reception area, a short narrow corridor to a small Conference Room, a further two offices and also two fully equipped bathrooms. One suitably converted bedroom was sub-let to an insurance company, represented by a smooth and extremely well educated Guyanese gentleman called Terry.

Our first week on Tortola was hectic. We were spinning between cocktail parties and dinner dates. It was *very* important, insisted Porky, we were known and recognized as representing the company as rapidly as possible, and in an attempt to display us to the expatriate community we were being exhibited nightly.

Porky expected me to make his breakfast, go to the office, spend the day being an efficient secretary, shop, return home, prepare a meal, wash up, iron his clothes, and attend company functions, while he sprawled in *my* lounge in *my* chair, a can of *my* Bud in his pudgy hand, gazing vacuously into space, or reading the newspaper. But since he was effectively my husband's superior I could only seethe in silent anger.

Exhaustion began to kick in. We had not recovered from our Tobago Carnival and island-hopping fatigue, yet we were expected to put in a full day's work, and acclimatize, and organize the apartment, and appear at these functions calm, composed and charming while trying to remember the names of everyone we met.

All this was organized without any reference to us, including our own cocktail party for sixty guests *"to reinforce your presence in the Territory"* explained the overly energetic over-ripe Porky. I began to find it all bit of a strain.

Sometime during this whirlwind of activity we went for our Immigration Medical at Peebles hospital. The Immigration procedure was a complex but carefully observed ritual, and we were keen to do everything exactly as required. It was the first thing a new arrival had to endure.

Dr. Bob Thomas (recently from UK and notorious for wild parties) gave us a card to take to the hospital and told us to be sure and have a stool specimen about our person. Fortunately Bob Thomas is the human face of the medical profession and wittily suggested we supply the required small sample in a matchbox and not, as had been known, in vast quantities in an 8 oz. coffee jar. This sample, it seemed, would show whether we suffered from any undesirable intestinal infestation, or in layman's terms parasites and worms.

Carefully carrying our bulging matchboxes, we dutifully delivered our samples, trekking up the rough dirt track towards the small white-washed building which was Peebles Hospital on the edge of Road Town. Two small rooms constituted the wards and the laboratory was a large open room with a fridge at one end and two bar stools in the middle. Having found the laboratory fairly easily, we settled ourselves on the bar stools and with some trepidation offered our arms for a blood sample. The little matchboxes were taken away with no comment and we presumed we could leave.

We were just wandering past what appeared to be a store cupboard when an arm shot out and grabbed my husband's sleeve. The cupboard was the X-ray room and the arm belonged to Hilary. It seemed she didn't get many customers and was therefore delighted to find two in one afternoon and she was not about to let us escape. As a result we also got an invitation to dinner at her house, a fair exchange we thought.

After our medical had been successfully negotiated and we were pronounced free from any 'infestation' we were required to present ourselves to the Immigration Office so that any police record could be checked. Searching the database the official could find no such records, which we innocently assumed was in our favour. Not necessarily so, apparently, and the efficient official insisted we produce a sworn Affidavit to the effect that we were neither criminals *'nor persons of a criminal disposition'*.

So we were obliged to find ourselves a lawyer. Fortunately for us a talented and likeable young lawyer had recently arrived on Tortola, Joe Archibald with his stunningly beautiful wife Inez. He had his office in the converted apartment adjacent. In fact I could climb out of my reception room window, hop across his balcony and in through his office window. A somewhat unorthodox method of entry but it saved me having to go down my stairs into the street then up the stairs to his office.

Having secured the Affidavit from Joe, which said we were honest, reliable and thoroughly dependable individuals, my husband and I retraced our steps back down Main Street to the Registrar. We were required to hold a copy of the Bible and repeat, very solemnly, some such words as *'I hereby swear that this is a true statement'*. The Registrar watched us with such great intensity that I was sure I would falter or stammer under his direct gaze and he would take this for admission of some reprehensible past, but all was well.

We finally had a Medical, an Affidavit, a return ticket, and a Bond (US$900 held by the BVI Government should they require funds to deport us). We had successfully negotiated Immigration Office hurdles and had permission to stay in the Territory for six months, or perhaps even a year. It felt marvelous.

The euphoria was short-lived. The next challenge turned out to be Work Permit approval. The Labour Commissioner had to personally decide whether or not we were allowed to work while we were in the BVI. We had naturally assumed the company had already taken care of the official requirements needed for working in the Territory and we were very surprised they had not already arranged Work Permits before our arrival.

Porky was fairly confident about acquiring a Permit for my husband to work for the company, but he was concerned that with my secretarial skills the Labour Commissioner would prefer me to work for the Tourist Board who were desperately seeking a competent Secretary. I would have liked to work for the Tourist Board very much and I felt slightly cheated Porky had not explained this to me before.

My passport put my occupation as Publicity Officer, and in his misguided wisdom Porky chose to play down my Secretary/PA skills, deciding instead to convince the Labour Commissioner that the company could not possibly operate effectively without the services of a qualified Publicity Officer. This was to prove a very unwise idea.

CHAPTER 8

WORK PERMIT AND DRIVING LICENCE DILEMMA

Immigration was absolutely no problem, but sorting out our Work Permits proved a more difficult experience. Porky had totally disregarded island protocol. It was quite obvious to the BVI officials that we had arrived on island, been paraded as the 'new' couple taking over the company office and had settled into work before being officially granted Work Permit and Immigration permission.

Unemployment was high in the BVI and it was completely reasonable that if someone already on island was capable of doing the job they should be given the opportunity. A white couple breezing in from the UK and taking two jobs was extremely irritating and not surprisingly the authorities were annoyed, and personally we entirely agreed with them.

The company had been arrogant and discourteous. They had failed to go through the proper procedure before we arrived and had taken BVI Government approval for granted. My husband and I were to experience the consequences.

Porky, pink and perspiring, directed us to the Immigration and Labour Office. He refused point blank to have anything to do with the Labour Commissioner and became quite agitated at the mere suggestion he should accompany us. We learned later that Porky had crossed swords with the Labour Commissioner before, but the details were unclear. It must have been a very hostile confrontation because Porky was thick-skinned and did not frighten easily.

Before we were abandoned to our fate Porky urged me to stress my accountancy and law qualifications, adding somewhat unhelpfully *"and then waffle"*. This advice made me nervous since I'm not a very experienced waffler!

Armed with all the requisite papers (Affidavit, return ticket, medical certificate and bond) we first of all presented ourselves to the Immigration Officer. He was chatty, convivial, helpful, and was just about to wield his official rubber stamp across our papers when he realized that we had not yet been approved to work on the island by the Labour Office. Big mistake. We were directed next door to meet the Labour Commissioner.

I was apprehensive. We tapped timidly on the door and entered. Small office, large desk behind which sat the inscrutable Labour Commissioner. But I felt encouraged when I saw on the wall above the Labour Commissioner's head a framed poster of *Desiderata,* the lovely poem by Max Erhmann in which we are all urged to *'Go placidly amid the noise and haste'* and I presumed that a man who could appreciate such sensible counsel could not possibly be as alarming a person as Porky had implied.

I was mistaken. The Labour Commissioner spent the next half hour ruthlessly interrogating me on the function of a Publicity Officer while my husband was obliged to sit as silent witness. It was not an easy question to answer and he became convinced I was some sort of Public Relations person.

It all got rather confusing but he hit the nail on the head when in conclusion he remarked astutely *"What on earth does your company want with a Publicity Officer? They used to have a Secretary, it seems to me they are using your qualifications to give them a cheap Secretary!"*

Well frankly I had to agree with him, but what could I say? I was feeling mildly dishonest and wriggled in discomfort.

My husband's permit was no problem. His particular qualifications and experience were much needed in the Territory and gave him instant acceptability.

In parting, the Labour Commissioner said he would sleep on my application and let me know. But I told Porky that if my Work Permit was refused I wouldn't work for the company. I had no intention of antagonizing the authorities and certainly didn't want to be shipped home as an *'undesirable'* for working without permission.

Over the following days I had several enquiries about my 'skills' from potential employers. If my Work Permit for the company was refused I would have no trouble at all getting other, more highly paid, work. Smiths Gore, the London Estate Agents, had an office on island and Derek Dunlop asked me if I would be interested in training as an Administrator, a very tempting offer. I began to wish I hadn't been so hasty in accepting Porky's proposition.

It took the Labour Commissioner several weeks to give us his verdict on my application for a Work Permit. The answer, when it finally came, was a resounding *'No'*. The company, he concluded, did *not* require the services of a Publicity Officer.

However he was prepared to compromise and generously offered us 'wriggle room'. If we redefined the job description to Secretary and advertised the vacancy, provided we could prove that I was the best applicant, then I could have my Work Permit. This solution sounded very fair to me.

Joe Archibald felt we were nearing a successful conclusion. He had been conducting an energetic campaign on my behalf by whispering into the ears of influential officials. I had been paying my Employment Tax regularly like a good girl. Since it only amounted to 3% of my month's salary and was paid for by the company it seemed a sound idea and I could be seen to be a good citizen.

So we placed an advert in the local paper *The Island Sun* for one week and waited. It's very easy to get an advert in the paper but not so easy to get it taken out. It ran for weeks. Each time I phoned the Editor, a rather vague but dear old chap, he apologized profusely said *"It completely slipped my mind"* and promised me faithfully that it would be removed forthwith. Forthwith, however, never seemed to come. But we did get one applicant.

She was a lovely girl who looked quite hopeful on paper, but sadly the interview was not a success. She would have made a great Receptionist but unfortunately she lacked the necessary typing and book-keeping skills to be of any use as a Secretary. At the very least my husband needed a fast, efficient typist.

When we phoned the Labour Commissioner with the result he appeared to have had a personality transplant. No longer the terse, monosyllabic, unapproachable official he acted as if I was his new best friend. He was chatty, understanding and *"only too delighted"* to give me my Work Permit. Joe had worked a miracle.

It was raining when I went to collect my precious Work Permit. When it rained on Tortola it really rained. The heavens opened and disgorged vast quantities of drummingly powerful water onto the earth below and it could fall from the sky for two days solid. It was relentless.

The previously parched hillsides were running with thick, gravy-brown water, the main street frothed and raced with it, the ghauts (normally powder dry gulleys) were plunging rivers. Since most properties were entirely dependent on cisterns to provide water we really needed this bounty. The flat roofs of the buildings collected the falling rain and channeled it down into the concrete cisterns underneath the houses. There was nothing as deliciously good as the fresh *'sweet'* rainwater in the cistern, straight from the roof.

Some of the homes close to the town centre had the benefit of piped water from the town well. The level and quality of the well water was checked regularly by the doctor. If the level got too low the water became saline and contaminated and the well was switched off until a heavy rainstorm had refilled it.

We were considered very lucky at Slaney because we had the luxury of both forms of water supply. We could take it from the piped well water or draw it up by pump from our communal cisterns. We preferred to use our cistern water as the well water flow was unreliable. Several times I was caught in mid-shower with a head full of frothy shampoo bubbles when the flow abruptly stopped.

Our electricity supply was similarly unreliable. We suffered sudden *'brownouts'* when the power dropped off, or dramatic instant groping blackness when it went altogether. However, both electricity and piped water from the town well were considered great luxuries and still something of a novelty on Tortola and so no-one ever dreamt of complaining.

Islanders preferred not to go to work when it rained and sensibly stayed at home. It was not much fun wading through the streets in almost bare feet with only a light summer dress and an old brolly or a paper bag on your head.

Our maid Blanche, however, was different. When it rained she would use her feminine charms to persuade a male friend to drive her up to our apartment in his car, and I would drive her home again afterwards. Having worked for the previous tenant Blanche was part of the package that came with the apartment. Since I didn't really need help every day we negotiated a twice-weekly deal. But as a result Blanche decided to find herself another job. Reluctant to leave me helpless she offered me the services of her good friend Rosalind.

Rosalind was a delightful, colourful character and totally unreliable. I adored her. She was unsure of her age but looked to be about fifty. Incredibly skinny, no teeth, and spoke very fast and somewhat incoherently when excited, smacking her gums rapidly together. Her black hair was turning a little grey and was plaited into tight, tiny tails wrapped up in a black chiffon scarf. She wore large heavy glasses and blinked shortsightedly through the thick lenses. She had come to Tortola from St. Kitts.

I could see that Rosalind was not everyone's idea of the perfect maid but I took to her immediately. She was so grateful to be employed and considered my wage offer very generous. We were both happy. I warmed to her when I saw her at the sink drying my cutlery with such tender loving care. I overlooked the fact that in her enthusiasm to please me she had unwittingly washed the pile of clothes meant for ironing, and had ironed the pile of clothes meant for washing. An easy mistake to make I thought.

We also had help cleaning the office. Mary was from the island of Montserrat and had been on Tortola for two years. She was cheerful chubby, middle-aged and instantly likeable. When I told her I was writing a letter to my mum she propped her mop against my desk, settled down in the chair opposite, and began to tell me, very confidentially, her life story.

Her father had died before she was born and her mother died when she was eight. She was then brought up by her stepfather's new wife. Stepmothers were *"wicked, wicked, people"* according to Mary. She launched into the story of Snow White and the Seven Dwarfs to illustrate her point, gesticulating with animated passion as the story unfolded. I was absolutely enthralled by the whole performance and felt quite emotionally drained when at last Mary finished and stiffly raised herself to her feet to shuffle off down the corridor with her mop and bucket.

Our friendship was cemented the day I bought her a fresh can of Vim. Her previous one went solid and unshakable with damp (she accidentally dropped it in the toilet). She was so delighted with the present that I dashed out and bought her a shiny new bucket to go with the Vim.

It was good working for my husband in the office. Once pesky Porky had departed the routine became relaxed and enjoyable. I was the company Receptionist, Secretary, Book-keeper and general factotum and sat in the front entrance office. The door was always open and while I worked I watched the world go by outside.

Terry, the insurance agent, slipped quietly in and out of his room at the back, passing me in reception, pausing occasionally for a polite word. For some reason he was deeply concerned about my health. He worried that I might be neglecting my vitamin intake. Vitamins, according to Terry, were absolutely essential to keep body and mind healthy, especially on Tortola. But above all I must never forget to keep my *eye-ron* level high. Keen to oblige, I rushed out and bought twelve huge cans of orange juice, although I don't think this was quite what Terry had intended.

During our first week on island we were told we needed a BVI Driving Licence. We were directed to the Police Station and told to ask the desk sergeant. The Police Station was almost directly opposite the office and was also the town jail and fire station. It was one of the oldest buildings in Road Town and looked as if it would be more comfortable as a desert fort in the Sahara.

The high white washed walls of the yard had two huge double doors opening directly on to the street. These enormous wooden gates were usually left wide open. It would take about fifteen men to push them closed and since the police force only numbered eighteen it would need the whole force plus some volunteers on each occasion.

We walked into the compound and up the stone steps into the small, Charging Room. A policeman was perched on top of the tallest stool I have ever seen. As he peered suspiciously down at us we explained our need for licences, and he asked us whether we had licences from our own country. We nodded. He then asked if we had any money to pay for them, again an affirmative nod. Things were going well.

Next he asked how long we wanted the licences to last. This was our big mistake. The usual Driving Licence was issued for a period of six months, but we decided it would be better to go for the full two years. The policeman shook his head sadly and said that if we wanted two years we would have to go to the Traffic Department. We were lucky, he added helpfully, the Traffic Department was open today, and he directed us down Main Street to the new recreation ground, a quick two minute stroll he assured us cheerfully.

Still unfamiliar with the layout of Road Town we carefully followed the directions, but when we reached the recreation ground all we could see was a small circular bandstand in the centre with two lonely figures leaning against it. The two figures turned out to be policemen, and on the floor of the bandstand was a chalked notice which read *Traffic Department*.

We explained we had been sent to them by the Police Station because we required a two year Driving Licence. They shook their heads. They were unable to help us, they did not have the right forms. In fact as we glanced around we could see that they did not have any forms at all, only the chalked sign and two chairs. They suggested we return to the Police Station, ask for the appropriate forms, bring them back and then the Traffic Department could consider our application. However, they warned us, it was not a forgone conclusion, it was quite possible we might be denied a two year Licence. If that proved to be the case we would have to return to the Police Station a third time and start again from the beginning.

We retraced our steps back down Main Street to the Police Station and tackled the desk sergeant once more. But he insisted that he didn't have the appropriate forms, Traffic Department did. We explained that the Traffic Department in the recreation bandstand was totally, completely and absolutely formless. So our helpful desk sergeant disappeared into the open cell behind him and rummaged about for a good ten minutes searching the pile of papers. He returned insisting that he most certainly didn't have the appropriate forms for a two year Licence and couldn't we just settle for a six month Licence and make life easy?

We were ready to capitulate after such a harrowing morning and agreed instantly. The desk sergeant looked so pleased we wished we had settled for a six month Licence at the beginning. With a flourish he produced a tiny piece of paper which was the appropriate form. In no time we were the proud owners of BVI Driving Licences, valid for six months. It was some weeks before we noticed, hidden in the small print at the bottom of the form, the note *'this form can also be used for any application longer than six months'.*

CHAPTER 9

CREWING FOR KEITH AND SUPPER WITH HENRICO

The Ridge Road of Tortola which extended the whole length of the island from West to East was a narrow mountainous spine. To reach it required an almost vertical drive. A heart-stopping, first gear, corkscrew journey up Joe's Hill behind Road Town went from sea level to 1,500 ft. in less than a mile. Not to be undertaken by the nervous or faint-hearted. But once on the spine the view from the Ridge Road across Road Harbour to the south and the Atlantic to the north was breathtaking, absolutely stunning.

From here you could see some of the other Virgin Islands in the group, scattered like casually tossed emeralds across the sparkling sea below. Most of them were uninhabited, mysterious and inviting. Dead Chest was one, a small bump lying in the shadow of bigger Peter Island where the wreck of *RMS Rhone* lay on the sea bed.

RMS Rhone sank during a hurricane which swept through the islands in October 1867. It was anchored off Peter Island when the hurricane struck. The Captain ordered full steam ahead and tried to ride out the storm. During the lull as the eye passed over them he decided to weigh anchor and head for open sea. Unfortunately the anchor and chain caught and broke away. As the *Rhone* steamed away the hurricane returned and with winds stronger than before forced the doomed ship onto the rocks where she broke in two. Out of 145 passengers and crew on board only twenty-two survived.

Another was Norman Island, named after a buccaneer and believed by some to be the location of the classic novel *Treasure Island*. A great place for underwater cave exploration. There was a local legend that treasure from the Spanish ship *Nuestra Senora* was taken by Tortolians, hidden on Norman Island, and still lay buried there.

Shortly after our arrival on Tortola we had a wonderful opportunity to explore the nautical highlights for ourselves. We were invited out by the illustrious entrepreneur Keith Maddox (the man instrumental in organising the extraordinary sale of 400 British Leyland Buses to Castro's Cuba in 1964). He now owned a garage and car sales company on Tortola and we were guests/novice sailors on his 35ft yacht.

Our first lesson on board was to tell the difference between a yawl and a ketch. The explanation went over my head unfortunately, but I remember it had something to do with the position of the mizzen mast. Keith's boat, I was assured, was a yawl. Next came lessons in furling and unfurling, and steering. To his absolute credit Keith remained patiently calm throughout the whole day with his clumsy landlubber crew.

It was an unforgettable experience and a delightful baptism into the pleasures of sailing. We sailed from the West End of Tortola and took a heading north. We didn't have much wind to help so we meandered gently along using the engine now and again to give us a little boost. Several islands lay scattered around us and we pestered Keith with questions about them all. Thatch Cay and Little Thatch, both uninhabited scrubby knobs, were believed to have been the haunts of the pirate Edward *Blackbeard* Thatch in the early 18th century. No real evidence supported this but the alternative explanation, that they were named after the *Teyer* palm found on the islands, just did not have the same thrilling appeal.

Keith told us that the island of Jost Van Dyke, a small three square mile replica of Tortola, was also named after a pirate, the 17th century Dutchman Joost van Dyk. Again no proof but it was fun to believe he might have hidden out there. There were no cars and no roads on Jost Van Dyke, only footpaths.

Jost Van Dyke's main claim to fame lay in the fact that the designer of the United Stated Capitol, William Thornton, was born here in 1759. William Thornton was quite exceptional. Not only was he an architect but he was also a qualified physician, an inventor (he was appointed the first Superintendent of the US Patent Office) and a talented artist.

The island of Little Jost Van Dyke nestled close beside big brother and this tiny islet was the unlikely birthplace of another famous man in 1773, the founder of the London Medical Society, Dr. John Coakley Lettsom. His father Edward, a Quaker, owned a sugar plantation on Tortola at Cane Garden Bay. Edward fathered seven sets of twin boys but only John and one brother survived. John was sent back to England at the tender age of six to study medicine, returning only briefly to Tortola after the death of his father and brother in 1767. He freed all his slaves before returning to England and beginning his extraordinary medical career. Fifteen years senior to his good friend William Thornton from Jost Van Dyke he was also a close friend of Benjamin Franklin, one of the Founding Fathers of the United States.

They say Dr. Lettsom wrote the following doggerel himself *'I, John Lettsom, blisters, bleeds and sweats em, if, after that, they please to die, I, John Lettsom!'*

We paused for a swim and a bite to eat off Little Jost Van Dyke and anchored the yawl before Tina and I set off in the tiny dinghy for shore. Being unschooled in the art of oarsmanship we found rowing a bit tricky, and to our dismay discovered ourselves inexplicably wedged under the keel of the yawl, with one end of the dinghy rising up at an alarming angle and the other stuck fast beneath Keith's boat. The men had already swum for the shore and it was up to Tina and me to tackle the problem for ourselves. We did eventually escape but had laughed so much we were quite weak from the effort.

So it was with great relief we landed on the sand and accepted the hamburgers, banana cake and coffee offered to us by the two inhabitants of Little Jost Van Dyke, Tony and Jackie Snell. While we sat in the shade of a coconut palm on the beach eating our meal Tony regaled us with unbelievable anecdotes which stretched incredulity to the limit. Did he really escape death from a German firing squad by jumping sideways at the last minute? Probably not we agreed. He was mentioned, he assured us, in a book called *'Escape or Die'* about heroic war stories. Whether truth or fiction Tony was highly entertaining. He explained he couldn't settle after the war and roamed England as a *variety artiste* before finding Little Jost Van Dyke and moving in.

The couple spend their time entertaining passing boats by offering food, music and convivial company. Tony's piano was strangely incongruous beside a palm-fringed beach under a hot cloudless Caribbean sky, but Tony and Jackie gave us a tremendous welcome and sang, played the piano and told jokes in the best music hall tradition.

We were very reluctant to leave this lovely couple but time was getting on and we wanted to do some snorkeling, swimming and sunbathing before turning the yawl round and returning to Tortola. By the time we eventually reached West End it was early evening and we were feeling totally relaxed and very comfortable, also a bit pink, matching the magnificent sunset. Not from too many rum punches but more from exposure to the sun.

We had to race back to our Slaney apartment to get ourselves ready for a dinner engagement, and a rather unusual evening began. Our dinner date was with a gentleman called Henrico Belmonte, the owner of the furniture shop beneath our office. Henrico was a Venezuelan who lived with his mother on St. Thomas, US Virgin Islands. He seldom visited Tortola but usually left the shop in the capable hands of his manager Joe Perera, a small nutmeg of a man with a heart of gold.

Henrico planned to collect us from our apartment and we were to be treated to dinner at his expense. We waited and waited and waited. When Henrico finally arrived it was 9.15 p.m. and our tummies were rumbling audibly. Henrico had dressed with enthusiasm rather than taste and startled us with his uncoordinated attire. Perhaps it was the South American part of his personality that had chosen the sandy suit with Al-Capone lapels, the red and purple shirt, bright blue tie, white shoes and last but by no means least the scarlet socks. It was to say the least quite wild and very dramatic.

Apologising profusely for the lateness of his arrival Henrico prattled cheerfully and volubly. He took us down to the shop first, in order to lock up. Most of the shops in Road Town did not close until late at night when the owners were ready for bed. Since the majority lived on the premises it obviously made sense to remain open for as long as possible. When Henrico returned to the car he had Joe Perera in tow and the four of us set off in search of supper. Henrico had nothing planned and it was now getting very late, so we decided to start at the top of the forage providers and if unsuccessful slowly work our way down the scale to the basic trough fillers.

Our first port of call was Fort Burt, definitely one of the finest eating places in town with the bonus of panoramic sea views. Built on the ruins of a 17th century Dutch Fort it sat high above Main Street on a rocky knoll. Owned by Paulina Stewart, the American DuPont heiress, it was renowned for its lobster dishes and rum punches. Alas however, though not surprisingly, by the time we arrived at 10.15 p.m. service had ceased for the night.

So we left Fort Burt and moved down the street to try the Harbourlights Restaurant. No luck here either. Despite the hour they were quite prepared to feed us, but had little to offer, so Henrico suggested we try the local diner on Main Street. This was a popular West Indian watering hole aptly named *Cell 5*. The entrance was dark and forbidding and by way of several slippery steps. The interior was dimly lit, small and utilitarian. It was deserted. But our arrival was welcomed with great enthusiasm by the owner and he greeted us with warm affection and friendliness.

Henrico seemed more comfortable here, and in the subdued light his clothes did not glow quite so brightly, allowing us a much appreciated visual respite. At long last we managed to order some food which was finally served, with great ceremony, at 11.45 p.m. We took pot luck from the kitchen since there was no menu as such, and ended up with lamb chops, bread rolls, gallons of wine and pints of coffee. Henrico was a great raconteur and chattered away happily. He owned several apartments and a house on St. Thomas, an apartment in Puerto Rico, and a house on Tortola as well as the shop. For some reason which he did not divulge all these premises (except the shop) were currently empty, and he was quite insistent that we should take the opportunity of using them. After a memorable meal and many hugs and handshakes we finally disentangled ourselves from Henrico and strolled home through the deserted town in the early hours of the morning.

70

Getting up for work the following morning was particularly difficult. It was not helped by the fact that when we stumbled downstairs to climb into the landrover we discovered a flat tyre.

My husband struggled with the spare while I watched sympathetically, only to find that the spare was also flat. Punctures are, if not a daily, then certainly a weekly hazard and the spare had been sent for repair and returned, apparently mended, only days earlier. A phone call to Keith and within ten minutes (just enough time to drink a strong black coffee) the cavalry arrived with a replacement. Half an hour later, as we were crawling up the office steps to do battle with the day's work, the garage boys roared up the street to deliver the two punctured tyres duly fixed. Joe stood in the doorway of the furniture shop and he waved, grinning. He looked as if his night on the tiles had left him with no after-effects whatsoever.

Thank goodness for Rosalind. At least I did not have to go home and start the chores as well. She was proving very efficient although strangely accident prone. We would return to the apartment to discover inexplicable mishaps and she was unable to offer any convincing explanation. She simply blinked myopically at me and shook her head as if she didn't fully understand my question.

So we had no answer to the mystery of how the mesh mosquito screens came off their runners, and what could have possibly happened to the curtain rail to leave it broken and hanging down. Rosalind would shrug, and smile brightly and mumble something I could never quite grasp.

Rosalind also suffered from *'bad knees'* and to demonstrate the point she would show them to me at least twice a week. Her knees were usefully blamed for many shortcomings and could always be relied upon to be the reason for something which was not done, or something which, unfortunately, was done. And they were a wonderful excuse for me to give her a *'drop'* into town after an arduous day of duties.

CHAPTER 10

HERBERT 'BABYCHAM' SHOWERING, SINNERS AND SAINTS

My husband was working closely on Tortola with the new owner of the Treasure Isle Hotel. The owner, Herbert 'Babycham' Showering visited the island periodically from his home in Shepton Mallet in Somerset. He was a delightful, charming and candid old country gentleman who seemed to me to be much more at home in the orchards of Somerset than in the world of high finance.

His main claim to fame was as the joint producer, with his brother Francis, of the popular tipple Babycham. He told us of the days of his youth when he and his brother used to gather up the fallen apples from the orchard and then produce cider. Later, using pears, Francis invented the popular bubbly drink Babycham.

The Treasure Isle Hotel was an attractive bougainvillea clad building nestling on the edge of town. It was small, but select, and was one of the nicest hotels on the island. The restaurant and bar were on a covered terrace beside a tiny toddler and plunge pool. It was friendly, comfortable, relaxed, and very popular with expats.

When the vast dredging and reclamation work in Road Harbour began a few years ago no-one anticipated that it might have an adverse effect on the shoreline lower down the coast. But Herbie Showering believed the dredging work was directly responsible for silting up the hotel water frontage and brought a court action. When the hearing began my husband went along to the Court House with lawyer Joe Archibald in case he was required as an 'expert witness' on behalf of the Treasure Isle Hotel. He had spent several happy hours in his swim trunks plumbing the depths in front of the hotel and charting the shallows for Herbie Showering.

The court was a single storey concrete box with red wooden shutters in place of windows and a heavy wooden door which opened from the court room directly on to the street outside. Overhead fans grumbled and clicked away on hot days. Whenever the court was in session the road would be blocked off and the traffic stopped because the Judge could not hear what anyone was saying over the noise of the occasional passing car.

Since Tortola did not have its own Judge the island had to borrow one, usually from Antigua. The Judge sat on a small raised platform at one end of the room. The lawyers faced him, adorned in their full legal regalia. Hot and pompous the show could go on for hours. The Judge himself laboriously took down verbatim all that was said. He would write slowly, carefully, with many requests for repetition.

Poor Joe Archibald was running with perspiration and his cropped tropical wig kept slipping over his head and resting on the top of his glasses. At appropriate intervals, while the Judge was writing, Joe would lift his thatch and mop his steaming pate with a white hankie, before returning his wig back onto his head. In court Joe was a flamboyant character and obviously enjoyed the thrill and drama of the court room. He gave a masterful performance but after two hours he was visibly wilting. As a mere spectator even my husband was ready to quit.

Herbie Showering had to wait several weeks before the judgment. The Judge read his notes most carefully, pondered at length, and gave his final decision from the safety of Antigua. When the verdict came it ruled in favour of Herbie Showering and he was jubilant, crediting particularly Joe but also my husband for his success.

Around this time a group of Revivalists from the US landed on Tortola for a weekend of gospel singing and heavenly praise. They pitched a huge tent on the flat ground behind our office and it was quite wonderful and uplifting to hear to the powerful voices of big burly West Indians belting out gospel. The hymns were fabulously stirring and the voices terrific. Crowds poured in to the tent for the meetings. Stickers appeared on local cars with pithy religious messages. My personal favourite was *'If Your God Is Dead Try Mine, He's Alive, I Spoke To Him This Morning!'*

While the gospel singers pounded out their praise to the rear of the office, out in front on Main Street there was a wedding in progress. Diagonally opposite the front of our office, beside the Police Station and Jail, was St. George's Church. It was an Anglican Church transferred from the diocese of Antigua to the American Episcopal diocese of the Virgin Islands in 1963. The walls were old and white-washed and the roof was corrugated iron painted red. A small garden bright with yellow hibiscus and pink bougainvillea was sandwiched between the building and the narrow Main Street. Worshippers walked the short path to the front steps of the Church and up through the red wooden doors.

The four bridesmaids, wearing long dresses of brilliant green, waited on the Church steps to welcome the bride as she arrived and two men in startlingly white suits solemnly followed the bride up the path.

According to Mary, who loved a wedding and had abandoned her cleaning duties in order to watch, these were the *Father Givers*. All the neighbours and well-wishers who had not managed to cram into the church lined the street for a glimpse of the proceedings. The service lasted about an hour and finished as dusk fell.

After the church ceremony tradition dictated that the newly married couple 'process' round the town, displayed for all to see, perched on the back of an open car, feet on the rear seats, with the bride's long train billowing out behind. The father givers were in the second car and the bridesmaids in the third. The cars snaked slowly through the streets of Road Town gathering more and more cars in the convoy to the accompaniment of horns hooting, banners waving, and lights flashing. The whole town joined in the celebration.

CHAPTER 11

SAILING ROUND TORTOLA AND WAVING TO ONASSIS

As expatriates we were called 'non-belongers'. Most of the expats were from the UK and helped to shore up the professional community of the British Virgin Islands. They were architects, accountants, bankers, teachers, lawyers, and at present all the senior Government officials needed to supervise the Island's administration.

These included Her Britannic Majesty's representative the Administrator, the Financial Secretary, the Attorney General, the Chief Medical Officer, the Chief Engineer, and so the list went on. Many expat residents in the BVI arrived on contract, liked what they saw, and decided to stay.

Some people simply passed through, stayed for a few weeks and then returned the following year, or the year after. Middle-aged men, young couples, boozy bachelors and 'independent ladies' made up a cross section of the community on Tortola and combined together to produce an eclectic potpourri of characters.

There was Dick, the Yorkshire electrician. We met him when he came to the apartment to fix our hot water. He had arrived in the BVI after thirty years with British Rail in England, and he fully intended to stay forever.

Our close friends and neighbours at Slaney, Pat and Bob with baby Simone, came from South London to manage the Ready Mix Plant on Tortola. They had bought a small plot of land and had begun to build their own house.

Terry and Pam, recently married, were working with construction company Wimpey on a contract which they intended to extend indefinitely, if at all possible!

Then there were people like Porky. The ones we suspected of enjoying a perks-paid winter sunshine booze-up while pretending to acquire business for their company. They were employees who had been banished from Britain for a few weeks so that the UK office could enjoy a bit of peace and quiet. They were viewed with deep suspicion and a certain amount of distaste. Porky, for instance, spent his time spinning in a social whirl, drinking too much, being entertained by dubious ladies, and dashing up and down the islands on the Company expense account. He called it *'company promotion'*.

When Porky arrived on Tortola on his annual *'company promotion'* tours he caused chaos. Porky continued to be a thorn in my flesh. No matter how hard I tried I simply could not like the man. He began, you may remember, by selling my washing machine and dragging us into the office at 8.30 a.m. the day after our arrival. From then on our relationship with him had deteriorated rapidly and was only bearable because while he was with us he would fly off on *'company promotion'* to visit exotic places like Mustique, Dominica, St. Lucia and Nassau.

Sometimes he would sit sullenly silent for several hours in moody contemplation refusing to talk, sometimes he would jabber and giggle uncontrollably (especially after a visit to the Sir Francis Drake Pub). He was an inveterate giggler after a few drinks and it became very irritating. But his worst habit was his compulsive midnight feasting. We would wake in the early hours to hear him crashing around in the kitchen, raiding the fridge and leaving a trail of disaster behind him, so that when I got up to make breakfast I was confronted with a work surface littered with bread, butter, orange juice, cheese bits, and escaped pickle pieces. Thanks to Porky we had the best fed ants and cockroaches on the block.

He took to playing tennis at 6.00 a.m. on the courts below the apartments. His partner an eleven year old child on holiday from her UK boarding school. She invariably beat him, nimbly smacking home her shots while poor Porky bounced breathlessly backwards and forwards. Tennis was quite obviously not Porky's sport, but the 'plop' 'plop' 'plop' of tennis balls at 6.00 a.m. incensed our neighbours who preferred to sleep at that time of the morning. Fortunately for my sanity Porky's visits were infrequent and most of the time he was a safe distance away at Head Office in the UK.

As well as business bums like Porky, we had our fair share of drifters. Free spirited nomads chasing dreams, sliding through on boats and stopping off at Tortola for a few days or a few months as they sailed around the Caribbean.

One such sea gypsy became a great friend. Ben had tousled blonde hair self-cropped and uncontrolled, wore a torn and messy red T-shirt with ripped and blackened shorts, and loped through town barefoot with a cheery grin on his face, all the while exuding an appealing boyish charm.

Ben came from a privileged background and his family in England were both irritated and frustrated by his unconventional attitude to life. He was an enigma, a 'Swinging Sixties' Peter Pan who didn't want to grow up. He had unplumbed depths and was really not as non-conformist as he would have the world believe. He built his own small boat and set sail from England and having successfully crossed the Atlantic single-handed he washed up on the shores of Tortola three years ago and had remained.

After much agonizing Ben had finally decided to sell his precious boat and move on with his life. He invited us to join him on a final sail around the island on Good Friday, an appropriate way to spend Easter and a fitting farewell to his beloved boat. He would sail her off to Miami the week after Easter to deliver her to the new owner.

The master plan in Ben's mind was a day sail, starting at sunrise from Soper's Hole and returning at sunset having sailed right round Tortola. The plan sounded good to us landlubbers and we were more than happy to deliver ourselves into Ben's capable hands, especially since he had promised on-board refreshments at suitable intervals during the day.

We arrived slightly bleary at 8.00 a.m. not quite sunrise but as early as we could manage. We left West End in perfect weather and in what Ben described as ideal sailing conditions. We intended to work our way down the Sir Francis Drake Channel keeping Tortola to our left and the scattered islands to our right. With a lot of luck we expected to be somewhere off Beef Island by lunch time so that we could streak back to West End following the North shore to arrive at sunset. An ambitious and bold plan.

We took off at a spanking pace and were soon passing Nanny Cay, a small and calm bay useful for overnight anchorage. Then past uninhabited Norman Island on our right with Peter Island alongside.

There were impressive schemes in the wind for Peter Island. An enterprising group of Norwegians planned to build a select holiday haven for discerning and wealthy vacationers. During the construction phase of the complex ordinary mortals like ourselves were encouraged to call, eat and admire, and a small boat was laid on by Peter Island to ferry us across from Road Harbour as and when required. But on this day we sped past, tacked and shot off on a heading to Brandy Wine Bay. We tacked only four times along the length of the south side and skimmed the surface of the sea at an excitingly acute angle.

Occasionally the water lapped the deck and if the boat had been in the hands of anyone less capable than Ben I would have been extremely anxious. It was during one of those dramatic moments when sailors jibe and dash from one side of the boat to the other that Ben decided to tell us about the time he and his boat turned turtle in the Bay of Biscay. He was, he says, asleep and strapped into his bunk at the time and fortunately the hatch was closed. The boat did the only sensible thing and turned herself upright again without any help from her Captain. But it was, said Ben, a very hairy experience to wake and discover himself apparently hanging from the ceiling.

We arrived off Beef Island and anchored temporarily at Marina Cay at about 3.00 p.m. And as the boat bobbed gently up and down, Ben set about supplying some sustenance for his ravenous crew, while my husband and I slipped overboard for a refreshing dip in the sea.

Ben decided to offer us spaghetti since, as he pointed out, it was fairly simple to prepare and was something of a specialty of his. We watched in admiration as he rinsed the cooked spaghetti in the sea over the side of the boat, and marvelled as he deftly tossed diced spam into a glue of indeterminate origin, and congratulated him on the final touch as he carefully ladled Parmesan onto the mountain peak heaped on the groaning plastic plates. Then we ate. The sea rinse had made extra salt unnecessary and added a special sort of flavour to the whole intriguing meal. To round off this mammoth feast Ben opened a can of sliced peaches and sprinkled the top liberally with dried milk. An unusual dessert born of expediency and all, he boasted with pride, his own invention.

While we ate Ben told us a little about the history of tiny, six acre, Marina Cay sleeping in the sun beside us. Apparently the author Robb White had brought his bride here some years ago and set about describing their trials and tribulations in a book he called *'Our Virgin Island'*. It was later made into a film starring Sidney Poitier and John Cassavetes. Today there was a small but very popular restaurant offering meals to passing yachtsmen, or to landlubbers prepared to hop across the narrow stretch of water between Beef Island and the Cay in the restaurant's little dinghy.

Replete and feeling satisfyingly stuffed we set off again, this time to cruise back along the North shore. We saw one or two small yachts gently enjoying a Good Friday breeze like ourselves, and then as we passed the uninhabited island of Little Camanoe, we saw a very large and impressive boat. An unusual sight for Tortola and implying ownership by someone used to ostentatious opulence, so it came as no surprise when Ben, who recognized it immediately, told us it was Onassis' yacht.

We waved as we swept alongside and from the deck someone waved back. Was it Onassis? We did not know but we liked to think so. But it wasn't his lovely wife, the famous Jackie Kennedy, she was probably sleeping off the effects of lunchtime caviar and champagne we decided.

It may have been our preoccupation with Onassis and his boat that caused a lapse in concentration, but my husband, who was in charge of the rudder, suddenly noticed that the clear crystal water below the boat held attractive and fascinating chunks of coral. He mentioned the fact quite casually and seemed happily unconcerned that we had somehow strayed onto a coral reef and were in imminent danger of grinding the boat's belly into driftwood. Ben leapt into action and expertly steered us clear with only six inches of draft to spare.

To me and my husband our unexpected slide across the reef was a bonus and gave us a chance to see the wonders and magnificence of that magic underwater world. We could see the reef fish very clearly as we peered over the side of the boat, they seemed so close I felt I could cup my hand and scoop them aboard.

We asked Ben if he had ever had any nasty experiences swimming amongst the fish on the reef and he launched into a graphic description of his close encounter with a shark.

It seemed he had been anchored off a reef some distance from shore, diving and spear fishing from his boat. His spear had got lodged between two coral outcrops and was stuck fast. Ben free-dived down to almost thirty-five feet in an attempt to free it but had to return to the surface three times after unsuccessful attempts.

On his fourth dive down he came face to face with a shark, literally eyeball to eyeball, and his instinctive reaction was to give it a hefty wallop on the nose. Fortunately for Ben the astonished shark shot off. Ben strongly believes that sharks and barracuda are simply curious and do not attack unless the swimmer panics. It was your fear, maintained Ben, which attracted their attention.

Barracuda look sinister with their long, lean silver torpedo bodies. They have a habit of swimming with their mouths open displaying a nasty set of teeth, and they hang in the water in a very menacing fashion. Barracuda are attracted by sparkling objects. The only attack Ben could recall had happened when a trapped barracuda, thrashing about in a small lagoon of sea water, had snapped at a ringed finger which was poked into his pool.

We continued our circuit of Tortola and goose-winged sedately past the small island of Guana admiring the deserted palm fringed beach with its virgin white sand. A solid looking square stone house was perched high on a hill overlooking the beach and we could see a tennis court beyond the palms. Apart from that it looked uninhabited. The house was built sometime during the 18th century by Quakers who settled on the island hoping to create a sugar farming community.

Ben explained that Guana now belonged to Louis and Beth Bigelow, a couple who offered member-only holidays to an exclusive selection of moneyed Americans. Laughing, Ben told us a story about Queen Elizabeth the Queen Mother who had once visited the Virgin Islands and had been invited to lunch on Guana. She royally accepted and the Bigelows were keen to offer her a pleasant, interesting and enjoyable visit. To this end, and knowing of the Queen Mother's love for shells, they scattered the beach with some extra shells from their personal collection, hoping to delight Her Majesty. However, when the Queen Mother arrived and strolled the sand, the shell she unearthed was not West Indian but had in fact originated in the Pacific and the knowledgeable Queen Mother instantly recognized it as such, to the embarrassment of the owners but the amusement of Her Majesty.

As the afternoon stretched into evening we passed some of the remote and inaccessible north shore bays on Tortola and yearned to pull in to explore further. Josiah's Bay, where the breakers were strong and the current dangerous. Then on past Brewer's Bay, very difficult to get to by road with a frightening roller coaster drive ending with a nose dive into the sea for the unwary. Cane Garden Bay followed, a beautiful long stretch of beach very popular locally with a small beach restaurant and mature palms ringing the bay. Then came Carrot Bay, Little Apple Bay, Long Bay and Smuggler's Cove, evocative names from the island's history. And as the sun set with breathtaking scarlet beauty over the sea, we came in sight of West End. Behind us the full moon was rising up over the ridge of Tortola, and in the velvet of the dark under the eye of the moon we slipped quietly into our berth.

It was the perfect ending to a perfect day.

CHAPTER 12

SIR ALAN COBHAM, ALAN WHICKER, AND BUILDING BOOM

The same weekend on Easter Sunday we were invited to an American-style brunch by Sally Bell, a delightful Bostonian lady who came to Tortola for the winter. One of the 'snowbirds' escaping to the Caribbean for some warmth and sunshine while Boston shivered under snow.

Sally lived in a unique and truly stunning house at Maya Cove set on the hillside overlooking the bay. It was designed by architect Mike Helm who was gaining a reputation on island for original and extraordinary house designs. In order to maximise the natural air-conditioning breeze which blew across the site Mike had designed a tower for the two bedrooms leaving an open patio between these and the rest of the rooms, which were arranged under three domed roofs.

One of the shower rooms was open to the elements and as someone pointed out, a lucky low-flying plane taking off from Beef Island would get a grandstand view of Sally performing her ablutions. Sally said she had carefully studied the LIAT timetable and had no intention of being caught out.

It was a very select party with about fifty guests. We arrived at 11.30 a.m. to discover that we were by far the youngest couple invited, with most of the 'brunchers' being retired. Rich 'snowbirds' who had holiday homes on Tortola. Usually these island residents kept themselves to themselves, rationing their public appearances and only emerging onto the social scene for Government House functions or special occasions. Sally's Brunch was considered one such special occasion.

Among the guests was Sir Alan Cobham. Now 76 Sir Alan was a hero from my father's youth and dad never tired of telling me stories of the daring exploits of this amazing pilot. He was an extraordinary man, an aviation 'pioneer' with a dare-devil streak that saw him take amazing risks. After WW1 he became a test pilot, but his wild adventurous spirit wanted something more exciting. He made history when he began flying long distances, London to Cape Town and back then London to Melbourne, Australia and back. If there was a flying challenge then Sir Alan embraced it with reckless enthusiasm.

In 1932 Sir Alan started his own 'Cobham's Flying Circus' and toured England entertaining the crowds with some terrifying stunts. My dad was an enthusiastic photographer and had captured on old 16mm film Sir Alan's aerial acrobatics from the 1930's, and each Christmas we were obliged to sit and view the yellowing, blinking reels to marvel yet again at the skill of this remarkable aviator as he flew his little plane down, down, down, to pick up by the wing a white handkerchief placed on the ground.

We were introduced to Sir Alan's companion and took an instant liking to her. She was the only other person at the gathering young enough to wear a mini-skirt. She was a wild, blunt and thoroughly down to earth Welsh girl called Bronwyn. There was, it has to be said, an age difference of about fifty years between Sir Alan and Bronwyn. Her job, she explained, was to keep Sir Alan 'company' and make sure he stayed out of trouble. She confided Sir Alan was a compulsive bottom-pincher and warned me never to turn my back on him. Good advice, unfortunately forgotten when saucy Sir Alan and I chatted later.

Sally's house was one of several new homes on Tortola. There had been a flurry of construction over the last few months inspired by the reclamation in progress on Wickhams Cay.

Down to earth no nonsense Bob Gray was one of the first to recognize the building boom potential of the British Virgin Islands, and he arrived on Tortola from Bermuda to start the Ready Mix Plant and a construction company.

One of his first projects was building the Slaney apartments and he lived in the block. Slaney was still unfinished and there was still much to be done by way of improvement to the site, but whenever Bob found he had a slack period, he roared into action on the home front. He had just replaced the cinder track to Slaney with a ribbon of concrete, and placed a cattle grid across the entrance to deter the roaming cows and goats. He promised us a swimming pool which (according to the grapevine) he intended to donate to the town. The noisy JCB had begun to scratch and burrow a hole beside the tennis courts below. It felt like a minor earthquake each time the bucket banged on to the hard, unforgiving ground.

Bob decided to beautify the area by planting small but vigorous coconut palms beside his new strip of road. A complete waste of effort for when I looked out of the window I saw a large and contented cow had managed to negotiate the trap of the cattle grid and had nonchalantly munched the last green sprout of the last green palm. Bob, not renowned for having a placid temperament, was absolutely livid. Born in the East End of London, with Irish ancestry, Bob had retained from his roots a colourful and forceful vocabulary capable of stripping paint, and he was not shy in using it, at full volume, if he considered the occasion demanded.

Any problems with our apartment and Bob would organize the remedial work. Our hot water cylinder decided to flood the kitchen shortly after it was repaired and Bob came in to inspect the damage. It was Sunday and he was on his way to Church. His grey hair was freshly cropped in a scalp tingling brush-cut and he was looking extremely smart in a new suit, white socks and black shoes. Seeing our amazed expressions he gruffly informed us that he was to be Godfather to someone's new baby and had needed to *"dress-up"* for the occasion. Squelching around in our kitchen had not been on his morning itinerary.

More construction was taking place on the hill behind the Treasure Isle Hotel where the Showering family were building some new condominiums. Herbie Showering asked my husband to design and supervise the building of a concrete road up through the estate to the new property, so we went to have a look round.

The condominiums were exquisite. Beautifully furnished inside with a truly luxurious feeling. They were very desirable and definitely the most exclusive and sumptuous apartments on the island. Everything was included, down to the last ash tray, and the

84

most attractive feature as far as we were concerned was the air-conditioning unit. I drooled with desire each time I thought of those palaces on the hill.

Herbie Showering also asked my husband to design and supervise the building of a jetty in the shallows in front of the Treasure Isle Hotel. He intended to use the jetty as a mooring area for the hotel's small launch and the sunfish which were available for guest use.

The pub I mentioned earlier, the Sir Francis Drake, was on the waterfront between our Slaney apartments and Road Town. It was a popular rendezvous for expats experiencing English Pub withdrawal symptoms. But it was hardly very English, with stroll-through arches open to the weather and Budweiser canned beer the standard swill, but it did offer fantastic Friday night *'all you can eat curry'* and a darts board.

Even the ladies had a darts team and I was cordially invited to join the *English Virgins*. We took our darts matches very seriously and the *English Virgins* were fearsome and had been doing remarkably well against the men. Employing tactical cunning we would wait until very late before starting our matches, thus allowing plenty of time for the male teams to over indulge their beer, giving us an obvious advantage over our inebriated rivals.

One Friday night we went down for our usual darts game to discover

Alan Whicker, the British journalist and TV presenter and his team of intrepid reporters tucking into a curry. They had arrived to film a documentary to be called *The British West Indies*. They intended to interview a representative cross section of expat Brits asking *"Why are you attracted to Tortola?"* and *"What do you think of the island?"*

They seemed to be hoping for genuine comment and spent much of their time at the Pub chatting to us all and winkling out potential contributors. They were to spend two weeks on Tortola before returning to the UK to cobble together a Whicker's World special about the island. It was difficult to find anyone coherent enough to express an opinion. When Alan Whicker approached Bronwyn and asked *"What do you think?"* she blew an enormous raspberry, which, as Mr. Whicker was quick to point out, was not

85

the sort of critical comment he could allow to appear on the program.

Although we did not have television we did have radio and could pick up the American stations from the US Virgin Islands and ZBVI, our very own local station which transmitted from a tiny pink concrete bunker beside the harbour in Road Town.

I usually listened to the American stations and generally only when they were broadcasting the BBC World Service. On a good day I could catch one word out of ten and managed to make some sense of most of the information coming across. The crackle and pops between audible words had a kind of music and were entertaining in themselves. It was quite irritating though, to find that the reception suddenly improved immediately the sports results came on air. We then had fifteen crystal clear minutes of *"Partik Thistle 1 Tranmear Rovers 2"*etc.

The American radio stations were a source of great, if unwitting, entertainment to me. Shortly before American Mother's Day the station was urging listeners to buy Mother a magnificent present, and the more magnificent the better. One recommendation ran *"Buy your mom a super present she'll never forget - get her a Toyota with one year's free maintenance, she'll love you forever."* I bet she would! Then there was this one *"Get your mom a fabulous transistor radio so she can keep up with all the latest records - so handy she can walk round the shops with it in her hand so she doesn't miss anything!"* No feeble flowers or pitiful chocolates for these indulged 'moms'.

I quickly became hooked on a fifteen minute radio soap that ZBVI broadcasted at 2.15 p.m. each day. It was called *'Portia Faces Life'*. Truth be told it was a slushy, painful, love story in the most awful bad taste but I found it made compelling listening. Poor Portia had been having a bad time of it recently and her sighs of anguish had almost reduced me to tears. Genial Bermudian Leo Mills, who ran ZBVI, took me into his little pink studio one day and showed me the huge records which arrived weekly containing the episodes. One episode per side. He could put it on the turntable and slip out for a late lunch while it played.

CHAPTER 13

FIRST TASTE OF ST THOMAS

My husband's salary was sent out from Head Office in England monthly in Sterling, and since the official currency in the BVI was the US dollar, he had to exchange his salary and in effect *buy* dollars each month. Of course the bank took a little commission on each transaction and as the dollar rate varied each time we converted, we never quite knew how much he was going to earn. Fortunately it only fluctuated a little but, as the investment advertisements say, *"it can go down and well as up"* and to our dismay occasionally it did.

Income tax was charged at 12.5% on money earned over and above $7,000. There was no reciprocal tax arrangement between UK and BVI and any money earned on island could be taken back to the UK as savings and was exempt from UK tax.

Our predecessor never paid any tax while he was in the BVI, and when he climbed on the plane to leave the island he must have thought that he had avoided payment. However the officials had been 'informed' about his departure and were waiting at the airport. They hauled him off the plane and refused to let him re-board until he had paid his outstanding Income Tax. Fortunately he had sufficient funds in ready cash to pay his debt and after a humiliating scene he was finally allowed back on board. Since we did not wish to be subjected to a similar indignity, we were being very honest with the tax authorities and paid our fiscal obligations promptly.

Our free-wheeling sailor friend Ben confided to me that he had been on Tortola for three years, started two different companies and was working as the official representative of a third but he had never had a work permit. He said that with a Bond lodged at the bank it was quite legal to stay for six months and when the first Entry Visa expired, he renewed it by hopping off the island for a day and coming back in. Provided you had a Bond all you were required to do was renew the Entry Visa every six months by taking a quick break over to St. Thomas. It was a loophole in the system. I asked Ben what would happen if he was discovered working without a permit and he shrugged, his answer was a cheerful *"everyone else does it!"*

We had heard so much about St. Thomas USVI that we decided to extend our horizons and see for ourselves this exciting, wild and exhilarating island. We went over for a couple of days to sample for ourselves the exotic pleasures and duty free bargains of the place.

We returned to the tranquility of Tortola in a state of exhaustion after a weekend of manic activity. The capital Charlotte Amalie was everything that was promised and some more.

For the journey between the two islands we chose the new, aptly named, *'Bomba Charger'* ferry from West End. It was a super, luxury, 65ft launch with two massive and energetic engines. The manufacturer in Louisiana said she was capable of speeds up to 32 knots and she certainly took off from West End Tortola like a bat out of hell. We shot into a crowded Charlotte Amalie in St Thomas harbour in just 45 minutes and discovered we had landed in an alien world.

Huge cruise ships tethered to the waterfront disgorged hundreds of passengers hungry for the duty free shops. All passengers appeared in the uniform of the American tourist, regulation Bermuda shorts (or knee length baggies as we preferred to call them), long white socks, spongy sneakers, little white sun hats, and of course all strapped with the fashion accessory compulsory camera. This uniform made it very easy for the vulture vendors to spot the tourist quarry and we were relieved not be so easily identifiable.

Bodies bustled and pushed along the crowded streets. The pace was fast and frantic. Cars, hundreds of them it seemed to us, raced along the waterfront with hands permanently on horns. We stood dazed and amazed feeling very much the country bumpkins.

The downtown area was a buzz of duty free shops in converted Dutch warehouses off narrow alleys. To our surprise most of the buildings were built with brick. The result, we were told, of bricks being used as ballast in the trading ships from Europe as they sailed across empty to collect the cotton, sugar, spices and other exports of the 18th century.

While Tortola had remained a small agricultural community, St. Thomas had turned to trading and the sea. And now it was a tourist hot-spot and thriving. We were intending to stay for three nights but in the event managed just two before we ran out of strength, money and enthusiasm. We were positively afraid to stay any longer in case we ran ourselves into debt. The temptation of the duty frees was more than we could resist. The greatest bait for us turned out to be jewelry, cameras and hi-fi equipment. The bargains were abundant and the traders happy to barter. And the culinary delights in every street and alley restaurant just too delicious to refuse.

In the evening we treated ourselves to expensive candlelit dinners and during the day stuffed our tums with waffles and syrup for breakfast and beefburgers for lunch. My husband bought himself a movie camera. I bought myself a Longines watch (having successfully convinced myself it was a good investment) new clothes, new shoes, new handbag, and new perfume. It was about the time that I bought the perfume we decided retreat was the better part of valour, and we should return as quickly as possible to peaceful temptation-less Tortola.

There were eighty-eight passengers crammed into the *'Bomba Charger'* on her return trip, and we were the only white couple. Hundreds of boxes and bags overflowing with food were squashed into every available space. We had been so busy trawling the duty free shops that we hadn't thought to buy food, but it was the main reason most people travelled back and forth between Tortola and St. Thomas. There was such a wonderful variety of fresh food and all at very reasonable prices.

When we landed at West End pandemonium broke out. We tried to disembark with dignity, but the rampaging Tortolians swept us aside. They knew that only one Customs Official was on duty and unless they could get through with speed they would be there for hours. The first day of the sales had nothing on this.

The noise was unbelievable, and as we spilled out onto the dock the harassed Customs Official was literally engulfed by a shouting, waving, pushing sea of hot and tired Tortolians who wanted to pass through and go home. Our two white faces were growing ever whiter amid this human flood, and we were spotted by the Official. As we were swept up to him by the jostling crowd he leaned forward and quickly chalked a white cross on my husband's suitcase. We were through, we were home, exhausted but triumphant.

CHAPTER 14

JOST VAN DYKE, CHASE MANHATTAN BANK AND BREWER'S BAY

Sometimes my husband needed extra help surveying or note-taking in the field and he took me along with him. On one memorable occasion we went on a 'site visit' to the little island of Jost Van Dyke. The trip was to make a final check on a bridge which my husband had designed and supervised.

'Bridge' was perhaps a rather grand description for the little structure which spanned the dry sandy ghaut. As there were no roads on Jost Van Dyke the bridge simply enabled donkeys to cross from one sandy patch to the other with greater ease, and without the possible indignity of falling into the ghaut.

We were collected from West End on Tortola by a delightful lad called Butch, who was using his father's speedboat to ferry us across the short stretch of water between Tortola and Jost Van Dyke. Butch was still at school and welcomed this unexpected opportunity to truant. He celebrated by driving the tiny, pitching speedboat at full throttle with exhilarating and nerve-jangling enthusiasm.

My legs were wobbly and refused to function normally when we landed, and I vainly tried to peel my plastered hair from across my face as I was formally introduced to the man who had commissioned the bridge. He must have been reasonably impressed with the work because he generously offered to sell my husband three-quarters of an acre of his twenty-five acre holding.

My husband also found himself involved in the building of Chase Manhattan Bank, one of the first structures on the flat plate of Wickhams Cay. Wimpey won the contract to build the bank, and because the reclaimed land was compacted sand, piles were needed to support the impressive structure.

As the supervising engineer my husband watched aghast as, with one delicate tap of the hammer head, the first forty feet long steel section pile went through the sand *"Like a knife through butter"*. The next pile did exactly the same. It was such an extraordinary sight my husband filmed it with his new movie camera, otherwise, he said *"No-one would believe me!"*

A special welder was flown out from the UK and he proceeded to weld another forty feet of pile onto the top of the submerged one buried in the Wickhams Cay sand. This time the hammer head gently tapped the second section down, down, down, to rest on the coral almost eighty feet beneath the reclaimed land.

In a particularly inaccessible part of the island, over the ridge and down into Brewers Bay, an American had bought a large plot of land. The area was rugged, beautiful, quite remote and extremely difficult to reach. But the American wanted a house built. He returned to his home in the US leaving the Brewer's Bay construction in the hands of a local group of very eager but somewhat inexperienced workers, and appointed my husband to oversee the progress of his secluded and isolated eagle's nest.

The boys who formed the construction team were enthusiastic, willing and very keen to learn. They were a happy group, with a lot of natural talent but little training or understanding of the principles of building. This meant my husband had to supervise very closely, advising frequently and teaching constantly. My husband liked them a great deal and it soon became his favorite site and he looked forward to his weekly visits with real pleasure.

Although the site was only about two miles away from our office the journey to get there was punishing. By the time the landrover had chugged up Joe's Hill, rattled and bounced along the rough ridge road, and then jerked and slithered in teeth clattering, bone cracking fashion down into Brewer's Bay, my husband felt as if he had been violently dismembered and then casually reassembled incorrectly.

However the expedition was always well worthwhile. During the previous week the boys would have encountered building problems which would have puzzled them, and after much careful thought they would have produced an ingenious, novel and quite surprising solution.

Initially it was hard for them to understand that sand taken from the convenient beach below the site was unsuitable for building, likewise the stones needed as aggregate, and even harder to appreciate that salt water from the sea was entirely unsuitable for mixing concrete. When such bounty was quite literally *'on the doorstep'* it was difficult to appreciate the need to struggle with *'sweet water'* in oil drums down a perilous hillside.

But the boys also had their own impressive and unusual skills they passed on to my husband. When the site was first cleared they uncovered a huge boulder set firmly in the middle of the planned property. The boys gathered up the rough bush they had already cleared and heaped it on and around the massive stone and set fire to it. For many hours they kept the fire stoked, while the rock got hotter and hotter. In the meantime the boys collected sea water in every container that came to hand, buckets, bins, and cans, and when the foreman deemed it right, they threw all the water they had over the rock as fast as they could. The sudden drenching of hot rock with the cold water cooled the boulder rapidly, it contracted and split into several managcable pieces. My husband was impressed. Without any mechanical means the boys had successfully removed a major obstacle.

Very occasionally the boys' unorthodox solution to a problem proved unacceptable. They had been waiting for my husband to approve their formwork before pouring the first wet concrete for the walls of the cistern and were extremely pleased with themselves and proud of their handiwork. They were confident that my husband would be, if not delighted, quite satisfied with their work. But in their efforts to keep the formwork rigid the boys had taken a piece of planking and hammered one end to the formwork and the other end to a handy young and somewhat willowy palm tree. To their credit the boys could quite see, when it was pointed out to them, that a swaying palm would do nothing to ensure the rigidity of the formwork.

CHAPTER 15

QUEEN'S BIRTHDAY AND SMUGGLER'S COVE

With the onset of summer the weather warmed and to cool off we oscillated between the air-conditioning of my husband's office and the beach.

The construction of our new swimming pool at Slaney was well under way but sadly not yet completed. A convoy of Readymix trucks banged, clattered and slurped deliveries of concrete from early morning until late at night, and Bob Gray could be heard bellowing instructions to his men.

On the first Saturday in June the BVI always celebrated Her Majesty Queen Elizabeth's Official Birthday. This was an annual celebration not only in London but in all British Protectorates and Territories around the world. It was the most official of the numerous public holidays enjoyed on Tortola and was an occasion of pageantry and ceremony.

The routine never differed. The morning always began with a parade on the new recreation ground and an inspection of uniformed groups of Brownies, Guides, Police, etc. by the Administrator.

During our first year, along with the rest of the island, we went into Road Town to watch. The Administrator was resplendent in his plumed pith helmet, white suit and ceremonial symbols of office. We had been told the official designation of 'Administrator' was soon to be changed and we would be required to refer to Derek Cudmore, the current Queen's representative on island, as *'His Excellency the Governor'*.

After the inspection came the ceremonial 21 gun salute by the police, all nineteen of them, immaculate in their white pith helmets, white jackets, and dark blue trousers with white-ribboned seam.

We had been told that at this point last year there was an embarrassing incident. As the rifles were solemnly lowered after the uniformed police had performed the traditional salute, another shot rang out. A ripple of panic ran through the watching crowd, word spread someone had been shot. Consternation and confusion followed until it was discovered that an unlucky policeman had accidently squeezed the trigger as he dropped his rifle to his side. Fortunately no harm was done.

The salute was followed the raising of the Union Jack flag while the British National Anthem 'God Save the Queen' was being played by the police band. We watched as the Union Jack rose slowly up the pole and was unfurled, and saw with dismay that it had been accidentally raised upside down, normally seen as an indication of a death or distress.

Most watchers were unaware that there was a wrong way to hang the flag, but the Chief of Police saw it. Taking command of the situation he quickly leapt forward and stopped the ceremony, and while the onlookers gazed in puzzlement, or smiled, or shuffled with embarrassment, or exchanged polite words, depending on our point of view, he managed to haul the flag down and re-arrange it so that the wide white diagonal hung, as it should, from the top of the flagpole. The ceremony was then allowed to continue.

The Union Jack had caused problems in previous years too. On one memorable occasion it stubbornly refused to unfurl. The honour of pulling the rope to unfurl the flag is a jealously sought privilege, and the young man who had been entrusted with the duty was not about to let Her Majesty down. On his second attempt, he pulled so hard that the flag broke loose and fluttered to the ground.

That afternoon we decided to escape from the heat of Road Town and the flush of Royal patriotism and joined a group of friends on the beach at Smuggler's Cove.

This was our first visit to Smuggler's Cove and our friends had given us precise instructions to follow. We drove along the coast road towards West End and just before Soper's Hole there was a rocky track which peeled away to the right. It was easy to miss for it looked more like a wide, if rough, path. Few people passed this way but a four-wheel landrover was the ideal vehicle for tackling any and all of Tortola's unmade routes, so we launched off the 'tarras' road happily confident.

A flock of turtle doves were resting in their dust baths and were most surprised at the intrusion. We bounced and rolled in four wheel first gear for a considerable time and began to wish we had taken the more usual route to Smuggler's, up and over terrifying Joe's Hill. We realized that a puncture, highly likely in this terrain, would leave us stranded and miles from anywhere in the heat of the day, picnic hamper notwithstanding.

However we rounded the final bend and below us stretched the small, sandy, totally secluded delight of Smuggler's Cove, with the very local and very basic beach bar nestling beside the sea grape bushes and almond trees. It was a picture out of paradise. Our friends Terry and Pam, Bob and Pat (and toddler Simone), Audrey and Nicholas (and toddler Thomas) were already established and we flopped down beside them. It was a glorious day and the perfect way to spend the Queen's Birthday.

Pam and Terry proudly announced that they were to become parents and we all celebrated with much clinking of Budweiser cans. Much to Audrey's consternation Pam had already made the decision to have the baby in Peebles Hospital in Road Town and she had already received her list of *essential items on confinement* (which, incidentally, included bringing in her own sheets.)

In Audrey's opinion any hospital which allowed chickens to wander round the ward could not possibly be hygienic and she urged Pam to reconsider and to return to the UK as soon as possible. Pam cheerfully explained that the new Chief Medical Officer on Tortola had been a Consultant Gynaecologist in London before coming to the Territory, and she was therefore absolutely confident she was in safe hands.

Audrey was often teased about her fastidious obsession with hygiene. She wore rubber gloves to change little Thomas' nappy, and regularly disinfected the stones on the path outside her front door.

"Germs in the tropics" Audrey told me earnestly *"can be very dangerous"*.

Our afternoon on the beach was wonderful. Smuggler's Cove was the perfect place for a family to swim, and the two toddlers Simone and Thomas thoroughly enjoyed themselves splashing in the clear blue shallows. The sand was soft and white and warm underfoot, and shelved gently into the water. There was a lovely coral reef just yards from the shore with shoals of fascinating fish in all shapes, colours and sizes. A baby turtle, about fifteen inches long, came to inspect the swimmers but was allowed to pass unmolested. The sea grape bushes gave just enough shade and the bar offered liquid refreshment and burgers at very reasonable prices.

Because it was a holiday the local children were also enjoying the beach at Smuggler's. Groups arrived from nowhere and raced screaming and laughing into the sea where they squirmed and ducked all day. Someone had brought a huge, inflated lorry inner tube and the children bounced in, out, and around it. The accompanying adults lay in the shallows and talked, and scrubbed themselves, and washed their hair.

The afternoon did produce one exciting moment, when a small earth tremour wriggled the beach like a wobbling jelly for a few seconds. Not an alarming experience, just rather peculiar and unfamiliar. The chairs shook and the sand trembled and we looked at each other warily, waiting, but the epicenter must have been far out to sea and all, except an agitated Audrey who remained on high alert, quickly relaxed.

We returned in convoy to Slaney to discover that the young foal, recently brought into the Slaney compound with his mother, had eaten all the potted plants placed outside the ground floor apartments, and was nuzzling my washing which was strung out on the line, with an obvious eye on dessert.

'Drummer' was a darling, a fawn coloured foal who had been adopted by Bob Gray's son, Bobby, but he did have a nasty habit of nipping you and then rolling his eyes in anticipation of a slap. The foal's mother Maggie was quite unsociable and bared her teeth at people she hadn't been introduced to before running away, as a result Bobby changed her name to Diana, 'fleet of foot'.

The Grays used to have a donkey. It was allowed to wander freely around the grounds. Before the cattle grid was in place the donkey loved to chase passing cars. He had been known to race all the way into Road Town if the car he was following particularly took his fancy.

But he had other annoying habits and was particularly partial to people's washing, which he would pull off the line and munch with delight. When, in protest, they stopped putting out the washing, the donkey wandered around until he found a bucket, or similar, which he would rattle loudly by putting his head inside. So they deprived him of all potential toys, and in an effort to gain attention he began the habit of falling into the well. This worked wonderfully at first since everyone was very sympathetic and murmured gentle, soothing words while he was being winched out. But then they covered the well in an attempt to stop him from throwing himself in. The final straw came when he took to *he-hawing* loudly at 3.00 a.m. every morning in the mistaken belief that he was a cock welcoming the break of day!

When Bob Gray's wife Maureen discovered that an exasperated tenant had attempted to strangle the donkey, she decided the only solution was to take the animal up onto the ridge and let him loose. It was either that, or an empty apartment block, all of us residents having moved out. The donkey was taken up to the hills and deposited alongside a group of friendly wild donkeys in the earnest hope that they would adopt him.

My maid Rosalind did not like animals and she was scared of both the mare and foal. She would arrive in the morning having been 'dropped' off from a car. She hovered, hesitated and generally hung around until one of the other maids arrived and they could walk together across the grounds and up the short stretch of road from the cattle grid to the apartments.

Our relationship had become firmly established into mother/child dependence. Leathery, lean Rosalind was mother and I the simple-minded woolly child. Most of the time Rosalind suffered me with benevolence, but got very frustrated when I had trouble understanding her speech. Her voice rose higher and higher and her speech would get faster and faster and the more excited she became the more unintelligible, until finally, with a huge gum sucking sigh, she would take me by the arm, sit me in a chair, and with a pained and saintly expression she would go over the whole sentence again, very slowly until light dawned in my eyes and I finally understand, or at least pretended to.

As I have explained Rosalind was extremely accident prone and recently had yet another accident in the apartment. It looked as if she had been involved in a fierce fight with a violent assailant. We arrived home to discover upturned chairs, cushions across the floor, the mesh fly-screen bent and broken and a general state of confusion and disorder, but no sign of Rosalind and no explanation.

The following morning Rosalind breezed in as if nothing had happened, rolled up her sleeves to tackle the washing up, and launched into a chorus of *Bang Bang Lulu* a popular West Indian song. A cautious enquiry on my part and she sheepishly admitted that yesterday had been *'bad'*. In what way *'bad'* she couldn't explain, shaking her head, lowering her eyes and shuffling uncomfortably, and I was left puzzling.

Until I checked the drinks cabinet, then I discovered Rosalind had been sampling the bottles. Variety rather than quantity seemed to be her maxim with a little sip from each, starting on the left and working to the right, rum, whisky, gin, Cointreau, vodka, martini, Kahlua, a lethal cocktail. Rosalind, I realized was partial to a tipple or two, or more. I was not sure how to handle this and took the cowardly way out, by temporarily ignoring it.

I was to learn that whenever the island had a holiday Rosalind celebrated by hitting the bottle, any bottle, and as a result would be suffering from *'poor health'* the following day and would not turn up for work. After something as special as the Queen's Official Birthday, Rosalind required an extra day to recover from her excesses and I had to tackle my own dirty dishes.

In contrast to Rosalind, Mary at the office was a model of propriety and an absolute treasure. Hard-working, helpful and a good friend. Her husband was a small inoffensive little man, who would sit on the stairs outside, patiently waiting for her to finish work. Cleaning our offices had now become a family affair with little Joseph, her youngest, helping by wielding a mop, twice as big as himself.

Mary offered to buy the office fridge. It sat in the corner, large and white, and generally empty. Mary negotiated a mutually agreeable sum we offered to deliver it to her home. Mary was thrilled.

We persuaded our friend Bob Woodage to help us with the delivery, and with accompanying grunts and groans my husband and Bob successfully negotiated the office stairs and finally heaved it into the back of the landrover. Mary had given us careful and clear directions to her home and we wound our way cautiously and slowly down muddy Huntums Ghaut on the outskirts of town. Several neat, traditional, wooden houses painted blue with red galvanized roofs, were cheerfully packed together at the end of the track.

Mary was waiting for us at the door of her small, single-roomed home. The children, playing outside, sprang forward in enthusiastic welcome and neighbours popped out of adjoining homes to watch the excitement, arms akimbo, smiling faces. Huntums Ghaut was a warm and kind community.

The one room acted as living and sleeping space for the four members of Mary's family and it was kept absolutely immaculate. On *'good'* nights Mary told me the children preferred to sleep outside.

The fridge was lowered from the landrover with reverence and carried ceremoniously inside. The neighbours were very obviously impressed and Mary swelled with importance as they crowded round her door to view the new status symbol. Mary explained that because she had no 'current' yet for the fridge it would be used to hold all the things that she didn't want the children to touch. Food, maybe, but other valuable things too.

"A sort of safety-deposit box?" I suggested, and Mary agreed, roaring with laughter. She was going to buy a padlock to make it more secure.

CHAPTER 16

SWIMMING POOLS, PRISONERS AND VI 999

Young Bobby Gray celebrated his 21st birthday recently. Bob senior intended to have the biggest and best party the island had ever seen and had hired a calypso band and caterers for the special occasion. He desperately tried to finish the swimming pool which he fully intended as the focal point to the whole event. But the weather was against the workmen, raining when they were trying to render. Bob appeared to have given no thought to the ultimate problem, the filling of the pool, and we all waited and watched with interest to see how he would solve this particular puzzle.

Water in the tropics was scarce and a valuable commodity and filling a swimming pool no small achievement. We had reckoned without Bob's cockney cunning. To him the answer was simple. He called out the fire engine and offered a free tanker full of water if they would pump the water stored in our cisterns into the pool.

The residents were quite naturally furious, but Bob sensibly reasoned that by the law of tropical averages it would rain soon and refill the cisterns. Anyway we could always turn to the town well-water in an emergency, or failing that, buy in a tanker load of water to see us through the dry patch or, he pointed out triumphantly, we could always pinch some back from the pool.

To Bob young Bobby's 21st birthday party and the filling of the pool were of paramount importance and despite our cries of protest Bob stuck stubbornly to his decision.

The island had one fire engine, VI999. She arrived last year. Before she came Tortola used to rely on a small red truck with miles and miles of snaking hose on board. The truck was a most inadequate firefighter at the best of times but one embarrassing incident, which may have been embellished over time, stood out in everyone's memory.

The story is as follows. About a year ago a fire broke out in a house at East End, near the airport, and a panic call was received by the Police. Four policemen ran out of the station to the bright red truck only to discover that it was locked. They ran back inside the station in search of the key, but the hook on the wall behind the desk was empty, a dusty outline, but no key. Then someone remembered that a few days earlier an officer had taken the red truck round town *'for a bit of exercise'*. Unfortunately the officer in question was not on duty at the time of the emergency, but a hasty search of his desk produced the vital keys.

The four policemen returned quickly to the truck, jumped into the cab, thrust the key in the ignition and tried to start the engine. Nothing, completely dead. A quick investigation and the exasperated officers discovered to their dismay that not only was the battery missing, but also the engine and certain other essential parts of the truck's insides. About the time this embarrassing discovery was made, a call was received from the scene of the fire reporting that it was now out. The emergency was over.

I am told that it was as a direct result of this unfortunate incident that the current VI 999, which is now so proudly maintained by the Police Force, was requested and its purchase approved.

The new fire engine was a grand old lady with a huge red belly. She was kept in sparkling condition and was cherished and lovingly maintained. She made rare public appearances and usually only on ceremonial occasions. She rested in state on a special concrete pad opposite the Police Station in Main Street. We passed her every morning and every evening on the way to and from the office.

When VI 999 arrived to pump our cistern water into the Slaney pool, she was accompanied by two police officers and one convict. The prisoner was brought along for muscle and did all the hard physical work. He connected the snaky hoses, ran backwards and forwards between the cistern and the pool, and frantically attempted to administer first aid to the numerous punctures and slits as the precious water fountained from the wounds in the hoses.

We watched saddened and mute as a substantial quantity of our valuable water poured down the hillside. It took some considerable time before our convict got the hang of things and the pool began to fill in earnest. It needed several long hot hours to fill the pool, and while they waited the two supervising police officers and their prisoner languished under a shady palm with several cans of Bud kindly supplied by Bob.

HM Prison housed only two convicts. This particular prisoner was serving a life sentence for murder. Apparently he had a disagreement with his son as to which of them was the better workman, father or son. The argument became more and more heated until the dramatic and tragic ending when the father finally lost control of his temper and in his rage murdered his son. After a long trial the father, our helpful and hard-working hose hustler and pool filler, was convicted of murder and sentenced to hang. Although Capital Punishment was abolished in the UK in 1965 it was still the law in the British Virgin Islands.

The sentence was to be carried out behind the white stucco walls of the Police Station yard, where a temporary gallows was built. But the construction must have been faulty because when the awful moment of the hanging came, the apparatus refused to function correctly, and after the third attempt it was abandoned and the prisoner's sentence commuted to life imprisonment.

Since he was a local man, he enjoyed special privileges, privileges not normally allowed to down-islanders or expats. He was allowed to help with odd jobs, like gardening, around Government owned property, always under supervision of course.

During the day the two inmates of HM Prison sat out in the sun by the huge gates of the Police Station, sometimes playing cards with each other, sometimes chatting to passersby or sometimes simply waiting to collect food from relatives. They both enjoyed a considerable amount of liberty. In fact the prison had acquired something of an international reputation. A recent report in the American press described the Tortola prison cells as *'cozy and generally pleasant'*.

It was a fairly new experience for the island to have anyone in the cells. For years they remained empty. Not because the islands lacked crime, but because punishment took on forms other than jail sentences. But the Judge who periodically passes through to try the more serious offences began to commit the offenders to prison. This caused a real headache for the already stretched police force, and in the end a bond of mutual trust was forged where prisoners have been allowed to roam freely around the police station area, provided they behave themselves.

However this relaxed attitude did cause an embarrassing incident not long ago, when under cover of darkness the prisoners let themselves out of their cells and walked down the street, broke into a supermarket and helped themselves to liquor and cigarettes, then returned to the jail for a night of drunken revelry. But as a general rule the system of allowing prisoners a fair amount of freedom seemed to work well, as was amply demonstrated when we needed one of them to fill the Slaney swimming pool.

I watched with interest the *'pouring of the pool'* from Audrey's balcony. Audrey had been our neighbour on the second floor, but she felt it was unsuitable for a toddler and had managed to exchange apartments with a sympathetic resident on the ground floor. But Audrey instantly regretted the move. She had a genuine fear of insects and an irrational horror of cockroaches and spiders. Up on the second floor she was protected to a certain extent from invasion, but on the ground floor, in an apartment built directly on top of the cistern, the bugs were abundant and brazen.

During her first week in the new apartment she had, she told me in stricken tones, at least twenty *"immense"* cockroaches scuttling across the apartment. The worst moment was when she disturbed one in the bathroom as it was picking its way through the debris on her husband's toothbrush. Audrey screamed in panic, ran outside slamming the front door, and then to her dismay realized she had accidentally locked it, with toddler Thomas still on the inside.

Her husband Nicholas was at the office but a frantic phone call from a hysterical Audrey in a neighbour's apartment brought him racing back home, to find Audrey had roused the whole block and was desperately trying to pick the lock of their apartment, watched by several anxious neighbours.

When Nicholas and Audrey finally burst in, little Thomas was discovered sitting on the floor of the kitchen rearranging the contents of the fridge and munching happily through a packet of biscuits. Of the offending cockroach there was no sign.

As Audrey and I watched the pool being filled, Audrey commented about the *'little wrigglers'*, the mosquito larvae that lived in the cistern, being sucked up and deposited into what would be our swimming water. She shuddered as she spoke.

When the weather was hot and the wind died we were plagued with sandflies and mosquitoes which seemed to be at their biting best around 6.00 p.m. Again poor Audrey had drawn the short straw since they preferred to hug the ground and seemed to congregate around her apartment. The mesh screens stopped the mosquitoes but sandflies were so small they simply flew straight through. A mosquito was big enough to see as it settled and a swift slap soon dispatched it, but sandflies were cunning and almost invisible and ate and departed before you were really aware of their presence. The best thing to do was stay inside, or wear long sleeves and long trousers and spray liberally with some powerful insect repellant. When a group of us gathered for dinner the collective smell of repellant was positively pungent.

After successfully filling our pool VI 999 was returned to her parking pad outside the Police Station. Later that week I looked out of my office window to see three policemen struggling to push the big red fire engine down Main Street. They had received an emergency call from the harbour. A small boat had been loaded with three large gas cylinders for the residents of Peter Island. When the Captain started his engine there was an almighty explosion. The Captain was thrown up into the air and somersaulted onto the dock. He had a miraculous escape with only shock, cuts and bruises, but his poor boat was ablaze.

Having discovered that the battery of VI 999 was flat the policemen were attempting to bump start the fire engine. Things went from bad to worse, when they finally arrived at the harbour they discovered the tank (so generously filled by Bob with our precious cistern water) was empty. Having pulled out the hoses, trained them on the blazing boat and waited, expecting a powerful blast of water, nothing happened.

A few moments of hurried consultation and an officer was dispatched to search out a suitable water supply close enough to hook up to and within the length of the hoses. Luckily a nearby house was able to offer ample supplies of water from its cistern and the hose stretched just far enough. But by the time the water began to flow the boat had long since disappeared, sunk to the bottom of the harbour, leaving only charred debris floating on the surface.

It may be totally coincidental but within days of opening the pool to the residents, the five children at Slaney were suffering various forms of sickness. It started with little Thomas, who was discovered to have worms. Audrey went into shock and was all for getting the first plane back to England, until a friend explained that youngsters in England also suffered, on occasion, from worms.

All the other mothers checked their children and the only other child suffering from worms was Jane, who played a great deal with little Thomas. Now whether Jane caught them from little Thomas or little Thomas caught them from Jane was not clear, and to everyone except Audrey totally irrelevant. However, two days later Jane's younger brother Shaun went down with enteritis and little Thomas complained of feeling sick. Audrey rushed him off to Peebles Hospital in a hysterical fit and was told *"yes, it was probably enteritis"*. She was seriously considering flight plans the following day when little Thomas toddled out saying he felt fine and could he please go outside to play.

Audrey was jubilant with relief for about two hours, until she was told that Christine (who had successfully negotiated both worms and enteritis) had just broken out with measles. This really was the last straw for Audrey because Christine, much older and therefore considered more responsible, had been playing with little Thomas. Christine knew she was in quarantine for measles but had *"forgotten"* to mention it. Audrey was beside herself with rage and if little Thomas does indeed go down with measles, which everyone now suspects he will, dire consequences will follow. Audrey will certainly leave the island, for good.

CHAPTER 17

HURRICANES AND MAIDS

As the weather got hotter and the trade winds dropped we entered the hurricane season. July to October were considered the risk months, but the acute period was probably August. During August the wind dropped away almost completely and the air became hot, still and very uncomfortable.

Officially the danger period was over by St. Ursula's Day, 21st October, a holiday in the BVI, but the powerful hurricane that swept through the islands in 1867 and sank the Royal Mail Steam Packet *'Rhone'* off Peter Island (and incidentally fifty seven other vessels at anchor in St. Thomas) arrived on October 29th, a week later.

As far as I can gather the last time a hurricane hit the Virgin Islands was in 1928 when St. Croix was more or less flattened. However each year, at the beginning of July, out came the Government circular on preparing for a hurricane.

I was instructed to stock up on food which could be eaten cold without preparation, buy in at least two days' supply of drinking water (in case the cisterns and Government well became contaminated by salt water), purchase or otherwise find, boarding materials suitable for protecting the windows, and so the list went on, with a final suggestion that I buy vast quantities of matches and candles. I duly stocked up with 48 tins of baked beans, 24 tins of new potatoes, 12 huge cans of orange juice and 18 pints of milk.

The circular was very informative since it gave a good detailed description of what to expect should a hurricane happen.

"A hurricane lasts approximately seven hours, during this time the wind blows very strongly from one direction and then there is

a pause of approximately half an hour, during which time everything is deathly still - on no account must anyone leave their houses during this time - after this lull the wind then begins to blow very strongly from the opposite direction."

The authoritative description of a hurricane. I rather think that the author underplayed the gravity of the situation. The Captain of the *'Rhone'* would argue that it was more than just *'blowing strongly'* in 1867.

According to the circular, a weighty tome and onerous reading, during the hurricane season I should listen to the daily radio broadcast on the hour, but this gave the situation throughout the whole of the Caribbean and tended to ramble on in a wearying fashion.

The Government of Tortola set up their own hurricane early warning system. In the centre of Road Town stood the Administrative Building. Not in itself a conspicuous construction but crouching shyly beside bigger neighbours. On top of the Administrative Building was a flag pole.

During the hurricane season the flag pole was of paramount importance and we checked it daily as we drove past on our way to work. A small red pennant flying from the top of the mast meant we must be on alert, ready for more news. One pennant meant that a hurricane was in the area, though not necessarily heading our way. Two small pennants with black circles in the centre indicated that there was a hurricane in the area and it was heading our way. Three red pennants with black circles in the centre flying from the pole told us, in essence, *'Tough, too late, hurricane about to hit'.*

The Governor, realizing that this form of warning was of limited value, promised to sound the mid-day lunch siren intermittently should a three pennant emergency be imminent. Confusion could arise if a hurricane arrived at mid-day, we wouldn't know whether to run for cover or stop for lunch!

My maid Rosalind went walkabout recently and disappeared. I shared Rosalind with a neighbour who explained that she had been caught helping herself to their drinks cabinet. After inspecting our bottles I discovered the rum had been reduced by almost half, and half a loaf was missing from the fridge. We assumed she had gone on an alcoholic binge and tentative enquiries confirmed our suspicions.

We both suspected Rosalind had a serious drinking problem after she confided to me about the nasty *'Jumbies'*, evil spirits she said, that came to plague people and drive them mad. She explained that the windows of our apartment had to remain open so that the *'Jumbies'* could come and go as they pleased. As far as I could gather she had been fighting with the *'Jumbies'* the day the window mesh had been wrecked in the apartment.

I couldn't be angry. I had a fleeting image of Rosalind with loaf in one hand and bottle in the other stretched out on my sofa jabbering irrationally to herself.

After a two week absence Rosalind returned. I was at the window and watched her arrive, striding briskly up the path. Suddenly she seemed to acquire an evil-looking limp. She made a great show of suffering as she came slowly up the stairs, struggling and still with a marked limp, huffing and puffing with pitiful little grunts punctuating her progress. She reached the door of our apartment, apparently exhausted, and smiled shyly when she saw me standing there. She began to mumble in a disjointed, gum smacking way about *'roomatik nees'*. No mention of the neighbour's missing gin bottle or my half empty rum.

"This time Rosalind you've gone too far, just too far!" I scolded. I explained that turning up out of the blue after two weeks absence was not just unreliable, it was quite unacceptable. I graciously forbore to mention the missing drinks but added that I considered *'roomatik nees'* was insufficient reason to land me in it.

To my great surprise Rosalind agreed with me, she seemed almost relieved to be dismissed. She wanted to assure me that she still loved me very, very deeply and always would. We came to the mutually agreeable decision that she must go and as she left (limp miraculously cured) she gave me a big hug of affection.

So I needed to find a new maid. I had one offer but it came with complications. Another middle-aged willing worker who seemingly suffered the same *'roomatik nees'* as Rosalind. Her son, (who drove a very flashy American car, a most unusual sight on Tortola) took over the responsibility of assessing my suitability as a potential employer. He explained to me that *'Momma'* would not take the job unless I was prepared to pay for a taxi to collect and drop her from Road Town to Slaney. *'Momma'* would not, he told me firmly, under any circumstances, be allowed to walk from town to the apartment. Since this little arrangement would cost me more than her wage (taxis being notoriously expensive) I was obviously very reluctant, no matter how highly recommended she came, and silently wondered why her adoring son could not 'drop' Momma in his big flash American car.

CHAPTER 18

SURVEYS, SUPERMARKETS, AND SUPPER

As well as being the office Girl Friday I was often used by my husband when he needed another body to help with his survey work. Since I proved incapable of working the theodolite I was put in charge of the 20 ft. steel pole and sent off in various directions, pole in one hand and wielding a machete to clear the way with the other.

On one occasion we were surveying a hillside site above Road Town and after half an hour of struggling through virgin bush I was so hot and bothered I stripped to bra and panties, hoping that none of the residents lower down the slopes were watching. I must have slipped and landed on my bottom a dozen times during the three hours it took to complete the laborious task. However we were blessed with a delicious compensation. We stumbled upon a big and generously productive papaya tree somewhere in the jungle. It was temptingly clustered with fruit, some still slightly green but some orange, ripe, and begging to be picked and sampled. My pole proved an invaluable scrumping tool. I deftly loosened six fat juicy paw-paw which my husband caught and we fell upon them with relish.

On a previous occasion when I accompanied my husband out on site it was quite a different experience. He was setting out a road at Belmont Estates near Smuggler's Cove. It was thick scrub and bush and the weather was unpredictable. We put on gum boots and had to wear jeans to protect our legs. We could hear the weather rumbling and grumbling and did wonder if we would complete the work before the heavens opened. But the bulldozer was due to begin clearing the following day and the route of the road needed to be marked. So armed with a machete in one hand and a can of red paint in the other my husband strode off. I was carrying the tape and the notepad as Assistant Surveyor. Needless to say we got about half way through the job and the rain simply fell out of the sky in a way that only tropical rain can, and we were absolutely drenched. We completed the job but looked like drowned rats.

His Excellency the Governor moved out of his three-bedroomed Official Residence on the hill in Road Town and moved into one of the brand new condominiums at the Treasure Isle Hotel. A temporary measure while Government House was undergoing renovation.

Government House was humble home with poor plumbing and other assorted problems, but His Excellency had decided on a complete refurbishment and refused to return until it was completed. His black official car, sporting a gleaming gold crown where lesser mortals have a number plate, cruised up and down Pasea Estate to the Administrative buildings in town, or to the supermarket.

The beautiful new Pasea supermarket had only recently opened and was of huge interest. It was one of my husband's jobs and we took a personal pride in it. At first the supermarket shelves were rather empty, waiting for the Booker ship that called every six weeks bringing supplies to the island. We all went there to enjoy the cooling breezes of the air conditioning or *'refrigerated air'* as my American friends called it. Since most of the shelves were bare we were not particularly interested in the stock, but I found myself tempted by the custard powder and chocolates.

I was struggling out of the door with my brown paper bag full of goodies recently when the Governor's chauffeur James rushed forward to help. Not only did he rescue me from the stubborn doors which refused to respond to my nudging bottom, he even volunteered to take me back home in the official car. Sadly I had to refuse, since the landrover was parked and waiting. But I had great pleasure in imagining the look on Bob Gray's face had I arrived (in T-shirt and shorts) in the Governor's shining black official car, sporting Union Jack pennant and gold crown number plate, with chauffeur James behind the wheel!

The supermarket with its potential Aladdin's Cave of groceries inspired me to screw up my courage and throw a dinner party for six carefully selected guests. Not an immense or daunting experience for most but I was very nervous.

I was quite happy to take people out to dinner and hostess a gathering of business guests while professionals rushed backwards and forwards with the appropriate dishes. But I didn't know whether I had the skills to cope with the culinary demands of the kitchen and make scintillating conversation, both at the same time.

I spent days pondering on menu, sequence of cooking, people to invite. Meat was very difficult to find on Tortola but I thought I would start off with soup or prawn cocktail, try and find a nice piece of pork for the main course, with apple sauce (tinned of course), potato fritters, tons of peas and carrots (all tinned), followed by Chocolate Instant Whip, and a strawberry tart (tinned strawberries of course) covered with a strawberry jelly and rounded off with coffee and some of Pasea supermarket's yummy chocolate.

My husband promised to be very liberal with the company 'drinkies' and assured me that by the time our guests sat down at the table they would be past caring about the food.

At first my dinner party looked to be doomed. I was suffering from exhaustion brought on by nervous anticipation. My husband had just returned from a site visit to Brewer's Bay bruised and battered, swearing he had been rearranged physically. One guest arrived having just lost his temper with another expat and was seething with suppressed anger. Another couple arrived and said they had just had a row, weren't talking to each other and were considering a divorce!

Under the circumstances I did wonder whether it was worthwhile continuing, but since the food was cooked and ready it seemed wasteful not to eat it. But in a surprisingly short time everyone was mellow and jovial, my husband was relaxed and hosting, and the arguing couple had made peace and were chatting.

Everyone said how enjoyable the evening had been and I glowed with pride. My very first dinner party was a success. My greatest compliment was paid when the wives expressed amazement that their respective husbands had remained awake throughout the evening, apparently an event unparalleled in either household. One maintained he had stayed awake, not because of the meal, nor the witty and entertaining banter, but because he was convinced my skimpy bolero top would prove inadequate to the task required of it, and that sooner or later my bosom would burst out of the restraining bands of material. He sat goggling with anticipation throughout the evening. Fortunately, he was disappointed.

CHAPTER 19

Cooper, Salt, and Dr. Smith's blood

During our relaxing weekends we enjoyed the delights of the outer islands and the glorious Caribbean that lapped Tortola's shores. The summer in BVI was so hot the only place to be was beside, in, or on, the sea.

We spent our free time swimming, basking and beaching so we were soon as nut brown and wrinkled as an old coconut shell. It was a great pleasure to gather up a few friends and disappear off to the beach or out on a boat. Convivial company and warm sunshine proved the ideal stress-buster combination.

It didn't always go as planned. On one occasion we went out with twelve friends in a boat to explore the outer islands, but although the weather was great there was a bit of a swell in the sea. After only five minutes two of the passengers complained of nausea and were sea sick, so we decided to visit closer Cooper Island instead of the distant Camanoe as planned.

Uninhabited Cooper Island had a good anchorage off Manchioneel Bay. We landed and built a BBQ on the beach and those who wanted to simply sat and sifted sand while the more energetic and adventurous went exploring. We climbed up the hillside for a better view of Sir Francis Drake Channel and discovered a lime tree laden with small green fresh smelling fruits.

The men took the boat across to neighbouring Salt Island and dived down to inspect one of the shipwrecks on the seabed there. It was the first sunken wreck my husband had seen and he was very impressed. Unfortunately there was little time for a good snorkel or dive and they decided to organize a return visit for a more thorough look.

Our friends at Slaney all had young children and their favorite beach was Smuggler's Cove. We would often accompany them and while the mums and toddlers enjoyed the shallow sea and warm white sand we would go off for a snorkel around the coral reef beside the beach.

On one memorable occasion we borrowed the Smuggler's Cove motor boat and anchored a little way offshore beside the outer edge of the reef. I stayed in the boat to make sure it did not drift, and to collect any shells, rocks or fish which might be handed into the boat by the plunderers. Finally, and most importantly it seemed to me, I was instructed to *"watch out for sharks"*.

Someone had idly mentioned that once, many, many months ago, a swimmer thought he had seen a shark off this particular reef. So I was appointed *'shark lookout'* with implicit instructions on what to do should a shark be spotted. They were terse and to the point.

"Pick up an oar and belt it over the head."

Fortunately on that occasion I saw no sharks but I was required to do some occasional baling as the slops in the bottom of the boat began to rise. I had a quiet and peaceful afternoon stretched out in the boat, bobbing in the swell, drifting and dreaming in the sunshine. Every now and then I was obliged to lean over the side to collect some treasure hoisted in by the divers. Their prize of the afternoon was a small lobster, but I took pity on it and let it go. When the snorkelers returned to the boat I had to pretend the lobster had jumped overboard.

The Chief Medical Officer, Dr. Smith, decided to organize a list of blood donors for the Territory. He used the local radio to explain to people about the necessity of having a blood bank and how a sample would be taken and checked. The Rotary Club had bought Peebles Hospital a small freezer unit and Dr. Smith wanted to encourage enough volunteers to enable him to hold a reasonable blood bank in case of emergencies.

The initial reaction was poor with only thirty people responding to the appeal. But Dr. Smith was determined and arranged to sit in the hospital laboratory every Wednesday evening between 6.30 and 8.00 p.m. in case any donors arrived. I decided to be a good citizen and jumped into the landrover and drove down to the hospital.

I was glad I did. Dr. Smith was sitting all alone twiddling his thumbs and humming to himself. He pounced on me with delight, plunged in for a sample and talked me through his laboratory test. Then, just to make sure, he took another sample. It seems I was somewhat unusual and he was so pleased at finding a donor with something other than boring 'O' that I felt quite thrilled and special. I left the hospital floating on a cloud and assuring the delightful Dr. Smith that I was there *'day or night'* if he needed me.

On reflection I could see that this discovery had a negative twist. While I was donating my precious and unusual liquid all well and good, but what if by chance I became the patient, who would donate to me?

We were off to a dinner party that night and the puzzle bothered me all evening, I kept wanting to ask everyone *"What's your blood group?"* not the most appropriate conversational topic for a rather formal dinner date. However I did manage to persuade some of our friends to go to the laboratory, primarily in the vain hope that one of them might have the same group as me. My husband, it transpired, was boring 'O'.

CHAPTER 20

GRISELDA

When an Englishman wishes to attract your attention he normally coughs loudly, or calls *"I say!"* or *"Excuse me!"* and if you are a long way away he might whistle. An American shouts *"Yo!"* or *"Hey"*, but in my experience a West Indian goes *"Psssst!"* in a conspiratorial and most penetrating manner.

I first discovered this when I was sitting quietly in the passenger seat of the landrover in Road Town waiting for my husband. A sudden shrill *"Psssst"* sounded in my ear. Startled I turned my head and found myself nose to nose with a very large West Indian lady peering in at my open window.

For a moment I simply stared wide-eyed, then she uttered another ear-splitting *"Pssst"*, this time her hand slipped in through the window and she gave me a quick poke in the shoulder. She wasn't smiling but yet she didn't look violent or threatening, just large and insistent. She had a shorter friend apparently glued to her side and they both stared at me. Big, round eyed, persistent stares. I felt intimidated and wasn't sure what was required of me and I said, rather timidly, *"What do you want?"*

My question unleashed a torrent of totally incomprehensible words from the extra-large lady who kept turning to stroke the head of her little friend and patting her on the shoulder. I understood that I was being asked something which related directly to the little friend, but the specifics escaped me. After the fourth repeat I grasped approximately one word in four. The story was that little friend, who stood at her side dumbly passive, was desperate for work, any work however humble.

Since I fired Rosalind I still hadn't found a replacement for my daily help and large lady's little friend needed a job. So impulsively I offered it to her on the spot. Extra-large lady was so ecstatic and excited I thought she was going to pluck me out of the landrover through the window. She hugged little friend and wobbled with pleasure and was so busy being grateful that she was almost run over by a passing truck.

I arranged to collect little friend, whose name was Griselda, from outside the office the following Monday at 9.00 a.m. sharp to take her back to Slaney where we could discuss money, hours, and duties. She looked relatively young and healthy so I presumed we would have no problems with either *roomatiks* or alcohol, and I reasoned that if she was so desperate for work she would try very hard to please me, at least for the first few weeks.

When Monday arrived they both turned up. Griselda said she needed her friend *'wit she'* for morale support. They squeezed with some effort into the front seat of the cab and as I drove the mile from the office in Road Town to the Slaney apartments we discussed money and hours. Griselda was disappointed to discover that her employment was not full-time, but she rallied when I promised to ask around the block with the possibility of finding extra work for her.

Extra-large lady was not happy about the bumpy ride in the landrover and her face grew longer as we covered the distance between Road Town and Slaney. She explained that Griselda, who remained silent on the subject, would not like walking all that way. Maybe, she wondered, glancing sideways at me as we lurched through another pot-hole, I would be willing to give Griselda *"de drop"* since *"ow you could expec' she ta wack dis lan lan way?"*

I carefully explained that the landrover belonged to the business (always impressive) and was not for my personal use. Griselda nodded vigorously in understanding but extra-large lady was still unhappy. However after some probing I discovered that Griselda lived in the same house as Blanche, and I suggested that the two of them could arrive together. Blanche had prestige in her house, and was held in great esteem by Griselda and extra-large lady because she had been employed for two years, no mean achievement on Tortola. Griselda was visibly flattered to discover that she had been elevated into the same working circle as Blanche.

Griselda was a 'down islander' from Grenada and was living with her boyfriend in Road Town. They already had two boys, left behind with relatives in Grenada and were planning to marry.

Unfortunately she proved not as efficient or speedy as Rosalind, and we had some problems with communication. Griselda could understand me if I spoke slowly and used only three or four words at a time, otherwise she smiled brightly and nodded but had completely misunderstood. She was charming and delightful but sometimes did the strangest things.

On one occasion she went to collect my sheets from the washing line and then toiled back up the stairs with a full laundry basket. Opening the door to the apartment she discovered to her astonishment it was bare. No familiar furniture, no books, no pictures. She went into the bedroom, it was stripped and empty. She rushed into the bathroom, a different shower curtain was hanging over the bath. Panic stricken she dropped the laundry basket and went in search of the phone. It was while she was searching for the phone that light slowly dawned. She realized that instead of climbing up three sets of stairs to our apartment, she had climbed only two and had mistakenly entered the wrong apartment.

Griselda thought this was so funny she laughed until tears ran down her cheeks and she clutched me for support as she repeated the story again, and again, spluttering hysterically. She really thought, she said, we had packed our bags and mysteriously vanished before her very eyes.

Griselda managed to find work with Tina who used to share Rosalind with me. As a result she was chirpy and merry and very grateful to me, and to show her appreciation she developed the habit of thumping me on the back in a playful but painfully powerful way, which she followed with a succession of loud giggles that were irresistibly infectious.

But I did miss Rosalind. When I saw her in town she would throw her arms round me and give me a bear hug of an embrace. Once she was wearing a brown paper bag on her head, and when I asked why, she said it was to keep off the rain, or to be more precise *'da wata!'* When I pointed out that it wasn't raining, and in fact there wasn't even the remotest sign of any rain imminent, she just grinned her huge gummy smile. Anyway, I said, if it did rain, her brown bag would go soggy and be no good at all, at which piece of information she looked thoughtful, and I am sorry to say, slightly depressed.

CHAPTER 21

BOATS, BLOOD, HERBIE AND SIR OLVA

You cannot live on Tortola within sight and sound of the beautiful Caribbean without succumbing to the overwhelming urge to sail.

Danny, the Manager of the Paint Factory, was no sailor but when his friends persuaded him to buy their small dinghy *"for a bargain price"* (they had graduated to a thirty foot Westerly and needed cash urgently) gullible Danny was assured that sailing was simplicity itself. If he bought their delightful little dinghy, they declared, he could look forward to hours, days, months of endless pleasure afloat. So Danny handed over the cash. Then, before he could get to use his new toy, he left for England for an extended holiday.

But Danny was noted for his generous nature, and during his absence he offered the use of the boat to my husband and his friends Terry and Bob. These three were probably the least capable sailors in BVI waters, even less able than Danny, if that was possible. At least Danny had weight, and therefore ballast, as an advantage.

The three friends were absolutely confident they could master the art of sailing by doing. How hard could it be? They knew the theory, all they needed was practice. So one afternoon they launched themselves off from the bay beside the Customs Shed in Road Town and headed across Sir Francis Drake Channel towards Peter Island.

I stood on our Slaney balcony and watched them head out across the Channel. They flapped and zig-zagged left then right, then left again, making slow progress until they became a tiny dot

122

bobbing far out to sea. I was alarmed. I feared they were three incompetent men in a very old dinghy, enthusiastic but incapable.

Nevertheless they surprised me, returning home hours later more or less in one piece and very triumphant. They were sunburnt, hot, hungry, thirsty and keen for a few reviving cans of Bud at the Sir Francis Drake pub. They were in the pub, recounting their sailing success to anyone who would listen, when they heard Leo Mills on ZBVI read out an urgent message over the radio:

"Will the owner of the boat anchored off the hospital kindly come down to the Customs Shed IMMEDIATELY. The boat has drifted, pulled down an overhead electricity cable and caused an outage covering half of Road Town. If the owner does not come at once the boat will be towed away and the owner charged accordingly."

They knew immediately it was Danny's boat that had caused the outage incident and overwhelmed with guilt they raced as fast as they could into town. Fortunately by this time it was quite dark and under cover of the darkness the three silently slipped out, retrieved the boat (which was in danger of grounding itself on the reef) and pulled it away to a mooring well away from the overhead electricity cable. Just to be certain they dropped overboard two anchors, then slipped just as silently back. No more was heard about the incident so they hoped Danny would never need to know how careless they had been with his precious boat.

After the excitement of the evening we all decided to have a midnight swim in the pool to unwind. The floodlights were on and attracted the attention of Grandma Gray who was visiting Tortola. She was a dear old lady, about seventy five, a bit unsteady on her 'pins' and had never learned to swim. But watching us enjoying ourselves brought her down to the poolside for a natter.

Within half an hour we had persuaded her to put on a swimming costume and levered her into toddler Simone's inflatable rubber ring. To watch her delighted face as she bobbed about in the pool, gin and tonic in hand, rubber ring supporting her weight, was an absolute treat. Whether she would have the courage to repeat the experience during the day and in front of the children remained to be seen.

Everyone ended up at our apartment for a final coffee and we tumbled into bed rather late that night. Which was why, when the phone rang at 2.00 a.m. my husband was rather befuddled and confused when he answered it.

Dr. Smith was calling from the hospital. Could my husband come immediately? They needed a pint of his 'O' blood for a young girl who was having a Caesarian. My husband was at the hospital within minutes and Dr. Smith was waiting for him on the steps.

I had just fallen back into bed when there was a knock on the door. It was the Governor's Secretary, who lived in the flat below. They had also been called to donate blood and should have accompanied my husband to the hospital.

They both returned half an hour later, looking very sleepy and realizing that for three very important reasons they could expect to donate, urgently and at uncivilized hours, rather frequently. One, they both had the common blood group 'O'. Two, they were both on the phone (still a luxury on Tortola) and finally three, both lived within minutes of the hospital.

A small price to pay for saving the life of a young mother and her baby.

When the weather is hot and the sun overhead the long seed pods of the Tamarind trees begin to pop, creating an interesting crackle and rustling sound. The pods were popping as we toiled up the slope from the Treasure Isle Hotel to visit Herbie Showering in his condominium. He had kindly invited us for tea and a chat and he was his usual charming self. He was full of grand ideas and became very excited about his plans. Although he had retired from the family business he was, as he put it *"running down, like a racer after the race"*.

It was impossible for such an active man to simply stop, and so he hoped to slow down gradually before finally coming to a standstill. He told us about Compton Castle near Yeovil with its 150 acres of grounds, his Caribbean interests, his marina and land somewhere near the Montague Estate in Southern England.

"On a clear day" he informed us *"I can stand at the marina, look through my binoculars, and see what people are wearing on the Isle of Wight!"*

He was very proud of his ownership of part of the New Forest, and of his association with the speedboats and racing yachts in which he had an interest as a sleeping partner. It hardly seemed to us that he was slowing down, especially when he added that he was returning to England in order to meet Sir Peter Scott so that they could discuss the possibility of making the grounds of Compton Castle into a wildfowl sanctuary.

As we were leaving he casually offered us one of his newly constructed Treasure Isle condominiums to rent, at an extraordinarily bargain price. I was absolutely thrilled. I had been an ardent admirer of the apartments since we first saw them, they were the ultimate in luxury living but quite out of our league, and we knew the company would never pay the high rent demanded.

But with such a special deal, we agreed immediately. We were more than happy to pay the difference in rent between the Slaney apartment and the Treasure Isle Condominium ourselves, which meant the company could have no objections to our moving.

The new apartment was still being finished and furnished and it would be several weeks before we could move in, plenty of time to adjust. We knew we would miss the Slaney atmosphere, but it was only half a mile down the road and we would be frequent visitors. And our friends from Slaney would be able to use the Treasure Isle Hotel facilities when they came to visit us. The hotel pool, the motor boat and the sunfish moored below the hotel.

The pool at Slaney was at the time temporarily out of commission. Bob Gray said it had an 'allergy' and needed attention. I went to look. Through the murky green water I could see a diver sitting on the bottom of the pool, his exhaled tank bubbles floated gently to the surface. He was patiently scrubbing the tiles with what appeared to be a 'brillo' pad.

Once the 'allergy' was cured Bob agreed to allow the pool to be used for sub-aqua lessons. A recently arrived Texan, George Marler, had opened up a diving shop on the waterfront beside the Sir Francis Drake Pub and he decided to offer SCUBA courses on the island. Only a handful of expats had shown any interest, my husband being one of them. SCUBA had more appeal to him than sailing.

Others who had signed up for SCUBA lessons with George on his first course included the dentist, the anaesthetist, an architect, and Pammy, daughter of our cheerful and gregarious friend Sally Bell and the only girl brave enough to take it on. It was to be a very thorough training with twice weekly three hour sessions. The practical to be held in Slaney pool, and the theory in the Pub, with various weekend excursions to practice the practicals and apply the theory.

In order to prepare my husband for his new hobby we decided to pop across to St. Thomas for a quick bargain buy of necessary kit. Flippers (fins), snorkel and mask, and a tropical wet-suit for those cooler evenings.

From our Slaney apartment we watched the USVI ferry *'Bomba Charger'* leave Road Harbour and as it sped out across Sir Francis Drake Channel we quickly finished our coffee, ran down to the landrover, and raced it along to West End. We timed it perfectly and as we pulled into West End and parked the *'Bomba Charger'* was just tying up at the dock ready to collect passengers.

It was fairly crowded, and as usual my husband and I were the only white faces on board. However we knew so many of the Tortolians very well indeed and it was a jolly, happy party that set off for St. Thomas, including our good friend Olva Georges and his wife.

Olva waved and indicated he wanted to talk to us. He left his seat and struggled across the boat towards us. We had first met Olva on the day of our arrival on Tortola and he had become a close friend. He owned the small general store on Main Street opposite our office. Every day he sat on a chair outside the shop entrance in the sunshine while his sisters floated around the dark interior, folding materials, sorting buttons and weighing sweets. We often chatted and he always had a smile on his face and would watch our comings and goings with great interest and amusement.

These days Olva, in his eighties, rarely moved away from home and it was most unusual to see him on the *'Bomba'*. He was dressed in a smart suit and looked slightly bemused and bewildered. As he reached us he held out his hand and grasping my husband's responding outstretched arm he shook it vigorously up and down.

Olva had received a knighthood in the Queen's Birthday Honours List and he and his wife were on their way to Buckingham Palace in London to meet the Queen and collect the honour. As the first British Virgin Islander ever to be knighted he was tremendously proud but very nervous indeed of the journey ahead.

We assured him that it would be a wonderful experience, nothing to be alarmed about. He seemed convinced that we had been somehow personally involved in his selection, and he was very disappointed we were not going on the same journey, able to accompany him all the way to England and Buckingham Palace. When we disembarked at St. Thomas he insisted on us joining him as we passed through Customs and Immigration. They were obviously expecting him and we were ushered through with a courtesy bordering on reverence.

It was hard to say goodbye, we knew in our hearts they were facing a stressful and difficult time ahead not only from the journey but the whole experience, but we also knew they would be very well looked after every step of the way. Olva wanted us to go with them but of course it was impossible. We said a warm farewell and grinning called them *'Sir Olva and Lady Georges'* for the first time, and waved them off in the direction of the airport.

While Sir Olva and Lady Georges headed for Buckingham Palace we launched ourselves into Charlotte Amalie. We had such a marvellous spending spree that we had to buy a suitcase to bring the goodies home. The *'Bomba'* back was solid wall to wall Tortolians with packages of every shape and size filling the gaps between bodies. We sat by the door and suffered the dreadful roaring engine noise all the way back. However it did mean that when the door was opened we were the first to stumble out into the Immigration shed.

We cleared Immigration quickly but then got snarled up in waiting for Customs. We waited, and waited, and waited. The afternoon was hot, sticky, stuffy and noisy. My husband watched the technique adopted by our Tortolian friends and copied them.

He picked up our suitcase and simply followed them through the shed, and out of the door, and into our landrover parked where we had left it early that morning, and drove home.

When we arrived home and turned on the local news we heard there had been a shooting incident in Charlotte Amalie while we were there. Apparently the St. Thomas police had been preparing to attend their Annual Ball. The officers were polishing up their shiny bits and pieces and organizing themselves, when two of them decided to have a competition to find out which one had the fastest draw.

According to the news bulletin both officers pulled their guns from their holsters but in the excitement of the moment one accidentally fired his, tragically shooting his draw partner. There was such a commotion afterwards that the Police Ball was, not surprisingly, cancelled.

The BVI police did not carry guns. The accidental discharge of a rifle at the parade ground during the Queen's Birthday ceremonial salute showed just how unfamiliar our boys were with firearms.

CHAPTER 22

SCUBA, GEORGE AND SHARKS

The underwater SCUBA lessons began very well. I sat and observed, either from the poolside, the beach or the balcony depending on the venue and my level of interest.

Because my husband was the lightest and slightest male of the group he was partnered as 'buddy' to Pammy. All divers, it seemed, had a buddy and my husband was more than delighted to be paired with small, gentle, quiet, shy, blonde and beautiful Pammy.

The group bubbled, sat on the pool bottom, exchanged masks and mouthpieces and learned all about nitrogen narcosis and hyper-ventilation. They also went to the beach and would take me along to perform sentry duty. From the safety of the shore I kept an eye on their clothes and an eye on them.

When they were tanked, masked and lined up for the dive it was hard to distinguish one from the other. Even Pammy could be Ken the dentist, or Paul the engineer, except for her height and the general air of anxiety which exuded through her pores. Pammy was not a confident diver.

I did feel rather stranded as I sat patiently on the beach watching the bubbles and I vowed to join the next group once George had officially stamped, approved and certified my husband.

George was an enthusiastic teacher. A long, lean, charismatic Texan who started diving at the age of sixteen in the freshwater lakes of his home state. He traded his Colt six-shooter for a scuba tank and was soon teaching diving at the YMCA in Fort Worth. George arrived on Tortola a month after us, accompanied by his bubbling teenage bride Luana. The lovely Lu was just as devoted to diving as George and together they hoped to make the BVI a prestige diving location.

They planned to chart and photograph areas around the islands aiming not only to find beautiful dive sites, but also to encourage appreciation and understanding of the undersea environment. The reefs surrounding the BVI were beautiful, and virgin, and both George and Lu felt it was part of their joint destiny to plot and preserve this unique heritage.

The most exciting dive was of course the wreck of *RMS Rhone* and George had high hopes that his first qualifying group would help him to explore, investigate and chart the wreck for future divers. The bow lay in 90 ft. of water and was mostly intact, a wonderful haven for an extraordinary assortment of beautiful tropical fish.

Currently there is no legislation in the BVI concerning coral, artifacts, shells or anything else found in the sea. However the US Virgin Islands, and in particular St. John, were planning to set aside small areas of sea as marine National Parks making it illegal to take conchs, coral or to spear-fish. George and Lu were hoping to encourage the BVI legislators to do something similar.

I went with them on a dive to Cane Garden Bay and they very generously allowed me to snorkel with them for a while. I turned back after half an hour so that they could concentrate on their SCUBA techniques. They returned to the beach and unloaded their equipment and stretched out to bask in the sun, chattering among themselves about the things they had seen. Communication underwater is limited to grunts and hand signals, so they couldn't wait to exchange verbal impressions and everyone started to talk at once.

They lyrically described a beautiful, colourful, quiet world of corals, fish, sand and sea. They raved about tube worms. They talked of feather dusters in colours from dark blue to creamy yellow and up to six inches across. Purple sea fans, willowy sea plumes, swaying sea whips with elkhorn, staghorn, brain and star corals in reds, blues, and a rainbow of other colours. Fish, large and small, colourful and curious. Puffer fish that blew themselves into a round ball. Sea urchins with black and spiky pins waving in the gentle current. Butterfly fish. Yellow and blue queen angel fish. Blue chromis and slender filefish that scattered in waves as they approached. Serjeant Majors, small and vulnerable, yellow and black, that swam beside them seeming to peer into their masks, secure in the knowledge that this 'big fish' afforded them protection.

Each of the group had a special observation to share with the rest. George decided to go back out to take some photographs and so my husband, Ken, Dick and myself put on our snorkeling gear and set off with him. George spotted a moray eel hiding in the reef with its mouth open and beady eyes watchful, and pointed it out to us. We saw several lobsters and chased one, but he was too fast and gave us the slip. And a tiny octopus, surrounded by small shells, allowed us to dive down and inspect him. We swam for almost an hour before turning back to the beach.

We thought George was following us but he had been tempted by just one more camera shot. As we sat in the surf removing our fins, George glided in towards us. He was carrying a baby nurse shark, only about eighteen inches long, grasped firmly in his hands. As we crowded round to look at the plump, creamy creature George explained that it had been resting on the sandy bottom, but with no sign of mama. He turned and swam back, carefully replacing the little shark where he had found it.

Cane Garden was a popular beach for local shark fishing. I had not witnessed a shark catch but Ken described how the villagers in the area dug a large pit in the sand and hauled the shark out of the sea, rolled it into the pit and piled sand on top. The shark, usually a sand shark, would suffocate and the following morning the body would be lifted out, cut up and shared amongst the fishermen as a wonderful and much appreciated source of food. To suffocate the shark was much simpler and more humane they maintained, than trying to club it to death.

George told us about the time he had been diving off The Indians, an area west of Pelican Island and about half an hour boat ride from Road Harbour. He was swimming around admiring the tall rock formations, when a shark appeared from nowhere coming rapidly in his direction. As it approached George gave it a quick wallop on the nose and it backed off, just long enough for George to turn back to his boat. He was almost there when the shark moved forward again, coming this time with an open mouth. George had his camera in one hand and the flash gun in the other and he quickly reached out and stuffed the flash gun into the shark's open mouth.

As he climbed into the boat he was aware of a broken bulb floating up to the surface, but as he said afterwards *"Better the flash gun than my leg!"*

The SCUBA group all successfully completed the first half of their test. They had to rescue a 'drowning' person, give them mouth to mouth resuscitation, dive into the pool holding fins, snorkel and mask and put them all on underwater. Then clear the mask, surface and clear the snorkel. All this followed by a half a mile swim, the equivalent of forty eight lengths of Slaney pool. At the end of this gruelling test they all looked absolutely shattered, but George was extremely proud of them, and my husband surprised himself by coming second in the half mile marathon.

The next test required them to take off their tanks underwater, buddy-breathe by sharing someone else's breathing apparatus and generally prove that they were capable of sorting themselves out underwater should something unpredictable occur. The final test was another written test on safe pressures, embolism, relative surface and depth pressures and a host of safety regulations. George was very thorough and very strict with them.

CHAPTER 23

EARTHQUAKE, SCORPION AND BABY SHOWER

The weather could be very unpredictable on Tortola with hot clear skies one minute and then, quite suddenly, heavy thunderstorms which passed across the island and were over just as quickly as they came. The thunder would crack and rumble virtually overhead and could be quite frightening. The whole room would tremble and vibrate in an alarming manner.

The first sign of impending rain was a strong wind which suddenly appeared from nowhere. When you looked up at the clear blue sky you could see, in the distance way out to sea, a black and ominous cloud heading directly for the island.

Then the saturated cloud hit the high ridge as it passed over the island and literally burst. The deluge which followed in the next few minutes was astonishing. Then the rain would stop as abruptly as if someone had turned off a tap, with a rush of wind in its wake, and then beautiful bright blue sky and hot sunshine again.

With five minutes of hard rain the roads were soon awash with mud and all the low lying areas became flooded. Then we all knew that within a few days the mosquitoes would be bad and biting, having quickly bred in the trapped pools of water.

I was alone in the apartment when I heard what I thought was the familiar sound of rumbling thunder, and the room began to shake. But on looking up I could see clear blue sky with no sign of a cloud. The rumbling continued and my pictures started to swing wildly on the wall and I assumed it was Bob's heavy JCB passing below the apartment.

Then, above the noise, I heard Audrey's familiar anxiety shriek. As I got up, the rumble passed away and the floor stopped wobbling. My pictures on the walls were hanging crooked, an ornament had fallen off the shelf and two glasses had tumbled from the drainer and smashed into pieces on the floor. I went onto the balcony to call out to Audrey below, but before I could she had come crashing through my front door, hugging a startled little Thomas tightly to her chest.

All she could say was *"Oh my God, Oh my God!"* in a strangled half-gasp. It took Pat, who was following close behind, to explain to me that what I had thought was thunder, or a JCB, was in fact an earthquake. We spent the next half hour trying to calm Audrey down. We heard later that the epicentre was out to sea but the earthquake had registered six on the Richter scale. We suffered high tides and rough seas but no damage to any buildings or people, except perhaps to Audrey's nerves.

After that we had several little tremors, usually in the early hours of the morning when the bed wobbled briefly and woke us. Or at the office, when the desk developed a tendency to shimmy for a few seconds, but nothing on the scale of that first earthquake which so terrified poor Audrey.

It was shortly after this experience Audrey discovered she was pregnant. Already in a heightened state of anxiety, she said nothing on earth would persuade her to stay on Tortola to produce the baby. So she and Nicholas decided to leave the island and return home to England. Audrey really missed England. She pined for supermarkets, buses, parents, cinema and TV (not necessarily in that order) and detested the mosquitoes, cockroaches, and germs in the BVI.

We hoped the decision to leave Tortola would help settle Audrey's nerves. But another unfortunate incident shortly after the earthquake threw her into total panic. Husband Nicholas, in his vague and nonchalant manner, had placed his shoes outside the back door of the apartment overnight. The following morning, still half asleep, he committed the cardinal error, he forgot to knock out his shoes before slipping in his bare feet. His howl of agony brought out not only a terrified Audrey, in her flimsy negligee, but

134

the whole apartment block. A scorpion was attached to his big toe and was most unwilling to let go.

We all, very unsympathetically, fell about laughing because the sight of Nicholas hopping and shrieking with Audrey swooning and flapping was very entertaining. And we also knew that this type of scorpion only inflicted a mild sting, not unlike a wasp, so Nicholas was not in any danger. But for Audrey it really was the last straw, she disappeared back inside and immediately began to pack.

As Audrey packed her crates to leave, Pam's pregnancy was progressing well. Pat and I decided to adopt an American custom and organize a baby shower for her. I volunteered to provide food and liquid refreshment for a host of girl friends who were to arrive in discreet ones and twos. When they were all gathered I was to go and find Pam and by some pretext get her up to our apartment. Then we would all shout 'surprise' and embarrass her with hugs, kisses, and presents for the expected baby.

Some of the English girls, unfamiliar with this American tradition, were slightly apprehensive and felt it would be more appropriate to wait until a successful delivery before celebrating the event, but Pam had a model pregnancy and we argued that there was no reason to suppose anything might go wrong.

When the day arrived everything appeared to be going like clockwork. Pat and I beavered away baking bits and pieces for the crowd. I used my bright red, lace-lined parasol upturned for all the presents and we decorated a 'throne' with balloons and ribbons for our guest of honour.

But at 3.00 p.m. Pam had not returned home, and by 3.30 p.m. we were all getting a bit fidgety and wondered if maybe she had decided to go shopping, or visiting, or was involved in something else equally inconsiderate to our surprise plan. Thankfully at 3.45 p.m. her little yellow 'moke' was spotted chugging up the drive and I was dispatched to lure her up. She swallowed my story and arrived at my door quite unprepared for the surprise, but she was absolutely delighted.

But it was a wonder the shock didn't start premature labour!

CHAPTER 24

POT, PARTIES AND FIREWORKS

Our close neighbours the US Virgin Islands were obsessed with the illegal narcotics trade which spilled in and around the islands of the Caribbean, but the BVI seemed to be immune and peacefully oblivious to such problems, or so we thought.

Unknown to us an FBI agent was working undercover on a yacht passing through the Virgin Islands on its way to New York. On board was an enormous quantity of marijuana, divided into large bags. The yacht was stopping off at isolated islands along its route and hiding bales of the stuff in secret places.

When the yacht finally reached New York the undercover agent was able to identify the islands and the FBI, together with US Customs, swung into action. They arrived on Tortola seeking the approval and assistance of our BVI Police and Customs, and swooped on a rocky outcrop we call Fallen Jerusalem.

I could see the chunky nodule of Fallen Jerusalem from our apartment. It looked less like an island and more as if a builder had tipped his rubble into the sea. Not the sort of place anyone would normally visit. Even cruising yachts passed it by, which is presumably why it had appealed to the drug smugglers as the perfect hiding place.

BVI Police, FBI and US Customs stepped ashore to search for the large bag of marijuana which according to the Agent had been hidden there. To their surprise (and delight) they discovered what they described as *"a pot party in full swing"* and joyfully arrested everyone. The huge bag of marijuana which had been dropped by the yacht was not to be found, believed to have been divided and distributed long ago, but the bonus arrest of a group of users was a triumph for our BVI Customs.

The day following this success BVI Customs threw themselves with enthusiasm into thoroughly searching the baggage of every LIAT passenger arriving at the airport. They were trying to impress the FBI agents who were propping up the wall, beers in hand, waiting to board the onward LIAT flight to the USVI.

I just happened to be in the airport building at the time, checking my weight on the LIAT baggage scales (the only sure way on island of checking your personal poundage!) I had just stepped down from the scales, definitely diet time, as the plane rumbled in. Customs sprang into frenzied action. It was a long, time-consuming exercise. Every item in every suitcase was picked through and closely inspected. No-one really expected to find anything but to Customs great surprise and excitement they discovered some marijuana in the suitcases of two incoming tourists. The FBI agents were duly impressed.

The BVI 'pot puffers' who were discovered partying on Fallen Jerusalem were all white expats. They were not Rastafarians with dreadlocks from Jamaica. There are no Rastafarians in the BVI at the moment.

Rastafarians, named after Haile Selassie, Emperor of Ethiopia (known as 'Ras' Tafari before his coronation) considered marijuana important to spiritual, mental and physical health. Rastas felt they had divine sanction from the Bible to use 'ganja' and therefore have no respect for a law which considers their 'herb' an illegal substance.

For a few days the jail was very full. As well as the two permanent residents at the prison, and the pot-party revelers, another young man had been arrested on a more serious charge.

It all started when two young men were driving in their car towards West End. Suddenly the tyre blew and the car slewed to a stop. Both climbed out to inspect the damage and agreed that one of them would have to replace the flat with the spare. Neither wanted to change the wheel and a heated argument broke out. They both lost their tempers. In the anger of the moment one of the young men reached into the car and took his spear-gun from the back seat. He pointed the gun at his friend and pressed the trigger. The harpoon went straight into the chest of his companion.

A passing motorist gathered up the injured man, spear-gun and friend and raced to the hospital. Although they quickly performed an emergency operation, the poor young man died from his wounds. The barbs on the dart had made withdrawal difficult, and there was nothing the doctors could do. So now the other young man was in the jail on a charge of murder.

By this time, almost a year into our contract on island, our own lives on Tortola had settled into a comfortable routine. My life was slightly less demanding than my husband's. He was obliged to stay at the office during office hours, visit sites, supervise constructions, draw drawings, calculate calculations and organize existing jobs and find new work. But I spent my morning in the office doing any necessary typing, chatting to friends who passed through, writing letters home, and making coffee. And then at lunch time we both came back home for a sandwich and snatched a siesta.

I had the afternoon off. Sometimes I visited friends, or they visited me. Other times I just plopped into the pool and cooled off. There were usually one or two other expats similarly plopping so the company was always pleasant and the afternoon very relaxed.

Evenings could be dinner parties, pub and darts, SCUBA in the pool, or drinks with friends. And weekends usually incorporated a beaching of one sort or another, again with friends. An occasional sail, BBQ, or visit to St. Thomas helped to add variety. There was little else to do on Tortola.

We once visited the local cinema, making up a foursome with the island dentist Ken and his wife. We were advised to wear long trousers tucked into tight boots and to keep our knees at chin level throughout the performance.

The reason became clear as the lights dimmed and went down. The noise made by scurrying cockroaches was so loud it could be heard above the sound track of the film. As the lights went on again during the interval, the dazzled cockroaches halted momentarily in mid-chew before scattering in all directions. Anyone with bare legs was likely to find a confused cockroach heading rapidly upwards in search of a dark hiding place, an altogether unnerving and unpleasant experience.

However the cockroaches were, we all agreed, slightly more entertaining to watch than the film which kept breaking, whining and bubbling. It was an experience we were not keen to repeat.

So on Tortola we relied on each other for amusement, which was why dinner parties and evening drinks were so popular. I found myself doing quite a lot of entertaining. After my tentative early starts I had become quite proficient and launched happily into dinner parties, coffee mornings and afternoon teas. We were invited out so often that I was forced into returning the favour. We couldn't keep taking guests out to dinner at expensive hotel restaurants. Pleasant though it was, the office budget wouldn't stretch. And having experienced some diabolical meals at friends' houses I realized that my cooking wasn't really so bad, and most people simply enjoyed visiting, chatting and boozing, the quality of the catering being fairly irrelevant.

I particularly enjoyed cooking for the bachelors, they were so grateful because anything I could produce was superior to the mess they usually prepared for themselves and they would shower me with compliments all evening.

Because we had to make our own entertainment it meant that any occasion which could be celebrated with a party became a popular island event. Which is why we made November 5th a grand and memorable evening by having a traditional British Guy Fawkes bonfire. It also served to show our American friends what a real fireworks party should be like. They made a great fuss on Independence Day, July 4th, but we were determined to show them how it should be done Brit style.

The Cable and Wireless expatriate employees organized it, primarily for their children. We were very pleased to be invited along. Generally the Cable and Wireless contingent kept themselves to themselves and did not often mix with the expatriate business community. Our invitation to join them was unusual and much appreciated.

To show my appreciation I made some traditional Guy Fawkes Yorkshire parkin to take along. Although I followed the recipe very carefully I think I must have done something wrong because the parkin my mum made never tasted like this. It was rock solid and such a dark brown it could have passed as black. I blamed the flour which was the American All-purpose kind, and I was not convinced that the shiny brown weevils I noticed wriggling in the flour hadn't created some sort of a chemical reaction with the other ingredients. But everyone was kind and tactfully disposed of their pieces when they thought I wasn't looking.

The Cable and Wireless Receiving Station was high up on the ridge above Road Town and was manned twenty-four hours a day, seven days a week, which meant some of the men did shift work and unsocial hours. One of the young men was therefore on duty when we had the Bonfire Party and unable to join enjoy the fun. Each time a rocket was prepared for flight we phoned him at the station before letting it off so that he could watch and appreciate.

We had a tremendous quantity of fireworks all stunning and impressive and it was a delight to watch the children's faces. Knowing that the whole island was probably watching the display from their balconies or local bars, my husband created an unusual 'double rocket' in a bid to outperform the American July 4th show. Although sound in principle it failed to perform in practice. The double rocket launched, raced for the sky, double somersaulted, ignited stage two, and then shot back down to earth at the speed of light. Everyone ran for cover. The children were delighted and begged for a repeat performance.

It was a fun evening and we met a whole new group of people who lived and worked on Tortola, all Cable and Wireless, mostly British, and several couples who had lived or worked in our own Surrey area before coming out to the BVI.

CHAPTER 25

BABY-SITTING AND ST. JOHN

Because most of my friends on Tortola had children they were determined to introduce me to the joys of motherhood. They persuaded me to sample their offspring for short periods and I seemed to be becoming an 'auntie' to several children.

Pat roped me in to help supervise Simone's third birthday party. It was an exhausting afternoon and I was amazed that I actually survived. Then Penny loaned me little Stephanie overnight and it was with great misgivings that I agreed. I wanted to help Penny but the responsibility of looking after someone else's child was daunting.

Penny had been unwell for some time. She travelled to Puerto Rico to see a specialist where they discovered her pituitary gland was not functioning correctly. A few months ago she was a well-proportioned lovely leggy blonde with model statistics, the sort of girl who should be on the front cover of a glossy fashion magazine. But she had been losing a lot of weight recently and was beginning to look gaunt and listless.

So when she asked me to look after 20 month old Stephanie overnight so that she and her husband could go with friends on a midnight sail, I simply couldn't refuse.

Stephanie was delivered ready for bed. She was so well behaved and angelic. I woke at 5.00 a.m. and had completely forgotten about our little guest, until a mumbling sound issuing from the spare bedroom reminded me. I was vaguely aware of having to put toddlers on potties, so I picked her out of the cot and plonked her on the toilet, and to my astonishment she performed a little miracle immediately. I returned her to the cot and promptly went back to sleep, not waking again until 9.00 a.m.

There was silence in the apartment and a tiptoe inspection revealed Stephanie happily playing with a coat hanger, one of my husband's socks and an empty egg carton, all harvested by her little hands through the bars of the cot.

I had no idea what to give a 20 month old for breakfast. Penny had failed to provide me with instructions and I should have phoned Audrey or Pat for advice. Being unfamiliar with the feeding of little people, I simply produced three servings of bacon, eggs and toast. Stephanie gazed at her plate and puzzled over this for several minutes before it occurred to me I should cut the bacon into tiny bits. She watched me with great interest, and when the plate was returned to her she heaped everything together with her hands and stuffed the combined pile into her mouth.

We were mesmerized. I was lucky she didn't choke. I realized I had a lot to learn about children.

We had returned Stephanie safely to her parents and were just recovering from the responsibility when the phone rang. It was the manager of Chase Manhattan Bank, on a Sunday morning. Not business this time but pleasure.

Ron had a small 'whaler' with an outboard engine, just large enough for three thin people to sit in comfortably, and he wanted to know if we would like to join him for an excursion across to the US Virgin Island of St. John. Although part of the US Virgin Islands, St. John was so close to West End Tortola that it seemed only a short leap across the dividing sea.

Of course we jumped at the chance. We never refused an invitation to go to sea. The water was flat calm and the weather perfect, and the trip from the rocks beneath Ron's house at West End across the channel to the peaceful Virgin Island of St. John was smooth and fast. We dropped anchor just outside the line of floats across Trunk Bay which cordoned off the new underwater conservation area.

Ron and my husband jumped overboard to swim for the shore and I was about to follow when I looked down and saw the dark shadow of a large flat fish, a stingray I thought. I hesitated, he was

142

almost 3 ft. across, even allowing for the magnification of the water, and he hovered just below the surface exactly where I had planned to jump. Ron and my husband, now some distance away, were treading water and calling for me to jump. So I did, on top of the stingray.

As I hit the water I felt something brush against my leg and I swam with manic thrashing speed towards the men. And the stingray decided to keep me company, flipping gently alongside me, teasing me.

I am a nervous swimmer. The sea is an alien and slightly frightening place to me. I needed the companionship of other swimmers to give me confidence. So instead of seeing the brush with the stingray as an exciting and wonderful marine encounter, I viewed it with panic and alarm.

Ron admitted to me later that he had seen the ray when he jumped overboard himself and his reaction had been somewhat similar to mine. My husband however, did not at first believe me and was then irked to think that he had missed the wonderful opportunity of coming face to face and swimming with such an elegant and beautiful creature.

Trunk Bay was completely deserted, only us three and our small boat bobbing up and down out to sea. We put on snorkels and masks and followed the underwater Nature Trail, the first of its kind in the world, which had been laid out along the ocean floor. It was fascinating, educational and very beautiful. My husband was hoping to see my graceful stingray companion as we swam slowly back to the boat, but he was disappointed.

Ron took the boat around the cove, moored offshore, and putting on our shoes we waded gingerly through a bed of spiky black sea urchins to the beach.

Viewed from Tortola, St. John always looked pristine and tranquil, the green hillsides rising up from the blue sea with not a single house or human intrusion in sight. The bays were ribbons of yellow velvet against the green of the slopes. Man had not yet polluted this beautiful place, all that was there was in harmony.

It was a supremely special island, an island of serenity. Ron wanted to show us the ruins of an 18th century sugar mill which was in remarkably good order. So we toiled up the hillside and it was certainly worth the effort. During the latter part of the 18th century Tortola (and some of the other islands like St. John and Jost Van Dyke) was very productive. Over one hundred estates or plantations were recorded, most growing sugar and many owned by Quakers. There are almost thirty places on Tortola where sugar mills and distilleries used to stand, but now were ruined sites. We had stumbled across one when we were exploring the ridge road above Road Town, and managed to identify the old coppers, pot still and coiled 'worm', all relics of the rum making equipment.

In the old days the hillsides of Tortola and St. John were covered with sugar cane which was cut during spring and hauled by mules to the mills. Rum made from pure cane juice was light and mixed well with ginger ale to create our favorite drink 'Virgin's Thigh'.

We completed our tourist trip to Trunk Bay and St. John by returning to Ron's home at West End, a large sprawling villa high on a hill looking out over the sea towards St. John. We sat on his stone patio beside a huge tamarind tree, listening to tree frogs and watching the red sun sink slowly behind the verdant hills of St. John, rum and ginger in hand.

Little did we know that one day, years later, we would be living in that very house ourselves!

CHAPTER 26

FRIENDS AND FAREWELLS

Most of our friends were, like us, expats employed on a contract basis, and the saddest part of our life on Tortola was saying goodbye to those leaving at the end of their contract period.

We seemed to spend a great deal of time driving along the bumpy East End road to Beef Island, crossing the narrow Queen Elizabeth Bridge and waving sadly to tearful buddies as the afternoon LIAT trundled down the runway for take-off.

Occasionally we would return with some of their discarded baggage. LIAT weighed both passengers and luggage, because if the DC3 was heavy it wouldn't manage to lift off and since the runway ended in the sea there was no second chance. As a matter of routine, each time the plane revved up for take-off we would cross our fingers and hope the calculations done by the friendly LIAT staff were correct.

Carol and Tony were two friends who had departed. Their gardening enterprise on Tortola had not been a success, so Tony cut his losses and returned home to England. Then Leone left, and Tony Norman too. Tony was a good friend. He was a young bachelor trainee architect who always seemed somewhat lost and quite lovable. We had to watch over him in the sea and the swimming pool because if he dived under water he lost his sense of direction and forgot which way was up, very alarming! He was also colour blind, not a problem as a general rule but it made for some hilarious suggestions when he was asked to offer his views as an architect on interior design.

Audrey also left, clutching little Thomas tightly to her chest but leaving Nicholas behind to sort things out before he too would leave. Understandably, the pregnant Audrey wanted to be home in England for Christmas.

The new condominium at the Treasure Isle Hotel offered to us by Herbie Showering was completed just in time for us to have our first island Christmas there.

We spent several days busily moving in. We managed to transfer our few belongings with two quick trips in the landrover, piling the back high with our bits and pieces. The condominium was stunningly beautiful and I was in heaven. It was on the first floor with two bedrooms, two bathrooms, a huge cool lounge with quarry-tiled floor and an immense pair of sliding glass doors to a large balcony with spectacular views over the shimmering Caribbean.

Standing on the balcony we had a full 180° view. The sheltered bay below rippled brightly with reflected light and was a joy to gaze on. The first thing we did was to paste paper butterflies onto the wall of glass to warn visitors of its presence. Friends stepped into the condominium, saw the magnificent view, rushed towards the balcony saying *'wow!'* and *'gosh!'* and *'how fantastic!'* and crashed into the dividing glass wall with painful consequences.

The second bedroom and bathroom were completely self-contained with a separate entrance that could be bolted off from the main condominium as an independent apartment. Very useful, we agreed gleefully, when Porky came to stay. When he wanted breakfast or a midnight feast he would have to gain admittance by knocking on the front door.

Mr. and Mrs. Hooper, the elderly couple who managed the Treasure Isle Hotel, were incredibly helpful and kind. They had been plucked from Shepton Mallet in England by Herbie who discovered them quietly running the local pub. They arrived with their son Mark who promptly took charge of the marine side of the business, and proved to be a real asset to the hotel.

Herbie Showering also found Mick, the general handyman on the Pasea Estate, working in Somerset and persuaded him to come out to Tortola. Mick was a real character, an extraordinary transplant to find in the West Indies. His soft Wiltshire burr and rural English ways seemed altogether contradictory on this hot, tropical West Indian island. He was a genuine piece of rustic England transplanted temporarily on Tortola, and we loved him for it. Like Mark and our good friend 'sailor Ben', he preferred to pad about in bare feet and ragged shorts. His broad shoulders bare to the sun, his hair tousled and tangled. He called me *'Blossom'* and I felt like one of his favourite Wiltshire cows. He had a habit of wandering into our condominium unannounced and at any time to fix the plumbing or have a gossip.

I happened to mention casually and in passing to Mrs. Hooper that the freezer compartment of my new fridge was smaller than the one I'd had at Slaney. Unknown to me the kind-hearted Mrs. Hooper promptly rushed out to buy me a replacement. The shop did not have the fridge Mrs. Hooper ordered, so they sent along the next size up. This meant that Mick, who was in charge of placing the enormous *'beast'* in my kitchen, was required to remove first the front door of the condominium, then the kitchen door, then the frame round the kitchen door, and finally remove the two doors of the new freezer and fridge, before at last managing to squeeze it, with just a hairsbreadth to spare, into my kitchen.

This took several hours and required many cans of cold Bud to lubricate the Wiltshire cogs as they wrestled with the apparently insoluble problem of getting the *'beast'* under control and into my kitchen. Mick was quite exhausted when he left, and swore me to secrecy. I was not to disclose ownership of the *'beast'* to anyone, because the other tenants, particularly those with families, would petulantly insist on equality, and poor Mick couldn't face going through all that again.

As Christmas approached inconsiderate Porky sent a huge pile of personal Christmas cards bundled together with an accompanying note which had the terse instruction *'please distribute personally'*. Did he really expect me to spend several days acting as postman calling on each addressee and handing over his card? Too tedious and time consuming so I put them in the local post with all the others, at 4c per letter I considered it money well spent out of the petty cash.

We decided the condominium should have a Christmas tree, but of course there were no traditional green firs available on Tortola. A number of homesick expats had brought a plastic apology for a tree with them but we decided to search out a Caribbean alternative to both plastic and pine. The obvious choice was the dramatic Century plant. It grew wild and in profusion on the island and shortly before its demise, just once in its lifetime, it produced a magnificent long pole of beautiful yellow flowers. This final effort proving too much for the waxy succulent and it then simply withered and died. But as the yellow flowers seeded and dispersed they left behind a tall and impressive woody stem of alternating arms. And this was perfect for decorating into a rather sparse but nevertheless exotic Christmas tree alternative.

We combed the island for an appropriate stalk, trudged through the undergrowth with our machete, then hacked and hauled our specimen home. Sprayed with silver paint and garlanded with ribbons it was the most beautiful Christmas tree in the whole world.

CHAPTER 27

PELICANS AND PEEBLES

One of my husband's jobs was the supervision of the construction of Chase Manhattan Bank being built on Wickhams Cay. They were nearing completion and piling was due to begin for the new Barclays Bank to be built alongside. These were the first two buildings to occupy the vast reclaimed acreage of crushed shells that was the Wickhams Cay site.

The island's Chief Electrical Engineer would take his golf clubs onto the Cay and rid himself of his frustrations by whacking balls left, right and centre. He thought the Cay would make a good golf course and suggested as much to the business community. They were not impressed.

One of Bob Gray's Readymix concrete trucks took a tumble recently. The driver was coming into Road Town with his heavy load rotating nicely when he misjudged a bend, slithered off the road and slid into the mangrove swamp. It was stuck fast and with such a heavy load presented something of a problem.

Bob was beside himself with anger when he discovered the mishap, and as the concrete in the drum started to harden he began to panic. There was no way the truck could be lifted out of the swamp and as time passed it became evident that the concrete inside was rapidly going off. My husband told me that in England Readymix lorry drivers always carried bags of sugar in their cab and if they wanted to stop the concrete hardening, for whatever reason, they would throw in the sugar.

But Bob's load of concrete went solid. And so it was that the poor driver was issued with ear muffs and a kango hammer and thrust into the drum. Finally, after a great deal of trouble, the truck was rescued and righted.

Bob had big plans for the mangrove swamp at Pelican Point below the Slaney apartments. The mangrove trees with their characteristic aerial roots arching into the water offered a safe haven for pelicans and other birds. It provided a picturesque buffer between the sea and the road. When we were at the Slaney apartments the mangroves below offered me hours of tranquil visual interest and entertainment as I watched the pelicans that roosted there rise, circle, and dive for fish.

But Bob intended to build a huge leisure development in the area and so the mangrove was destined to go. Already a D8 bulldozer had mashed and mangled its way through the outer stalks, crushing the mangrove onto the coral reef beneath. It may be the price of progress, but we were saddened to see the destruction of this natural habitat. It was another reason why we chose to leave our Slaney apartment and move to the Treasure Isle condominiums.

Griselda came with me to our new home. She was delighted to be asked especially as we were closer to her room in Huntums Ghaut. She had finally married the father of her two boys but since he was unemployed Griselda's salary was keeping the household going.

Griselda had explained to me that as a 'white lady' and her employer my wedding present to her would need to be seen to be extravagant and generous. *Very* extravagant and *very* generous she added with sly emphasis. It would be a sign to her friends that she was held in high esteem. I was uncertain of her expectations but knowing that her future husband was unemployed I gave her cash since I thought hard cash would be appreciated.

Just before the wedding Griselda discovered a flimsy white negligee in my wardrobe. She begged me to let her have it to wear as a wedding dress. How to explain, as tactfully as possible, that it was not a dress but a nightie? Transparent, figure hugging, and provocatively designed to expose sexy female features as seductively as possible, it was far more appropriate for the honeymoon night than the wedding aisle. Also, and the argument which finally convinced Griselda it was inappropriate, it was far too small for her. Her rotund little body would never have squeezed into it. She was crestfallen and very disappointed.

Around this time Griselda developed a craving for my Rice Krispies. She would tuck into my box of cereal by the handful, and I became convinced she was pregnant. As the wedding approached she began to balloon and my suspicions were confirmed. Given the circumstances, we both agreed, my negligee would have been the least appropriate garment she could have chosen to wear on her special day.

The day before Pam's baby was due she and Pat called in for a cup of coffee. Instead of driving up and around by the Pasea Estate road, they decided to park by the Treasure Isle Hotel at the bottom of the hill and walk up by way of the 1001 steps through the hotel gardens. When I caught sight of them, halfway up the hill, Pam was leaning against a post puffing like a beached whale while Pat massaged her back and clucked encouragingly. Pam finally made it to the apartment and collapsed onto a chair. We gazed anxiously at her wondering whether, after the exertion of the climb the baby might decide to pop out there and then.

But Pam recovered and after an hour she was back to her placid, kindly self. The locals say babies are born with the full moon and it was a full moon that night. They also have a saying that life on Tortola is so relaxed and slow it takes eleven months to have a baby here!

The following day Pam produced a bouncing baby girl. We said it was the full moon, but she said it was all on account of the gruelling climb up those steps from the hotel. She thought something was beginning to happen then, and she was right. All through that night she had what she called *'funny feelings'* and by mid-day she thought she had better make her way down to Peebles Hospital. And three hours twenty minutes later out popped a beautiful baby girl.

Great celebrations during the evening with massive back slapping for the triumphant dad and huge cigars all round. Dad Terry stayed around during the whole proceedings, and such was his interest that he had to be forcibly pushed out of the way during the crucial moment of birth. I raced down to the hospital to see

Pam and new baby Sophie within minutes of the news, and there was Pam sitting up in bed all pink and smiling and glowing with maternal pride.

The food at Peebles left much to be desired and so Pat and I took it in turns to provide meals on wheels, preparing and taking in Pam's lunch and dinner each day. Pam enjoyed Peebles so much she stayed four extra nights and only decided to leave when another patient arrived. A young Tortolian who needed her appendix removed.

The new patient did not suffer stoically and in silence. She moaned, cried, screamed and wept loudly and persistently, her voice seeming to gain strength as the anaesthetic wore off. After several hours of *'Oh my God'* and *'Mummy, mummy'* at an ear-splitting decibel high, Pam could no longer bear it, and discharging herself went home.

CHAPTER 28

THE INFIRMARY PATIENTS

When the BVI Red Cross Society, presided over by the Governor's wife Vrai Cudmore, decided that the island Infirmary was well overdue for some attention they begged some pots of paint and a handful of brushes from one of the Road Town stores, and six of us volunteered to spend a few hours of our time brightening the place up a bit.

The volunteers included me, four of the young Cable and Wireless wives and one freshly qualified American lady doctor, Yana. We unanimously elected a slightly reluctant Yana as the leader of our little team having agreed she was both more mature and more qualified than the rest of us.

'The Infirmary' was rather a grand name for the small dilapidated hut on the hillside behind the morgue in Road Town. There were six permanent residents, four men and two women. They were considered harmless but helpless and, except for visits by the doctor or the nurses, were left alone and unsupervised throughout the day.

They spent most of their time sitting peacefully on the wooden porch which ran along the front of the building. Sometimes they just sat on their beds, in a world of their own, waiting for a nurse to bring medication or a meal from the hospital below.

The Infirmary was reached by taking the narrow stony path to the right of Peebles hospital. The winding path went up past bushes draped with hospital sheets drying in the sun, and continued in front of the tiny one-roomed morgue and on past a well to the three-roomed wooden hut of the Infirmary.

Beyond the Infirmary the path meandered on and upwards through the scrub and bushes of the hillside to end at another hut, home to one man and one woman on *'welfare'*. Both were considered to be mentally backward but quite capable of looking after themselves, so they lived together in the hut while the six patients who were unable to look after themselves lived in the Infirmary.

When I first saw the Infirmary my heart sank. I thought we must have been sent to the wrong building. It needed more than a lick of paint to make it habitable, it needed flattening and rebuilding.

Mary was the first resident we met. She was the most lucid of the six inmates at the Infirmary and was the one in charge of getting drinking water for the others. She would drop the old paint can by its string into the well to haul up the water.

It was Mary who saw us climbing the hillside on the very first day. She was standing barefoot on the verandah in a tight, faded summer frock both too small and too short for her, surrounded by chickens. She watched in obvious consternation as six white women of assorted age chattered together as they wound their way in single file up the stony path towards her. She began to cluck and cackle as we came closer, flapping her arms in apprehension.

John, another resident, was inside but hearing the noise had crawled to the door to look. Unable to walk normally because of a limb deformity he moved along by shuffling on his bottom. At the sight of us he retreated rapidly back inside the Infirmary.

We set down our pots of paint and went inside to see what we were up against. Up the steps onto the wooden verandah, through the open wooden door. The entrance widened into a small room with a table and a TV. However the TV, we soon discovered, did not work. But the radio did and played away continuously in the corner of the room. This was the room used by the mobile inmates for their meals.

Straight ahead was a door. When we investigated we discovered a small and very smelly toilet. To the right was the ladies bedroom where Mary and Evangeline both slept, and to the left the male bedroom just large enough to take four beds. This was where William, John and the two other men slept.

We six volunteers were quite useless as painters but we were very enthusiastic hospital visitors. We discovered to our surprise that the six inmates did not talk to each other, did not even seem to notice one another. But they were very keen to talk to us and their chatter, though mostly incomprehensible, was incessant.

Mary was the first to be won over. Liz and Maggie kept up a non-stop, cheerful and loud conversation directed at Mary as she inched closer and closer to inspect the paint cans we had put on the verandah. As the lids were levered off and the colours were disclosed, Mary's curiosity overcame her anxiety. She particularly liked the bright canary yellow and as soon as she understood what we intended to do she pulled on Liz's arm and dragged her into the ladies room. Gabbling with gusto she pointed first to the canary yellow and then to the walls. It was crystal clear that she wanted the walls of the bedroom vivid canary.

As we finished opening the donated cans of paint we discovered with disappointment that the colours were quite unsuitable. Wild, and certainly not coordinated, we seemed to have been supplied with odd cans surplus to requirements, rather than colours chosen to be appropriate to a hospital environment. Morbid mud brown, vibrant canary yellow, startling salmon pink, and a revolting, quite disgusting, ghoulish green.

Yana took command. She demonstrated the rudiments of decorating to us lesser able helpers. She patiently explained the need for rubbing down and washing down, and also the differences between water-based and oil-based paints. A lesson which must have fallen on deaf ears since she subsequently discovered Maggie and me puzzling over a brush which stubbornly refused to be cleaned but simply coiled its left-over paint into disgusting blobs, no matter how hard we thrashed the bristles.

We amateurs were reluctant to bother with the rudimentary rub down and pre-wash that Yana felt would produce a more professional finish, so poor Yana found herself undertaking that boring part of the work. She also found herself volunteering to paint the fiddly bits of woodwork while the rest of us grabbed a brush and a pot and set to work on the larger items.

When it came to painting some of us showed a distinct lack of natural talent. Maggie was the worst and proved a very mucky painter. She had absolutely no idea and slopped and slobbered paint all over the walls, the floor, and herself, with great enthusiasm but no technique. But to her everlasting credit she did volunteer to paint the toilet when no-one else would go near it. Yana, holding her nose, quickly assessed the situation and agreed it was probably pointless trying to rub and wash down the toilet and therefore allowed Maggie the freedom to dash and splash at her own reckless pace.

Thanks to Maggie the toilet was transformed into a ghoulish green cubicle with amazing speed. But we spent almost half an hour trying to clean Maggie afterwards. She resembled a green gremlin with paint in her auburn hair, down her arms, her legs and her T-shirt. It was generally agreed the T-shirt was beyond help and Maggie decided she would dispose of it when she reached home, but Yana had an inspiration and asked if we could use it to clean the brushes and so it was generously donated to the cause!

I had the muddy milk chocolate brown and decided to tackle the outside shutters. John came out of the men's bedroom to watch me and shuffled so close to me and my pot, I was worried he might get covered with paint, due to my inexpert wielding of the brush. He studied me intently. His eyes followed my every move, the brush into the pot, up into the air, and down the wood. In, up, down, slop, dribble. Each time he caught my glance a huge grin split his face from ear to ear. Soon he was jabbering away and each time I chatted back he grinned and nodded vigorously. I certainly didn't understand a word John said to me, but somehow it didn't seem to matter. I doubt very much whether John understood me. However he and I quickly developed a very special bond.

Liz discovered a similar bond developing with Mary. But Mary was easier to understand and some sense could be made of her conversation. It was Mary who told us what little she knew of her companions. Since we could only understand about one word in ten of Mary's garbled conversation, the knowledge was incomplete, and the nurses we questioned are unable to fill in the gaps either, which is why we did not know the names of the old man and the young Tortolian in his twenties who shared the male bedroom with William and John.

The young Tortolian man was perhaps the saddest case. He sat on his bed gazing into space, rarely speaking and seeming totally unaware of our existence. He lacked physical co-ordination and so attempts to do anything for him, or with him, were very time consuming and laborious. Apparently he had been involved in a car accident and although he survived he was now in a mental world of his own. Once a week he received a visit from a Tortolian lady who sat beside him on the bed and read the Bible to him. She never acknowledged him, nor spoke directly to him, and once the weekly passage from the Bible had been read, she would rise, smooth down her dress, and leave. The young man did not seem to notice the woman or anyone else, but Liz and Maggie made a point of chattering away to him as they worked round him. He would run his fingers up and down the blanket on his bed restlessly, rhythmically, staring vacantly at the wall.

Liz was wonderful with them all but William was her favourite. Her light-hearted banter kept him smiling and nodding as he sat on his bed. He never left the bedroom but sat on his unmade bed, clad only in rumpled and ancient striped pyjamas with an old, battered brown felt hat on his head. He was devoted to his filthy hat and it was evidently his most treasured possession. He would watch out of the window but never moved from his bed.

It was difficult to put an age on William with his wrinkled brown face and gnarled hands, we guessed somewhere between forty and fifty. We discovered he had a passion for cigars and cigarettes and he was quick to identify the smokers in our group. We dared not leave him alone in the bedroom with a lighted cigarette, so one of us would stay beside him while he puffed away, his eyes rolling blissfully with each lungful of smoke.

The last man at the Infirmary, and the oldest, was grey haired and wiry. He hovered anxiously, grunting with unease and protecting the small cupboard beside his bed. Initially alarmed and disconcerted by our presence it took a little longer to win his trust. He turned out to be something of a perfectionist and became very agitated at our lack of skill. He would sidle up to each of us in turn, closely inspect our handiwork, and with grunts and noises of disgust point out our inadequacies, of which there were many!

Evangeline was the final resident. She could not speak recognizably but simply grunted and nodded. She was always barefoot and wore a simple cotton frock which like Mary's was too tight and too small. She didn't bother with the zip and her dress hung limply open down the back. Evangeline was perhaps about thirty, and was more mentally disturbed than the other residents. She disliked the men intensely and kept away from them. Within minutes of our arrival we realised that her sexual preference was for women. She showed an instant partiality for Maggie and tried to pin her into a corner in the bedroom, but a loud and firm *"No Evangeline!"* was normally sufficient to stop her advances.

We agreed between ourselves that the cupboards beside each bed should be left untouched. They held the few personal possessions of each one, and we did not want to invade their only privacy.

CHAPTER 29

CARIBBEAN CHRISTMAS

Our first Caribbean Christmas went by in a fast blur of parties, food, drink and jollity. A festive week of late nights and very little sleep. We alternated between exhilaration and exhaustion.

The celebrations began in earnest on Christmas Eve when we went to a Cable and Wireless party which never really finished. At about 2.30 a.m. we reluctantly decided we had better leave and we wound our way home, falling in to bed at about 3.00 a.m. to the sounds of a traditional fungi band struggling to play *'Away in a Manger'* in the road below.

When we finally surfaced on Christmas morning I suddenly remembered I was supposed to be at the hospital with the Red Cross, carol singing for the patients. Nursing a hangover I raced up to Peebles Hospital and arrived just in time to stand demurely beside His Excellency the Governor as he solemnly dispensed Christmas greetings to the handful of invalids unfortunate enough to be interned in the hospital over the festive season.

An American priest had been invited along to read cheerful and appropriate passages from the Bible, and then the ad hoc choir of fifteen motley volunteers, myself included, launched into our unique rendition of several popular Christmas carols. Liz and Maggie had also managed to struggle in after the Christmas Eve party and the three of us tried hard to look appropriately pious as H.E. led the singing.

Having finished our duties at the hospital, a small group led by the Governor's wife wound its way up to the Infirmary to distribute presents and kind words to the six inmates. Our friends Mary, Evangeline and John were lined up and waiting nervously in the small entrance room, herded together by one of the nurses. All except William who had stubbornly refused to get dressed and was hiding in the bedroom in his pyjamas.

They looked perplexed and quite bewildered by this unaccustomed attention but then they saw Liz, Maggie and myself and grinned in happy recognition, babbling in greeting.

They gazed uncertainly at the rest of the visitors. Having been groomed by a nurse earlier and pressured into behaving by Dr. Smith, they were obviously unsure what was happening and very apprehensive. Mary, wearing her one and only dress, looked scrubbed and neat. All of them were, as usual, barefoot.

The Governor's wife solemnly handed each inmate a small, prettily wrapped parcel, working her way down the line, offering a limp hand and murmuring appropriate Christmas greetings. Evangeline was the last in line and she gazed blankly at the Governor's wife as she leaned forward to present the Christmas gift.

We three could sense that Evangeline thought something was expected of her, but what? Remembering Evangeline's little weakness for women, we looked at each other in alarm. To our horror Evangeline suddenly lunged at Vrai Cudmore, flung her arms around her and squeezed the breath out of her with a rib crushing bear hug. Liz and I leapt forward knowing from personal experience what was bound to follow Evangeline's initial hug. We couldn't possibly allow His Excellency's wife the indignity of being publicly fumbled in an inappropriate place by an inmate of the Infirmary!

With admirable poise the Governor's wife deftly parried Evangeline's attempted grope, while Liz and I neatly caught the offending arms and pinned them to Evangeline's side. And we held on, very firmly, until the Governor's wife, acting as if nothing had happened, marched quickly and safely out into the sunshine and away.

Evangeline clucked and grunted happily while Liz and I tried desperately to control our giggles. We refused to release our hold on her until all the official visitors had left. Evangeline was *very* taken with the Governor's wife and seemed genuinely distressed when she left.

After that incident we affectionately nicknamed the Governor's wife Vrai Cudmore *'Cuddles'*.

We stayed behind for an hour to give our own presents to our friends, and to hang some Christmas decorations. We thought it would cheer the place up a bit. William had his promised cigar which we lit for him and supervised, and Mary was given a red straw hat which she put on and then refused to remove, even during Christmas dinner. We had asked Dr. Smith if we could give them a small sip of rum as a special Christmas treat. He thought it would perk them up wonderfully and wholeheartedly approved, adding as an afterthought *"So long as you don't get them rolling drunk!"*

So we found their enamel mugs and poured a bare quarter inch of Cane Garden Bay rum into each. They were thrilled. Even the sad young man sipped at the rum when Liz held the cup to his lips, and he turned his eyes to look her as the burning taste of the drink revealed itself in his swallow. This was wonderful, it was the first responsive sign we'd had from him.

William beamed. Sitting on his bed in his disreputable pyjamas wearing his disgusting hat, he was in heaven puffing on a huge cigar and sipping rum. When he held out the empty mug and grunted, it seemed unkind to refuse him another. When the nurses climbed the hill with Christmas dinner, we thought we had better leave, but we promised to see them all in the New Year.

We had invited Bob, Pat and little Simone, Terry, Pam and new baby Sophie, Nicholas and his sister Caroline (who had arrived to keep Nicholas company in Audrey's absence) to join us for Christmas dinner and we agreed to combine our talents and produce the feast together.

Tortola's favourite Christmas songs were *Frosty the Snowman* and *I'm Dreaming of a White Christmas* which were played on the radio *ad nauseum* but we had real difficulty relating to snow, snowmen, and frost when basking in temperatures of 80°F. It didn't seem appropriate to tuck into a traditional Christmas dinner under the sweltering heat of a mid-day tropical sun so we decided to delay the actual festive banquet until the cool of late evening.

We had the full Christmas dinner works, turkey, fancy hats, crackers and Christmas pud. And then the men staggered out onto the tennis court for a frivolous game of tennis, paper hats and all. We should have visited two more parties on Christmas Day but there is only so much anyone can pack into twenty four hours.

Boxing Day found us sleeping in. We discovered later Mark had called twice, banging so loudly on our door that he woke both sets of neighbours, but not us! He was heading off in the hotel boat to Cooper Island and wanted to invite us along. But instead we drove down to Josiah's beach on the north shore and enjoyed some peace and solitude and having regained a modicum of sanity we returned to yet another Cable and Wireless party, not leaving until the early hours.

Having the landrover meant we could find beaches inaccessible to others and Josiah's beach was one of our favourites. With a clean crescent of pure white sand it was always deserted, always refreshing, and because it was the north shore, a sea that surfed into the beach.

The following day we thought a walk up Sage Mountain might clear our heads and so we rumbled and bounced along the ridge road until it dwindled into nothing and finished. And then we took to foot.

No-one rode the spine of the ridge road regularly. The condition of the road and the access up Joe's Hill made journeys to the ceiling of Tortola special and infrequent. Maybe this inaccessibility was why Sage Mountain had remained so natural and enchanting. It was the highest point on Tortola, rising to over 1,700 feet and an extraordinary contrast to the scrub of the surrounding hillside and the sandy bays below. Traces of primaeval rain forest had been found on its slopes and to hike through the area was to slip temporarily into the fantasy world of Tarzan and Jane.

The Sage Mountain people were friendly and charming with a quiet, reserved dignity. I was talking to an old gentleman who told me he only went down to town about once in four months. He gave the distinct impression that Road Town was a den of iniquity and best avoided if at all possible.

On an island which takes perhaps two hours to drive round in a landrover it was interesting to hear someone refer to the country and the town in this way. Some of the country people came into town once a week for the Saturday market, carrying hands of bananas, paw-paw, sweet potatoes and yams on the backs of their donkeys. They brought fresh produce to the town to sell and bought their supplies of flour, sugar etc.

We were invited to share a Christmas drink of illicit local rum, made by one of the families in the hills. Perhaps not the best idea after all the festive celebrating during the previous forty eight hours. One sip and it hit my insides like a ten ton truck. We would have been better advised to try the local *'Mawby'* a drink made from the bark of a tree and flavoured with orange and cinnamon.

We managed to start the climb through the rain forest and were enchanted by the extraordinary contrast to the rest of the island. Beautiful swinging lianas, tall trees, dark and beautiful. But we lacked the stamina to continue and were obliged to turn back too soon. It could have been the rum or the exhausting hike, but we were so tired we just wanted to collapse onto our beds.

So we returned home for a couple of hours rest before going on to yet another party. This time outdoors on the tennis courts at Slaney. We had to keep diving for cover as rain showers disrupted the dancing, but it was another hectic night and again we crawled home in the early hours. And then a breakfast of black coffee on the balcony watching shimmering green humming birds delicately dip those long, long beaks into the hibiscus flowers. They preferred the red hibiscus, and it must have been the colour which attracted them since I found one persistent little humming bird hovering beside my red pegs on the washing line.

There was a turpentine tree beside our balcony with smooth and shiny light brown bark. It attracted a variety of birds, particularly the mocking birds and noisy pearly-eyed Thrashers. But the little turtle dove, my favourite bird, preferred to sit in the dust of the road rather than perch in the trees.

CHAPTER 30

ORDEAL AT VIRGIN GORDA BATHS

Christmas brought some distinguished visitors to the BVI. Most arrived on their private yachts and anchored in the harbour only coming ashore for brief excursions or to provision.

Rockefeller moored his pretty blue boat in the bay below our condominium for a couple of days before sailing on to his Little Dix Bay resort on Virgin Gorda. And we literally 'bumped' into Dr. Spock, illustrious author of several child-rearing manuals, as we walked along the narrow quay beside George and Lu's Underwater Centre. We chatted for a few minutes and considered inviting him up to talk to Pam, now that she had a new baby we thought perhaps he could give her some useful advice on child psychology and valuable guidance on rearing. But he was obviously preoccupied, bumbling along in white shorts, tight T-shirt and grubby sneakers and somehow it didn't seem an opportune moment.

Two of the snowbirds wintering in the Caribbean and staying at the Treasure Isle Hotel wanted to visit Virgin Gorda, and so Mark agreed to organize a day trip for them, travelling across to Virgin Gorda in the hotel speedboat.

This lovely craft had a flying bridge and room for several people. It was fast and fantastic, equally suitable for deep sea fishing or shopping trips to St. Thomas. It was a new Herbie Showering indulgence and our good friend Mark had been appointed Captain. When Mark took the boat out for hotel guests or on hotel business and he had space on board, he invited us along for the ride, which meant that when he arranged the visit to Virgin Gorda he asked us to come along and we jumped at the chance.

Columbus is said to have called it Virgin Gorda (*the fat virgin*) because he thought the outline resembled a fat lady lying on her back. The central peak which rises to about 1,300 feet could possibly, with an active imagination, be seen as the large stomach of a fat female. Locally people believe that Virgin Gorda was probably the island originally named St. Ursula, the saint after whom the Virgin Islands is named and who, according to legend, was martyred with her 11,000 virgins. Covering an area of just eight square miles Virgin Gorda is the third largest of the British Virgin Islands, smaller than Tortola but larger than Jost Van Dyke.

It surprised me to learn that Virgin Gorda was the original seat of government until it was transferred to Tortola in the early 18th century. A census of 1717 showed a white population on Virgin Gorda of 317 but only half that number on Tortola. Now Virgin Gorda's population was less than 1,000 people and it had a relaxing, tranquil atmosphere where the pace of life was much slower than on Tortola.

The Government maintained a Rest House on Virgin Gorda, a very basic small cottage, so that 'rock happy' civil servants could slip away from the pressures of Tortola to restore their sense of balance in the peaceful surroundings of Virgin Gorda. The Governor Derek Cudmore and his wife were frequent visitors. And Rockefeller's prestigious Little Dix Bay complex was on Virgin Gorda. The luxury Resort brought wealthy Americans to the island where they could enjoy the Caribbean sunshine in peaceful pampered luxury.

Although Virgin Gorda had many charms, including beautiful beaches and an old copper mine, the main tourist attraction was undoubtedly an area called 'The Baths' on the southwestern side of the island. It was a most unusual natural phenomenon. Massive granite boulders lying randomly on top and alongside each other to a height of several hundred feet formed a fascinating labyrinth of caves. The sea flowed in and out of sandy pockets between the mammoth boulders creating cool, quiet, shaded chambers where shallow pools of salt water gently lapped the white sand. Some said the water had therapeutic properties, The Baths certainly seemed to possess an unusual and mystical quality.

Unfortunately, when the morning of our trip to Virgin Gorda dawned, my husband found himself too busy in the office to afford time off. But I really wanted to go and asked Mark if I could bring along a girl friend for company.

The day began well. The journey in the boat across was exhilarating and by the time we arrived on Virgin Gorda the six of us on board had developed a friendly bond. Together we took a taxi to The Baths, dropped our towels and snorkeling gear on the deserted beach beside the boulders and set off in search of the entrance to The Baths proper.

The boulders were unbelievably massive and locked together in a crazy geometric jumble. The bases of the grey granite had been eroded away by millions of years of sea action and the tumbled cone rose upwards finishing in a vast, flat plateau high above. The entrance was difficult to find and it was my friend Caroline who discovered it first. By squeezing through a small, triangular gap at the base of two boulders we found ourselves suddenly inside the magical, ethereal, chambers of The Baths.

Serene, silent and dimly lit, the first main cave was about twenty feet across. Directly ahead of us a shallow pool of sea water lapped gently backwards and forwards between the bases of two enormous rocks. The soft sand was cool on our bare feet, and smoothly unmarked. The six of us stood inside the tranquil cavern and gazed in wonder. High above our heads the body of the boulders closed in over us and the sunlight bouncing through and reflecting down gave The Baths a subdued surreal atmosphere.

Some of the smaller boulders looked temptingly easy to climb as they disappeared one after the other into the distance. Bending low and peering through the tight triangle of space at the base of the monolith in front of our watery pool, we caught a fascinating glimpse of other dim pockets of sand and water, guarded by cool grey granite, shafts of sunlight sparkling off the ripples of the undulating sea.

The other four, having seen and admired and taken some photos, waded in the pool and picked some small shells as souvenirs, then decided to retrace their steps back to the beach. They were impatient to have a swim before spreading themselves beneath the hot sun for an hour or two of bronzing.

Caroline and I thought it would be fun to explore a little further into the bowels of The Baths. So barefoot and in bikinis we scrambled up the lowest boulder in the large entrance cavern, and then stepped across onto the boulder beyond. As we stood on top of the second boulder, we saw below us a sandy lagoon, trapped until the next tide, glass clear and pure. We jumped down and realized that by wading through the pool, crouching down and wriggling between the rocks we could enter yet another enchanting cave. We moved on, and on, passing through a series of fascinating grottos of massive balanced boulders and sandy caverns. By climbing, sliding, wriggling and squeezing we discovered more and more of captivating interest.

I'm not sure when we came to the realization that we were lost. I remember Caroline saying she was getting a bit thirsty and perhaps we should turn back and join the others. And when we found ourselves scrambling back into unfamiliar hollows and pockets we were not particularly worried, just a little confused.

It seemed obvious to us that the beach and entrance were *'back there somewhere'*, the sea was *'over there'* and the granite rocks were *'up there'*. Neither of us had a watch, so we had no idea how long we had been aimlessly exploring. Around us all was thick silence. We could neither hear the sea nor any voices.

Soon it was very evident that we were hopelessly confused and our sense of direction had gone completely. Time and again as we dropped down onto a sandy floor, a large boulder blocked the path, too big and smooth to climb, so we had to retrace our steps and try another direction. We called, shouted, whistled, but there was no response. We were scratched, bruised and thirsty.

We sat down and forced ourselves to think logically and calmly. After some consideration we hit upon the idea of climbing up to the very top of the boulders. We thought that if we could come out at the top perhaps we would see the beach, or the sea, and at the very least it would help us get our bearings back again.

The boulders were weathered smooth by many millennia and we were not equipped for mountaineering. Our bare feet began to bleed, our hands were sore, but we persevered and slowly managed to climb higher and higher. We consoled ourselves with the thought that Mark would have missed us. He would have seen our towels lying on the beach and he would return to The Baths to search for us.

We were making quite good progress when, about twenty feet from the top plateau, our boulder stopped. We had two choices. Either we could work our way back down and start all over again, or we could summon up the courage to jump across a one hundred foot sheer drop onto the adjoining boulder to continue our climb. We rested for a few minutes, trying not to panic, trying to ignore our thirst, trying to remain calm and composed. Caroline was a Pan-Am air hostess trained to react with authority in an emergency. She grinned sheepishly *"Now if this was an aircraft I'd know what to do…"* she trailed off.

We looked at each other and decided to go for the jump. Tomorrow's newspaper headlines flashed through my mind *"Two British Girls Fall To Death in Caribbean Tragedy"* but I pushed the vision firmly away, took a deep breath, and jumped.

I fell on my knees on the hard granite and my right foot slipped away from me, kicking a pebble down into the chasm where it bounced and rattled against the sides of the boulders until, an age afterwards, silence. Under the circumstances I thought it was very courageous of Caroline to follow, but she did, and we lay gasping with relief on our new boulder.

Our euphoria was short lived. We discovered to our dismay, as we finally reached the summit of our boulder, that far from giving us a clear 360° view high up over the sea, beach and land, we had simply arrived at the top of a granite outcrop that extended as far as the eye could see. We appeared to have emerged onto a grey rock pavement crossed and re-crossed by black fissures too wide and too deep to be jumped by two barefoot, exhausted girls in bikinis.

We sat down and could have wept with despair. By now we were seriously worried and getting increasingly anxious. There was absolutely no way we could escape The Baths from up there, and the hot rock was beginning to burn our bottoms and our cut, bare feet. We held a council of war for two. Reluctantly we decided to go back down into the belly of The Baths. If, once down, we could hear the sound of the sea and work our way towards it, we could climb up again to come out onto a boulder directly above it. There should be boats moored off-shore, and perhaps swimmers, or at the very worst we could jump in to the sea and swim round the point to the beach. We surmised the beach was perhaps half a mile away *"Over there somewhere... I think!"*

It was a slow, tortuous and painful return trip down through the labyrinthine tomb of tumbled rocks. We didn't speak, just crawled, slipped and squeezed lower and lower. We perfected a technique using two smooth boulder faces, bum and back against one, feet and hands against the other and slowly inched down. When we were about fifty feet above the floor of a small pocket of sand, we found a flat-topped boulder and sat down for a rest.

And then we gasped in utter astonishment. A small blond-haired boy was standing in the circle of sand below us. We jumped up and called, shouted and whistled to him in delighted relief. The little boy did not appear to have heard us. He made no sound and no movement. We clambered across to a lower boulder, then onto another, and for a few moments the cup of sand below us was temporarily obscured from view. But as we scrambled closer we kept calling, expecting to hear at any moment an answering shout.

We were now immediately above the sandy pocket, and jumped down without too much effort. But our golden-haired cherub had disappeared. He had simply vanished into thin air. We stood staring in bewilderment at the high grey walls which circled the small strip of sand. There was no apparent entrance or exit. A set of small footsteps stopped at the face of a ten foot high sheer-faced boulder.

All we could conclude was that either our child had sprouted wings or had been lowered and then lifted again by someone leaning down from this boulder. We called and shouted in desperation. Why didn't the little boy answer? We strained for any sound. We thought we heard, very faintly, the murmur of the sea.

Caroline, being shorter than me, climbed on my shoulders and I pushed her up and onto the boulder. She lay flat and reached down to help me follow. Again we found ourselves surrounded by row upon row of round boulders. There was no sign of our cherub, and if indeed he had 'escaped' this way there was nothing to indicate which direction he might have taken.

Again we listened intently and heard the swish and roll of the sea to our left. Hopping carefully from rock to rock we worked our way towards the sound and as it got louder our spirits began to rise, until suddenly we were again faced with a rising blank wall of granite, with the sound of crashing surf beyond it.

We stood forlornly on a tiny strip of sand. Lying flat on our stomachs we peered through a small gap between the towering boulders. The space was no more than one foot square, and it separated us from a much larger cave where the sea rushed and gurgled in and out. We knew that the next cave must border the sea, and we were determined to crawl through the tiny gap. I wriggled through first wincing in pain as I scraped my spine on the rough granite. Struggling and grunting with the effort Caroline squirmed through after me.

We were right. This new cave was the final one before the open sea. But it was not the gentle, calm sea we had met in the entrance, this was a strong sea that crashed and foamed into the cave at speed, and sucked and pulled away again. The submerged rocks in the open sea looked rugged and unfriendly. If we wanted to escape this way we calculated we would have no more than five seconds to get through the gap between the rocks before the surging sea raced in again.

I am not a strong swimmer, and Caroline confessed neither was she. The headline in my mental newspaper changed to read *"Two British Girls Drowned in Caribbean Tragedy"*.

This time the odds were against us, it was just too risky. Blood from the graze was trickling down my back, our raw hands and feet were stinging with the spray, and we felt hopelessly and helplessly alone. I tried to stop the rising feeling of claustrophobia. Caroline confided afterwards that at this point she was bordering on hysteria. Her holiday of a lifetime was fast becoming the stuff of nightmares. Pan-Am had not trained her for anything like this.

We decided we wouldn't risk the five second dash for freedom, it was simply not long enough. So we agreed to climb upwards once more. We toiled slowly with great effort, leaving wet footprints on the smooth rocks, up and up. Two or three times we had to retrace our steps to try easier routes, it was a case of two steps forward one step back. Finally we emerged into the afternoon sun and scrambled from rock to rock to the sea edge.

We discovered we were some fifty feet above the waves, perched on a boulder that dropped away in a curve beneath us. The sea hissed and spat between the boulders below. There was absolutely no way either of us was about to jump into that churning, powerful water.

I remembered a friend on Tortola saying that the only place he had seen sharks was off the rocks at The Baths in Virgin Gorda, and looking down at my bleeding wounds the final headline swam mistily before my eyes *"Two British Girls Eaten By Sharks in Caribbean Tragedy!"*

Of the beach there was no sign. We must have been round a point some half mile or more down the coast. We were in a small, enclosed and rocky bay. All we could see were waves crashing against jagged rocks below, and two yachts, riding at anchor about half a mile away, out to sea. There was no sign of life on board, but we waved, shouted, and jumped up and down, before collapsing into a despairing heap on top of our boulder. And so we sat for a considerable amount of time, unsure what to do for the best, just waiting. We tried to calculate how long we had been wandering around in The Baths. We must have been lost for several hours because the sun was looking suspiciously like its mid-afternoon self and we had arrived mid-morning.

The sun would go down abruptly at about 6.00 p.m. which meant we had, if we judged correctly, about two or three more hours of daylight. Surely Mark must have organized a search party by now, and they were at this very minute systematically combing The Baths looking for us.

The sun was hot, the boulder hard and our thirst monumental. We both felt very miserable. Were we doomed to spend the night on this boulder? Where was Mark? If only my husband had come along. I managed to convince myself that it was all his fault and nothing to do with my own stupidity.

To pass the time Caroline told me about her plans to travel round the world, courtesy of Pan-Am. She explained the company was in deep financial trouble and was desperate to find ways of saving money. They had hit upon the idea of offering flights

171

anywhere in the world to employees who were prepared to take unpaid leave of absence. Caroline had taken up the offer and was soon to be off on her world tour. She rattled off a string of exotic place names she intended to visit, from Bali and Bangkok to Seattle and Sydney, and for an hour we travelled the world in our imaginations.

We were beginning to get very uneasy sitting helplessly on our rock, and wondered whether we should pluck up our courage to jump into the sea, striking out round the point and hopefully finding the beach before darkness came down. Night arrives very suddenly in the tropics, one minute it is light and bright and within half an hour velvet darkness has descended, made all the more dense because of the absence of lights. But I did not know how well Caroline could swim, and although I was fine with fins and mask, stripped of them, I lacked confidence. And the sea below looked intimidating and unfriendly.

Caroline saw them first. Four snorkelers slowly and purposefully working their way round the point, four lovely strong snorkelers, three men and one girl. We leapt to our feet and shouted, yelled and frantically waved our arms. But snorkelers keep their heads down, they concentrate on studying the sea below and the fish beside them, and the noise above the surface doesn't reach them and doesn't disturb them. And they were quite a distance away. Like our little golden-haired cherub they simply did not hear us.

We feared they might snorkel straight past our bay and we could have wept in panic. Whether it was that final despairing wail from Caroline, or a touch of heavenly intervention, we shall never know, but the girl lifted her head out of the water and across the intervening swell and roll of the waves she saw us. She tapped her companion on the shoulder and then he lifted his head. They all stopped, treading water, and looked in our direction. We shouted ourselves hoarse, we waved our arms, and they waved back.

For a few chilling seconds the horror that they might just wave and move on struck us, and tears began to pour down Caroline's face. I think she might have thrown herself into the sea there and then if they had swum away. But one of the men began to swim towards us, resolute, smooth and powerful strokes and within a few minutes he was treading water below us, calling up. Our super-hero was an American. We shouted down to him, explaining as lucidly as possible what had happened, and he suggested we should jump into the sea from our rock, and they would help us back to the beach.

His companions had joined him and they formed a circle, urging us to leap into the centre. We really had no choice. I went first. I slithered gently down the boulder, trying to keep some friction with my hands and bottom, and then suddenly I was slipping and I had to push away from the side and leap for the circle in order to avoid the jagged points of rock directly below. I was scared. I was bleeding. I was sure I was about to drown. I plunged into the water and was immediately dragged down and backwards in the powerful swell and suction of the sea. I was gasping for breath. I came up and then went under for a second time.

Struggling against the pull of the current that was trying to force me down, I surfaced for a third time, and a strong hand caught hold of my bikini bottom, plucked me out of the surf and literally threw me away from the dangerous rocks. Superman had saved me. He pushed and pulled me into calmer water by the entrance to the bay. I was swallowing water and he rolled me on my back so that I could float and gather my strength. I tried to look for Caroline and saw her, supported by the other three, being brought out of the bay.

I could see immediately that Caroline was a poor swimmer. Thank goodness we had not tried to jump without help, we would most certainly have been drowned.

It was a long haul back to the beach but my American super-hero was wonderful. He volunteered his fins but they were several sizes too large for my little feet. The girl had given her fins and mask to Caroline and this was a tremendous help. Caroline retained her triple escort and they kept close behind us. We struggled slowly on, clearing the point and aiming for the tiny sandy speck that never seemed to get any closer.

My super-hero stayed very close and did not take his eyes off me. There was a fleeting moment when I thought I saw a distinct leer on his face as he watched me. My bikini was particularly skimpy, more suitable for sunbathing than swimming. Even under normal circumstances it had only a tentative hold on my bosoms which resented the restraint and would try to burst free at every opportunity. I concluded my American super-hero was simply enjoying the view.

Mark was on the beach and he saw us coming, he was smiling as he splashed towards us.

"Hi!" he said jovially *"Where have you two been? We thought we'd lost you!"*

I could not believe my ears. We had been missing presumed dead for over four hours and all Mark could say was *"Where have you two been?"*

Our rescuers explained in graphic detail our ordeal and Mark looked horrified. It turned out that he had indeed noticed our absence, seen our towels by the entrance, but assumed we had gone back to the marina for a long lunch. He was just wondering where on earth we could have got to, just experiencing the first niggle of concern, when he saw us swimming in from around the point with *'our friends'*.

Caroline and I were so weak that we just lay in the shallows, unable to rise, unable even to crawl out of the water, totally exhausted. Our legs were so wobbly they wouldn't function and we were carried up the beach where our wounds were dressed.

When we returned to the boat and finally arrived home we were still feeling weak, bruised and very foolish for having got ourselves lost in the first place. And my husband refused to let me out of his sight for several days.

I never knew the names of the Americans who rescued us, they disappeared quickly and quietly back to their yacht, but I will never, ever, forget them.

CHAPTER 31

MORE ABOUT THE INFIRMARY

My old maid Rosalind called in to the office to wish us Happy New Year. It seemed she was still somewhat inebriated from her celebrations because she got half way up the stairs before she collapsed in an untidy heap and had to sit and rest for a few moments.

When I went to rescue her she flung her arms around me in greeting, gave me a big hug and a kiss and together we stumbled up the last steps before she crashed down giggling into a chair in the reception area.

As usual she wore a brown paper bag on her head but with the addition of a plastic bag over the top of it. She explained that if it rained the plastic bag would keep the brown bag, and therefore her hair, dry.

"Why both bags?" I asked, *"Wouldn't the plastic bag be sufficient by itself?"* A question she puzzled over but was unable to answer.

Rosalind was a proper tonic, such a pity she was an unreliable alcoholic with a Jumbie fixation, I would have loved to have her back working for me.

We six Red Cross volunteers returned to the Infirmary after the Christmas break. John was watching and waiting for us, sitting on the verandah steps. As soon as he saw us climbing the hill from the hospital he pulled out a harmonica from his pocket and with a smile that almost split his face in two he began to blow. The noise was not, as far as we could make out, a recognizable tune, but it was very pleasant and was obviously performed especially for us.

We spent the afternoon chatting to them as we painted the benches salmon pink and slopped yellow squares on the brown shutters of the window. Mary, John and Evangeline followed us around while William called out to us from his bed and watched through the window, and the old gentleman we had nicknamed *'The Supervisor'* closely monitored every brush stroke.

We were sorting out the paint pots at the end of a painting session when *'The Supervisor'* sidled up to Maggie who was in charge of a can of canary yellow. He pulled at her sleeve, jabbering. He was agitated and secretive and it was clear that he wanted Maggie to follow him into the men's sleeping room. Not sure of his intentions we all followed Maggie and crowded together in the small room. We were curious to see what this wiry old man, the one most jealously protective of the Infirmary, wanted. Still pulling on Maggie's arm he led her towards his iron bed in the corner, stopped and then pointed to his small cupboard.

Puzzled, we gazed at it. Frustrated by our obvious incomprehension he grabbed the paintbrush still in Maggie's hand and poked it at his cupboard. We all started talking at once. Suddenly it was quite obvious to us that he was asking Maggie to paint his precious little bedside cupboard canary yellow.

We thought this was a marvellous breakthrough, and immediately set to work with unrestrained enthusiasm to paint first his, and then by asking for permission, all the other cupboards. Six inmates, six painters, six cupboards, perfect.

I found myself entrusted with Evangeline's cupboard. She stood beside me twittering and grunting as I slowly and carefully explained what I was going to do. She seemed to understand, and so I gently lifted the picture of Jesus off the top of her cupboard and placed it reverently on her bed. She instantly sat on her bed and plucked up Jesus, cradling him in her arms. I put the plastic mat which had been under Jesus beside her on the bed and then I began to paint. Evangeline cackled and grunted as she watched, clutching Jesus and rocking gently backwards and forwards. Every now and then her hand shot out and a finger lovingly stroked the newly painted cupboard.

I tried to explain about sticky wet paint and the need to leave it alone until it had dried. I showed her how her hands were turning canary yellow. But Evangeline was bewitched by the change taking place before her very eyes and continued to touch and test as I painted. I had just finished the last triumphant brush stroke when I heard Mary calling.

A stranger she did not recognize was climbing the hill towards the Infirmary and Mary was afraid. The young man struggling up towards us looked more like a bundle of rags. He was thin, weak and dirty, and as he reached the steps of the Infirmary he collapsed. As we came out to investigate, a frightened Mary hid behind us, clucking with concern.

After a quick inspection we decided that as far as we could tell the young man looked relatively OK, probably drunk we agreed, best leave him to sleep it off. Satisfied, we went back inside to continue with our painting.

In my brief absence Evangeline had put Jesus and his mat back on top of her cupboard, and as I tried to peel him off to repair the damage I discovered he was well and truly glued to the surface. Evangeline loved the tacky, scratching sound the mat made as I attempted to lever it off and clapped her hands in delight. I tried to explain once again about leaving the paint to dry. Maggie was having similar troubles with *'The Supervisor'* who kept trying to replace the cupboard drawers.

But outside Mary was getting very distressed about our unexpected visitor. She had decided he was harmless but now she wanted to help him. She came into the bedroom and took my hand, pulling me towards the door. She was sure he needed a drink and she handed me the can on the string and led me to the cistern. I dipped the can down into the water and filled it, then, with Mary twittering beside me, held it to his lips. He rallied with the drink of water and begged for food. We gave him a sandwich left over from our lunch picnic and he wolfed it down.

A nurse came up the path from the hospital and seeing him lying on the steps of the verandah tried to shoo him away. But he lurched just a few yards and then refused to move.

The nurse became quite angry with him, explaining to us that he didn't deserve our sympathy since he was on welfare and from the house up the hill. She explained he was mentally ill but was considered by the authorities to be well enough to live with a female patient in the house higher up the hill behind the Infirmary.

Unlike our Infirmary patients, the two sharing the house were judged to be physically capable of looking after themselves. As far as we could see this poor man certainly was not looking after himself. The nurse was disgusted with him. Our ragged young man positively stank and she maintained he couldn't possibly be hungry because the hospital was feeding him.

After the nurse had gone our visitor crept back and this time tried to talk to us. He said he wouldn't go back to the house, the *'odda parsin'* the woman he was sharing with, had chased him out the night before and had threatened to kill him if he ever returned.

Because I had given him the drink and offered him the sandwich the young man was appealing to me. He was difficult to understand but I translated what he was saying for the benefit of Mary who was still very concerned for him. For this reason Mary got it into her head that he was my brother, and she meant 'brother' in the familial sense. Nothing I could say would persuade her that he was not related to me, not a member of my family, so in the end I told her that he was probably my brother *'in a sense'*, a brother *'in spirit'* and she seemed happy with that explanation.

Meanwhile Evangeline had put Jesus back on his mat on the cupboard and they were stuck fast to the wet surface, and there was yellow paint on her hands, face and down the front of her dress. It took us a long time to clean her up and I don't think we were very popular with the nurses, adopting a mental welfare patient and painting an inmate of the Infirmary canary yellow.

Our efforts to brighten up the Infirmary with a coat of paint had produced something resembling the Gingerbread House but everyone agreed it was a fantastic improvement. And fresh new curtains had been hung at all the windows.

Mary followed Liz everywhere, keeping up a constant chatter or occasionally whispering confidentially. One day she confided to Liz that her dearest wish was to go to Church one Sunday. Liz instantly volunteered to take her the following week but Mary shook her head and shuffled uncomfortably. Liz gently probed and discovered that Mary was too embarrassed to go into Church. She had only one dress which was too short and too tight, and although she quite understood that God would not mind how she looked, she was fully aware that the rest of the congregation would. Her new red straw hat given to her by Liz was her most prized possession.

We talked together and decided to buy Mary a dress to match her beloved red hat, and new shoes too, so that she could have her wish fulfilled and go to Church.

Mary confided to me that she was sure her family would come and get her soon. But except for the nurses, and the weekly visit from the Bible-reader, no-one visited the Infirmary.

CHAPTER 32

THE RED CROSS, GOVERNMENT HOUSE AND PATSY

The Red Cross, under the Chairmanship of the Governor's wife Vrai Cudmore, held their monthly meeting at Government House and these meetings could last three hours.

There were about thirty members in total but only seventeen 'active' ones. Among the active ones were a handful of 'working volunteers' including myself, Liz, Maggie and a new arrival to the Territory, a young Austrian/American woman called Ulrike. Ulrike was married to the Architect son of the owners of Guana Island, the exclusive resort for moneyed Americans. Ulrike was like a breath of fresh air, blonde, bubbly, worldly, well-groomed and thoroughly likeable. We instantly became best friends.

'Cuddles' (the Governor's wife) took on a dictatorial role, sending each of us our instructions in hastily written notes via James the chauffeur. The lovely James was inordinately proud of being His Excellency the Governor's chauffeur. He would drive up in the official car, Union Jack pennant flying, and with great ceremony deliver the message. If James couldn't find me at home, he drove to our office in town and made a great show of parking outside (much to the delight of Olva sitting in his chair beside the shop) before climbing the stairs and delivering my note with a grin and a flourish.

As Red Cross volunteers we were well known visitors to Government House. There was a green sentry box beside the entrance gate and visitors were required to pass beside it to walk up the drive. It was a steep climb up the short drive to the house with beautiful bougainvillea and hibiscus bushes lining the way.

PC Sylvester was my favourite on sentry duty. He was built like a telegraph pole, so tall he couldn't actually stand inside the box but had to prop himself up outside.

The official Visitors Book was kept inside the sentry box and anyone who didn't know the Governor well enough to phone up and say *"Hello Derek I've just arrived in the Territory for a holiday/business trip and I'd like to come up and see you sometime?"* would creep up to the sentry box and sign the Visitors Book (not forgetting to include dates of arrival and departure) which was whisked away daily and checked.

If you were socially, politically or commercially interesting, then you would probably receive an invitation to visit Government House before you left the island.

Whenever Porky came to the BVI his first mission was to dash to the sentry box at Government House to sign the Visitors Book in hopeful anticipation of an invitation to meet the Governor. To his frustration he had never been granted an audience and really resented my numerous visits. But he lived in hope, and when he was on the island he always insisted on stopping off at the sentry box to perform the ritual of the book-signing ceremony. Fortunately Government House was conveniently placed between the centre of Road Town and the Pub, a route used frequently by Porky.

Government House was not an imposing mansion, it was more a comfortable family residence. Substantial, when compared with the basic and humble dwellings of us lesser mortals, but not by any means an overwhelmingly impressive place. It had recently been re-plumbed and renovated and Cuddles was very pleased with the results.

Halfway up the drive the Governor's loopy but lovable golden Labrador would burst round the corner to welcome us. Bruno was allowed the freedom of the house and grounds and bounded around in gay abandon. He was adored and thoroughly spoilt, but such a gentle giant with a wonderful personality.

Bruno got very excited and quite out of control in the spring when the south-westerly winds blew across the Government House grounds carrying with them the delectable scent of bitches in heat. Then Bruno would be confined to the house. He had to be forcibly restrained from breaking out and hunting them down. In fact on one memorable occasion he managed to do just that.

It was about 6.00 a.m. and the sun was just rising. Road Town was quiet and Bruno was sniffing the air. He caught the smell of a hot bitch and his natural urges overwhelmed him. Unseen, he managed to escape and left the house moving at the speed of light down the drive and out through the gates. The Governor saw him, and in pyjamas and dressing gown, shot off in rapid pursuit. Bruno was oblivious to calls and whistles.

I knew about this naughty behaviour by Bruno because a friend just happened to be passing Government House at the time and witnessed the whole thing. The Governor was spotted racing after the errant Bruno as he sped out of the gates and down the road. Most Tortolians have a fear of dogs, and the policeman on duty in the sentry box was no exception. So it was left to the Governor in his *'pyjams'* to chase after the passionate Bruno, dressing gown flying, lead held high, calling loudly to the unheeding dog. Dog and Governor finally returned, both panting, both exhausted.

The Red Cross meetings at Government House were always very informal. Discussions tended to wander around circuitously with no real direction. Cuddles herself was full of dynamic enthusiasm and had a powerful personality, preferring in the end to dictate rather than debate, so we never really had a consensus of opinion, although we went through the ritual of a vote. Cuddles appointed me Red Cross Honorary Secretary. As well as being the Secretary and having to organize publicity and fund-raising, I found myself coerced into helping with the Junior Red Cross.

I thought it would be useful to teach the youngsters basic skills like cookery, dressmaking, cleanliness and first-aid, but Cuddles had different priorities. She wanted the Red Cross Juniors to exchange scrap books with an English group. But since we only had three Junior members my first priority was a membership drive. I was working against strong opposition from the Girl Guides who were both popular and powerful on Tortola.

Most of the time the meetings were a wonderful opportunity for a good winge and grouse, and we would muddle through the first half listening to each other's moans, but then the highlight of the evening, refreshments!

Government House hospitality was legendary being particularly noted for very generous alcoholic libations. We would be liberally supplied with our alcoholic beverage of choice and then pressed into having refills and of course none of us would dream of offending the Governor by refusing.

So the second half of the meeting was always extremely relaxed and pleasant, and this was the time Cuddles reserved for what she called her 'happy news'. At our last meeting she hushed us all to silence for *"an important announcement"*. She waited until we had put down our glasses and she had our full attention. We stared at her in anticipation. She took a deep breath, paused for effect and solemnly informed us *"the islands are to be honoured"* an even longer pause for further effect *"...by a Royal visit!"*

This news was received with varying degrees of excitement by the inebriated committee. Individual enthusiasm seemed to vary in direct relation to the nationality of the member. We four British people were, naturally, overwhelmed with the honour. The Tortolian contingent slightly less so, and the Americans didn't appear to be bothered one way or another.

Cuddles continued and explained that in order to celebrate the 300th anniversary of the British interest in the Virgin Islands, HRH Princess Margaret had been invited for an official visit, and *"had graciously accepted"*.

Cuddles was very excited and hoped to press-gang Princess Margaret into attending our Red Cross Annual General Meeting and perhaps presenting a few medals at the same time. This gave me roughly two months to try and swell our current Red Cross membership into a respectable size, a daunting task.

But there was more. We 'working volunteers' were also asked to paint some of the wards in Peebles Hospital. Word had got round about our amazing success at the Infirmary. But some of the Red Cross committee were unhappy about the proposed hospital painting. They felt it had been organized in order to impress Princess Margaret, and believed it would be far more appropriate for her to see the hospital *"as is"* and not *"tarted up"*.

But Liz, Maggie, Ulrike and I wanted, at the very least, to paint the children's ward. There was one little girl to whom the ward was home and for her sake we wanted to put a fresh, bright, coat of colour on the currently depressing, dismal walls. So we headed into Road Town begging pots of paint, brushes, sandpaper and all those essential things decorators need.

The children's ward was normally empty except for one little nine year old girl called Patsy. When Dr. Smith first arrived on Tortola little Patsy just lay in her cot in a corner of the children's ward, or was occasionally lifted out and strapped into a high chair. She had tiny wasted arms and legs and Dr. Smith was told that she had Muscular Dystrophy and would die within the year.

Determined to help her Dr. Smith managed to find an expatriate who was a physiotherapist and she worked with Patsy for twelve months. She managed to get Patsy to do exercises and finally succeeded in getting her to 'walk', a major triumph.

But when the physiotherapist left Tortola, little Patsy was returned to her cot. The Salvation Army hospital in Jamaica offered to help Patsy and she was sent to them for further assessment and treatment, but later was returned to Tortola.

Patsy's mother was still on the island but was not interested. Peebles Hospital was the only home Patsy knew. Cuddles decided to take it upon herself to help.

Patsy's case had a profound effect on Cuddles. She was absolutely determined to try and organize a proper mental health policy in the Territory. She was genuinely distressed that the residents in the Infirmary, and Patsy, and others in similar situations all over the BVI, did not have proper access to the facilities and care they so desperately needed. At the very least she wanted to start a little school for disabled children who currently received no education.

Cuddles was a crusader and we knew this dream of hers would one day become a reality. The first step was to raise funds for her scheme and so she decided to organize a Red Cross Ball to coincide with the Queen's Birthday Celebrations in June

We working volunteers also took over the production of bandages for the hospital and met once a week in each other's homes to cut gauze and roll cotton wool balls.

Liz had a fluffy white carpet (and a cat) and six of us would sit cross-legged in a circle with the vast tube of cotton wool placed in the middle. We plucked, pulled, rolled and tossed each little ball into a mounting heap in the centre of our circle. It was difficult to distinguish between cotton wool and carpet and I was convinced a great deal of Liz's white carpet (and cat fur) strayed into the mound.

We sincerely hoped our efforts were sterilized before use.

CHAPTER 33

A MARRIAGE PROPOSAL AND FATHER VALENTINE

Our friends Bob and Pat decided to buy a small plot of land, a tiny site that had been chipped out of the vertical face of the steep hillside above Slaney apartments.

A bumpy access track had been bulldozed out of the cliff and Bob would try to chug up to the site in his little yellow 'moke'. The effort always proved too much and the poor vehicle coughed, spluttered and wheezed. The track had been cut with two tight hairpin bends to accommodate the steepness and even our landrover could only just manage to turn the corner.

It was easier to climb up to the site on foot, huffing and panting and collapsing into a perspiring heap on arrival. My husband had offered to help Bob cast the cistern, build block walls and put in window frames. All was going well until Pat and Bob were given notice to quit on the apartment they were renting and they had two weeks to complete the build and move into their new house.

It was nowhere near ready for occupation and resembled an untidy building site. We desperately tried to help them lay floor tiles, plaster walls, put in louvre windows, and at least make one room habitable. But there was still no electricity, a major drawback.

One day, when I arrived at the site, I heard a strange scuffling sound coming from inside the house. I tiptoed through the rooms until I came to the one which the following week would become little Simone's bedroom. There, comfortably curled up in the corner where Simone's bed would go, was a family of wild goats.

Nanny goat saw me first and took a flying leap out through the window frame. Fortunately for her there was no glass in the panes.

186

Her kids tried desperately to follow, bleating pathetically for mum. They scrambled, fumbled and struggled to get over the sill and teetered for a moment in mid-air before falling down onto the balcony the other side.

I glanced around to check for any damage and to my horror I saw a large scorpion on the floor, about two inches away from my bare feet. It had its long tail lifted up and over its back and the pincers at the end of its long arms looked decidedly nasty. As I backed off the scorpion followed and I shrieked in panic. Bob rushed in and instantly dispatched the creature with his hammer and I felt miserable all day thinking I had been responsible for its death.

Some of the children who lived at Slaney came up to the site, curious to see how we were getting along, and later in the afternoon Bob volunteered to pile them into his 'moke' and take them back down the hill, promising to bring us back some ice cold Buds on his return.

He set off, overloaded with children. In the open 'moke' they spilled out over the sides without restraint. We watched Bob race off, bumping and banging round the rocks on the track and saw him arrive at the bottom. He disgorged the children and shot off again towards his apartment.

But instead of stopping outside as we expected the 'moke' kept going and careered off the road straight into a palm tree. From our vantage point high up the hill we watched helplessly, but fortunately Bob was not injured and it was with great relief that we saw him climb stiffly out to inspect the damaged 'moke'. The front wheel had simply come away from the axle and lay there, like a sick doughnut, in the middle of the road. Thank goodness it hadn't happened on the trip down or Bob would have surely gone over the edge of the hillside with a car load of children.

It was a relief to get back to our beautiful condominium at the Treasure Isle, grab an ice cold Bud from my enormous fridge and step into a nice hot shower.

Our water supply has been unpredictable lately. Mick was not quite sure what was causing the problem. I had just lathered up in the shower and had a head full of frothy bubbles when there was a 'phut' and a 'phizz' and the water just stopped. I wiped the foam from my eyes and padded to the phone to ring Mick, and he was at the front door so quickly I had hardly time to wrap myself in a towel. He just laughed and laughed when he saw me and suggested I should walk down to the Hotel pool to hose off, but I decided to wait for the repair instead.

Liz, Maggie and I called in to see our friends at the Infirmary again and they were sitting on the steps waiting. They have come to expect a weekly visit from us on Thursday afternoons and the nurses tell them when we are due. We sneaked in some rum again and gave them liberal splashes in their enamel mugs. Liz had bought William a new hat, a sort of natty pork-pie felt thing. While she held the new hat out to show him, she gently removed the old, smelly, stained, broad brimmed brown one from his head, placing it carefully in his lap.

We crowded round to watch the transformation and saw for the first time that William had a thick crop of strong grey hair. He looked very apprehensive and would not let Liz take the foul felt one away but hung on to it, cradling it in his arms. Liz carefully placed the new hat on his head and found a mirror. When William saw himself in the mirror his eyes lit up, his face broke into a vast gummy smile, and he burst into a convulsion of giggles. For the rest of the afternoon he studied himself in the mirror from this way and that, laughing and mumbling to himself, the pork-pie hat perched at a jaunty angle on top of his grey mop of hair.

When Liz gave him his mug of rum, he proposed to her, sitting there on his rumpled bed with his new hat on his head and wearing his old striped pyjamas. Liz explained that she was already married but William persisted, two husbands were better than one he argued. But Liz shook her head and said her current husband wouldn't approve of that arrangement, so then William turned and proposed to Maggie instead.

Mary was almost hysterical with laughter by this time. She had been standing in the hallway (Mary and Evangeline were forbidden to enter the men's room) and could hear everything that was being said. In the end William seemed to accept that both Liz and Maggie were 'spoken for' and if only he had arrived on the scene a little earlier maybe things could have been different!

Liz and Maggie decided Mary, Evangeline and John would benefit from a change of scene. After asking permission they took them out of the Infirmary for a short car ride.

It was a massive undertaking. Just the effort of getting John, disabled and unable to walk, down the hillside to the car was quite a challenge. Liz was not sure whether she and Maggie had bitten off more than they could chew and when the car developed a puncture just before they were due to return, she became really worried. They had to flag down a passing motorist to help them change the tyre, and it meant taking the three Infirmary patients out of the car and sitting them beside the road while the change took place.

Still, in the end it was a triumphant success and according to Dr. Smith it was a fantastic morale booster and very much enjoyed by the three. Dr. Smith said he hadn't seen so much activity, laughter and happiness at the Infirmary since he'd arrived.

But we have just been told that there are plans to demolish the Infirmary. The island intends to build a brand-new beautiful hospital to be sited next to the Mortuary and the Infirmary stands in the way. No-one knows where the government will put our Infirmary friends, but we were confident Cuddles would demand a good exchange and most certainly much improved facilities.

Cuddles adopted me as her personal assistant and took to phoning me up at all times of the day with urgent errands for me to perform on her behalf. She did not take 'no' for an answer and juggling office work for the company, volunteer work for the Red Cross and responding to Cuddles' demands was sometimes difficult.

One urgent phone call instructed me to rush immediately to St. William's, the Catholic Church in Road Town. Cuddles informed me that a new Roman Catholic Priest had just arrived on the island and I was to welcome him on behalf of the Red Cross. I dutifully gathered together Liz, Maggie and my new best friend Ulrike and we sped off in the landrover to find the new Priest.

St. William's was a small, brown, rectangular, unprepossessing building on Main Street diagonally opposite the more popular, vibrantly extrovert, red and white Anglican Church of St. George's.

Liz, Maggie and I were 'non-denominational', in other words nothing in particular, but Ulrike was a lapsed Catholic and she made us swear not to divulge this to the new Father. She said she didn't want to be pestered by some Bible-bashing priest after her soul. As it turned out nothing could have been further from the truth.

I had been told by Cuddles that the new Priest was living in a room at the rear of the Church. We didn't feel comfortable traipsing down the aisle of the interior so we decided to go round the back. This part of Wickhams Cay, behind the Church, was still rough and stony and waiting to be developed and seemed to attract all the rubbish that blew across the Cay. It was, frankly, a bit of a dump and we had to pick our way carefully to the back of the building.

We were not familiar with St. William's but we supposed that the door in the back wall of the building must somehow lead to the Priest's living quarters. We shrugged and banged on the door. To our surprise it was whipped open immediately. A middle-aged man, short and stocky with a round face sparsely topped with tufty grey hair and skin as pale as flour stood framed in the doorway. He was wearing a light blue, short sleeved, open necked shirt and baggy black trousers several sizes too big. He beamed down at us. Could this possibly be the new incumbent?

He must have wondered what four young women were doing knocking at his back door within an hour of his arrival. News travels fast on Tortola. We quickly introduced ourselves as representatives of Red Cross welcoming him onto the island, and he shook each of our hands vigorously and enthusiastically.

"I'm Father Valentine" he said, with a slight hint of an Irish brogue. The name amused us and we laughed out loud.

"That's O.K" he grinned as we tried to hide the smirks *"everybody thinks it's funny!"* and he invited us in.

There were no steps to the back door of the Church and it was a long drop from his floor to the rough ground we were standing on. He had to lean down and haul us in one by one. When we were inside it was hard to know what to do. The room was smaller than a cell and in it was an iron bed and a cooking ring. He waved us genially on to the bed so we sat down, lining up to face him.

Unfortunately this meant there was nowhere for him to sit but this didn't matter as he began to busy himself making us a coffee. The room was divided from the main body of the Church by a curtain, and Father Valentine explained that this was where the Priest would normally robe ready for the service and as such was little more than a cubby hole. That this poor man was expected to live in here horrified us, but Father Valentine was quite jolly about it.

To our great surprise he informed us that the Roman Catholic Church considered Tortola a mission church, so he was here in the capacity of a Missionary. He had previously been in San Francisco working in the red light district and also in Puerto Rico, helping with the drug rehabilitation clinics, and Father Valentine confessed he was more used to pulsating city life with its iniquity, than the quiet drift of a tropical island like Tortola.

He was amazed to discover that none of us were Catholic (Ulrike kept quiet). He had initially assumed that we were most likely visiting him through church duty, and he was delighted to find that we were motivated purely by good neighbourliness. We refrained from mentioning it was also by the command of the Governor's wife. We shared the two mugs of coffee he made, passing them along between us, and listened to Father Valentine as he talked, and talked and talked.

Father Valentine had sparkling blue eyes and a wonderfully dry wit and it was not long before the little room was reverberating with gales of laughter. I just hoped none of his congregation came visiting through the front of the church, because they would have wondered what on earth was happening, the new Priest in his robing room with four young women and a lot of hilarity! His reputation would have been ruined before he began.

His particular Order did not allow a priest to have personal possessions so he had arrived on Tortola with a single, very small, suitcase. But he was allowed to bring an archaic typewriter, given to him by one of his previous parishioners, and it was his pride and joy.

One day in the job and he already had big plans. He hoped his stay in the 'back room' of St. William's would be brief. He wanted the congregation to help him construct a single-storey building on the ground beside the church so that he could live in it but also use it as a hall for church recreational purposes. He would not, he said firmly, be wearing his *'uniform'* around town. He would be dressed in a blue short-sleeved open necked shirt *"Like everyone else!"*

CHAPTER 34

WHALES, JACK COUSTEAU AND OTHER VISITORS

We spotted the first humpback whale of the season recently passing through the Sir Francis Drake Channel and Jack Cousteau arrived on Tortola to film the migration.

This was the time of year when the whales slowly and leisurely made their way back up through the Caribbean to Arctic waters where they would spend the summer. The Caribbean was the nursery of the humpback and they came each year to breed. As soon as the calves were strong enough, the pods, in groups of three or more, began their long journey north.

Everyone looked forward to seeing the whales. They were a magnificent and awe-inspiring sight. Sometimes a small pod of whales would stay in Sir Francis Drake Channel for two or three days, just diving deep beneath the surface or playing. We tried to respect them by staying out of their way but it was a great temptation to jump into a boat and go 'whale-watching'.

Lu and George took their small boat out and dived in the water to watch at close quarters. Lu said there was a mother, about 35 ft. long with her calf, a mere 10 ft. They played together in the shallows off Nanny Cay for two days.

Calves are born once every two years, and then only one at a time. A humpback takes three years to reach sexual maturity and ten years to reach its average twenty-nine ton weight and 40 ft. length. From our balcony at the Treasure Isle we could see the tremendous spout of water as the whales blew, surfacing after a dive of ten to fifteen minutes. And then, as they dived again, up came the tail, way out of the water, a quick wiggle in the air and the tail smacked down onto the surface of the sea leaving a frothy shower of spray. Ten minutes pause and *'there she blows'* again!

Watching the whales was tremendously calming. It was tragic to think that these imposing animals were hunted almost to extinction. At the beginning of the 20th century there were an estimated 100,000 whales and now figures were estimated to be under 7,000. The films made by Jack Cousteau helped people who would never have an opportunity of seeing the humpback for themselves, enjoy and appreciate this beautiful majestic mammal.

Sadly another, less welcome, migratory species arrived in the islands with the whales. The lesser and totally undesirable, to be avoided if at all possible, friend of a friend who arrived on Tortola with the aim of 'looking you up'.

Friends back in England who had at first been horrified at our bold decision to uproot and head for the Caribbean now viewed us differently, we had become a very desirable potential holiday destination. And this interest had a ripple effect, extending out to their own friends, most of whom we had never met.

One such couple was Philippa and Henry. Recently married, the newlyweds had chosen to honeymoon in the Caribbean by sailing their pretty little yacht (a wedding present from daddy) from Southampton to Tortola. Philippa was the apple of her father's eye and he had hired a two-man professional crew to make sure his little girl arrived safe and sound at her destination.

I heard Philippa before I saw her. I was sitting at my desk quietly sifting papers in the front office at work when I heard a very English, very affected, falsetto girl's voice working loudly in a penetrating monologue. As I raised my head I saw a very large, bright red, straw sombrero coming up the stairs from the street.

The wearer rose into view. I blinked, before my eyes was an uncoordinated colour blind fashion disaster. Huge sunglasses, lacy pink blouse, vivid salmon-pink baggy shorts, and with legs so white they glowed blue. This was Philippa. In her wake struggled what appeared to be a large teddy bear. It had tousled brown hair, a bulky, flabby body (totally out of condition judging by the panting and sweating that accompanied the climb) and a very red complexion which incidentally coordinated perfectly with its owner's shorts. Red, it seemed, was the *de-rigeur* colour for tropical kit!

Philippa paused in the doorway and saw me sitting at my desk. I smiled politely in greeting. She stopped for breath and studied me over the rim of her sunglasses, silently inspecting me.

I was to discover that Philippa ranked people according to their social status and usefulness to her and I must have scored pretty low on her scale because without a word she turned abruptly to my husband who had emerged from his office at the sound of the shrill tones. I was given a dismissive glance and dissolved into an insignificant little heap behind my desk.

A limp hand was offered to my husband together with an ingratiating smile. Unlike me he had apparently scored high on Philippa's usefulness list and was about to experience the full force of her manipulative powers.

Unfortunately for us it turned out that Philippa's daddy had powerful influence with our company boss and he had been assured of our total cooperation and support. We were instructed to be nice to Philippa.

My husband, she decided, was to become her personal chauffeur during her stay on Tortola and she desired to have a tour of the island, immediately. Philippa was used to having her every wish fulfilled. Office work was an irritating incidental which could easily be put on hold she told him firmly. My husband stalled, procrastinated, refused, but Philippa easily beat him into submission.

It was obvious from the outset that neither of us was a match for the formidable Philippa, friend of a friend with an influential daddy. As she matured she would become a terrifying and indomitable lady and she was practising hard in anticipation. Husband Henry had already succumbed. He followed meekly and passively in her wake punctuating her monologues with deferential mumbles. We pitied him, and the two-man crew, trapped afloat with no means of escape from Philippa for the transatlantic trip.

As soon as she had stepped ashore Philippa's priority was to sign the Visitors Book in the sentry box at Government House. One needed to let it be known to the Governor that one had arrived in his Territory, one could then confidently await a personal invitation to visit.

My husband was simmering with suppressed fury when he set off with Philippa (sombrero still firmly on her head) beside him and the large teddy bear squeezed between Philippa and the passenger door. Three people in the front of a landrover. It meant a very uncomfortable journey with my husband crouched to avoid injury from the sombrero which swung left and right as Philippa drank in and verbally regurgitated what she saw. Her conversation was loud, inconsequential and constant. When she opened her mouth the most extraordinary nonsense poured forth, at full volume.

"Why" she asked in astonishment *"are those awful people allowed to build their awful homes beside that beautiful beach?"*

She was referring to local fishermen's houses that had stood beside the bay for hundreds of years.

Philippa laced her comments with superlatives and everything was prefixed with words like *'fantastic'* (views), *'astronomic'* (car hire prices), *'incredible'* (people).

The two-man crew having been dismissed, Philippa and Henry intended to use their boat as a charter yacht for a couple of months hoping to raise sufficient money to live in the BVI for a while. Philippa was a weekend mariner more familiar with the Solent and giving orders than crewing in the Caribbean and we anticipated problems but refrained from comment.

I was alarmed when it was taken for granted that I would organize the administration of the chartering. I discovered Philippa had already plastered posters around town with my phone number prominently displayed. She had variously described the yacht as *'fabulous'*, *'superb'*, *'prize-winning'*, *'fantastic'*, *'wonderful'*, *'brilliant'*, *'amazing'* and *'marvellous'* and we were expected to agree when we admired the craft for ourselves.

We were ordered to attend for dinner on board after my husband had completed their round-the-island tour. A duty he accomplished in record breaking time!

The thought of dining on board a boat confined with Philippa and Henry was horrifying to us, but in the heat of the moment we were unable to think of a plausible excuse. Nothing short of our imminent deaths would have been sufficient justification to decline Philippa's order.

With gritted teeth we prepared to endure dinner on board but to our surprise and great relief it was not as bad as anticipated. Henry turned out to be a passable chef and the wine was flowing freely. And with Philippa's verbal marathon in full force we were not required to speak, all she needed was the occasional nod of encouragement. So we were able to withdraw into a pleasant alcoholic haze of our own and enjoy the meal if not the company.

Philippa positively revelled in showing us her Visitors' Book and was quick to point out that only titled persons were permitted to sign. This meant, of course, our instant disqualification. She carefully read out, as distinctly as alcohol would allow, all the names she felt would impress a provincial couple like ourselves, and peppered her conversation with references to people like *"Daddy's good friend the Prime Minister"* and *"Lord and Lady Sainsbury whom we met in Antigua"*.

Henry was busy indulging himself. Firstly with the food, secondly with the wine, and had little contribution to make to the evening. He roused himself just once to tell his new wife that she was *"The worst name-dwopper in the world"* remembering to add the mandatory *"dah-ling"* a few moments later. It had, of course, absolutely no effect whatsoever on Philippa.

Through one of my remarks (instantly regretted) they discovered that my friend Ulrike's parents-in-law owned the private island of Guana. Philippa was thrilled. Confident of a warm welcome (after all she had met Lord and Lady Sainsbury) she decided she would sail across to Guana to introduce herself.

But we knew that Bill's parents Louis and Beth Bigelow fiercely objected to uninvited visitors arriving on Guana, and if there was one type of person they *really* disliked it was the pushy, self-opinionated, pretentious British colonial snob which Philippa personified. We tactfully explained that it was a private island and without an invitation she would be trespassing.

Her reply was typical.

"Well, it isn't as if one would do any damage, one simply wants to land and look around. Surely they can't object to that!"

We warned her that the last boat which had landed uninvited for a *'look around'* Guana saw the barrel of Bill's father's rifle. His hostility was well-known locally. On that occasion it was fully justified, the trespassers had brought their dog with them and while they ran up and down the beach the dog relieved itself in the bushes.

I'm not sure how we managed to get back after our dinner without capsizing the dinghy. Henry was not very good at handling alcohol, nor anything else for that matter. He wasn't really in a fit state to be in charge of a bouncing boat on a dark night off an unfamiliar coast. Fortunately for us the dinner in our stomachs stayed down, but my husband and I were both feeling more than a little bit green by the time we finally crawled out of the dinghy onto dry land.

CHAPTER 35

LICENSE PLATES, BLOOD AND BLACK PUDDING

Vehicles in the BVI were taxed each January, and every car and every bicycle in the Territory had to be able to show a new license by the end of March at the latest. For the duration of the three month period the Police Traffic Department set up business in the little circular bandstand on the recreation ground, usually two police officers and a mechanic.

Their day alternated between frantically busy and chaotic as vehicles queued for attention, and boredom when no-one came. Getting a new vehicle license was a tedious and time consuming procedure, an experience which had been known to drive normally relaxed and docile people beyond the brink of reason.

My husband decided to take our landrover very early one morning. At first he was quite hopeful, only two cars in front of him and the mechanic's inspection was cursory to say the least. The two cars ahead were quickly processed and tax discs stamped and supplied.

Then the mechanic sauntered over to the landrover, and strolled round it, kicked the tyres, gazed at the lights as they were flashed on and off, tried the horn and wandered to the rear. The back number-plate of the landrover was a large, white metal square. The mechanic studied the number plate and slowly shook his head. White and square was bad. Yellow and oblong was good. The white and square plate was the original and had been passed as acceptable for several years. My husband remonstrated and demanded to see the appropriate order in the official Police Manual. But the Manual was missing, probably back at the Police Station.

Wisely, the officers on duty advised my husband to humour the mechanic, and suggested that if he wasn't prepared to have the number-plate reshaped, at least have it re-painted yellow, then the mechanic would pass the landrover as roadworthy. Agreeing, my husband drove immediately to Keith's garage and explained the problem. They laughed and laughed.

One of Keith's mechanics decided to phone the Police Station to get an administrative ruling *'from the top'* on the question. After some discussion the Station Officer decided that they didn't really care what shape or colour the number plate was, in fact, he admitted the police vehicles and the fire engine were all displaying rear number plates which were white, large and square, just like our landrover.

But for the sake of a quiet life my husband asked the garage to paint the plate yellow while he waited, and then he retraced his steps back to the bandstand. The Traffic Department, rocking back on their chairs under the cupola roof, were impressed with the speed of the transformation and came down from the podium to admire the handiwork. A license was granted and they climbed back onto the stand to complete the paper work.

After a great deal of searching through bundles of paper on the table, the officers came to the conclusion that they must have run out of tax discs, so one of the men was dispatched to walk to the Police Station for some replacements. It took only a matter of minutes and the intervening time was spent pleasantly enough with a cold beer from the little shop opposite.

However, when the constable returned he was most apologetic. The Station had also run out of the relevant stickers and no-one seemed quite sure when the replacements would be available. So, although the landrover was officially taxed we had no sticky disc for the window, no problem!

My husband had only just returned to the office after his encounter with the Traffic Police when the phone rang. It was the hospital wanting a pint of his blood urgently. He ran down the stairs, leapt into the landrover and in less than two minutes he was walking into Casualty at Peebles Hospital. As he settled himself on the couch a needle was plunged into his arm. Four nurses who had been folding bandages and chatting, fluttered around him waiting for the suspended bag to fill. The bag was about three-quarters full when someone came into the room to say that there was a phone call for the nurse in charge. She sailed off, leaving my husband with his fast filling bag, and three nurses.

The bag began to bulge. The nurses watched anxiously and nudged each other. No-one seemed to know what to do. My husband was beginning to feel slightly peculiar and the bag was almost full. One of the nurses asked him if he was OK but he couldn't answer. Just before he passed out he glanced at the bag again, it was so full the seams were straining.

One of the nurses had run out to find someone to take charge, another searched for a clip to put on the tube. The third produced a bottle of smelling salts and tried to bring my husband back to consciousness. In her haste she inadvertently poured the smelling salts onto his face. He regained consciousness spluttering and gasping with a violent stinging in his eyes, blurred vision and the solution up his nostrils.

A doctor arrived in a whirl of panic, pinched the tube and unplugged him while the nurses dabbed at his face and trembled apprehensively. One brought him a glass of orange juice to take away the taste of the fluid, but as he tried to sit up and sip, he passed out again. The same solution was used to bring him round a second time, but fortunately this time the liquid stayed in the bottle. They helped him to his feet and carefully guided him out of the hospital and propped him gently behind the wheel of his landrover.

Beaming with pride the doctor told him that they had achieved something of a record as two pints of his blood had been squeezed into the one pint bag. Useful for the patient to be transfused but debilitating and possibly dangerous for my poor husband.

How he managed to get back to the office I do not know, but as he came up the stairs he teetered on the balcony and then gracefully slid into unconsciousness again. A client who had been patiently waiting to see him, helped me to rouse him and he was part-carried, part-hauled, down the corridor into his air-conditioned office and laid out on the floor for a few minutes.

As he came round my husband said he thought he must have got an air-block or something. But I reassured him, saying soothingly it was probably just that they had drained so much blood out of him, all he needed was a quiet rest, and he would be as fit as a flea in no time. Fortunately the client accepted our explanation that my husband had been blood-doning and was not heavily under the influence of an alcoholic lunch.

A week later the navy arrived on Tortola and the hospital vampire was on the quay as the ship docked waiting for the ship's Doctor. When she found him she persuaded him to volunteer the whole crew, with the promise of a tot of whisky or rum if they would be prepared to donate a pint of blood to the hospital.

The new Roman Catholic Priest Father Valentine had become a regular visitor to the office. He would wander in mid-morning, just in time for a cup of coffee. I would offer him a cigarette and we would have a long chat. He seemed to be settling into Tortola well. But with no transport he was rather limited and depended to a large extent on his flock for occasional dinner invites and trips out of Road Town.

He would bring me books to read which I appreciated very much. Most people read for relaxation in the evenings and we ran an unofficial library between ourselves. The Road Town Library, although quite small, was very well stocked but the books were old, well-thumbed, and worn-out so when a visitor came along with fresh new novels they were pounced upon with delight.

Ron, the Manager of Chase Manhattan Bank, had a whole wall of paperbacks in his lounge which he gladly lent to any starving bookworm. He said he had read every one. As he lived alone up on his remote hill, I could only suppose he had nothing else to occupy him during the long evenings.

Father Valentine told me his wardrobe consisted of a few light blue, open neck, short sleeved shirts and a couple of pairs of baggy black trousers. I told him that we were expecting a Royal visit soon and he would no doubt be invited up to the cocktail party at Government House, and what would he wear then? He screwed his nose up (the Royal visit did not impress him) and said they would have to accept him as he was!

On one visit he explained he had just been shopping. He was carrying a brown paper bag containing his groceries. He delved deep into the bag and showed me, one at a time, each of his purchases. He had two black puddings (discovered in the freezer of the little supermarket down the road) but wasn't sure how to cook them. He asked my advice but I was no help, never having eaten black pudding let alone cooked any. I told him I thought they were edible raw, but Father Valentine shook his head doubtfully. Father Valentine was from Irish stock and I told him that he, better than anyone, should know what to do with a black pudding.

Another recent visitor to the office was Griselda's new husband. Thin and quiet, shy and humble. He came very slowly up the stairs and paused for a long time on the balcony outside, hovering uncertainly. I watched, puzzled, wondering if he was going to come in. He appeared to be talking to himself, but I couldn't be sure. Then he plucked up courage and slipped in through the open office door.

"Mistress" he whispered quietly *"Griselda, she wan' she manni"*.

Griselda had been missing for weeks and I had resorted to using Risa who worked at the Treasure Isle Hotel as my maid. Since Griselda had married and become a 'Madam' she was distinctly unreliable. I asked her husband what had happened to her but he just shrugged and spread his hands. I did owe Griselda some money, so I gladly gave it to him. Poor man, he seemed far too gentle to have been saddled with a strong-willed Griselda.

Risa was as different from Griselda as chalk from cheese. A pretty and polite little thing with a natural grace and a charming manner she worked for Herbie Showering when he was in residence at the condominiums.

CHAPTER 36

ARK ROYAL, BARRACUDA AND CONCH

The Royal Navy had been on a war games exercise off Puerto Rico and arrived in the BVI to use the smaller uninhabited islands for Marine manoeuvres.

When we looked out from our balcony we thought for a moment that several new islands had erupted from the seabed overnight until we realized that the largest hump was the massive aircraft carrier *'Ark Royal'* and the two smaller humps beside her were not rocky outcrops but *HMS Fearless* and *HMS Dreadnought*.

For three days Tortola swarmed with sailors and marines, all of whom fell passionately in love with the place and likened it to Malta, one of their most popular ports. Some of the men were still engaged in the war games and were required to crawl through the rough bush in remote areas on their bellies trying to shoot each other. Fortunately for us they were using blanks but apparently the Puerto Rico exercises required the use of live ammunition.

Three of the marines were dumped on Beef Island but one got bitten by a spider and another hurt himself, so they were lifted off leaving the lonely third marine to handle the training alone.

All the navy top brass came ashore, including the Admiral, and moved into the Treasure Isle hotel below us, along with a journalist and photographer from the *'Soldier'* magazine.

The place hummed with activity. It was one long party for us with interesting and exciting people. Strangers became close friends. It was like the island had become one big happy family, and the warmth and friendliness of everyone was an absolute tonic.

The *Ark Royal* was enormous. Her huge flat deck had to act as a runway for the Buccaneer aircraft on board, and she looked like a vast floating airfield. We were told, unofficially, that off Puerto Rico over the deepest part of the Puerto Rican Trench, one of the Buccaneer's slipped from the deck and fell into the sea. The incident happened during the night and by the time a rescue had been scrambled together and they dragged the ocean, the only thing they managed to retrieve was the airplane nose cone. Someone had not secured the chain and the navy lost £1.5 million of hardware overboard.

Apparently they lose about eight planes a year, though not necessarily by dropping them into the sea, usually accidents happen on landing, or taking off.

The Traffic Department gave up the recreation ground temporarily so that it could be used as a helicopter landing pad, ferrying the navy men backwards and forwards between Tortola and their ships.

The helicopters arrived by the dozen.

They throbbed and spluttered rising from the deck of the ships and then appeared to be aiming directly for our condominium balcony. The huge plate-glass sliding doors which separated our lounge from the balcony vibrated alarmingly and I found myself ducking involuntarily as they hammered towards us. They would fly straight for us until, only a matter of yards away, they swung abruptly to the right to follow the main road to the recreation ground.

The recreation ground was used at weekends by our football teams. A local team were playing a rival team made up of expats. In the middle of the game a policeman ran on to the pitch waving his arms. The puzzled teams stopped the game and seconds later a navy helicopter swooped down to land in the middle of the scattering players. Several important but unidentified personages stepped out, solemnly shook hands with each of the players, stepped back on board and throbbed off. The match continued in some confusion with the Tortolian team finally winning. The expats rather unsportingly complained that their concentration had been thrown by the interruption of the chopper, and requested a replay.

The *Ark Royal* Marine Band came ashore and gave us a wonderful open-air concert on the recreation ground. It was very informal and everyone was welcome. It was great fun and much appreciated. They played a wide variety of music including some stirring marches. A brilliant performance and the atmosphere was electric. The highly polished brass instruments flashed and sparked with reflected sunlight, dazzling both the players and us.

We spectators were all sensibly dressed in casual shorts and T-shirts, unlike the poor band. Towards the end of their performance they were perspiring visibly under the hot tropical sun, even though a temporary awning had been stretched out over their heads. The final marched Retreat was a splendid affair, only slightly marred by the drummer who accidentally flicked his stick in a double somersault and was unable to catch it again. He kept going, using only one stick but earnestly pretending to drum with his empty left hand. We rescued the stick for him and piled some of the band into the back of the landrover to take them off for dinner.

Socially it was something of a marathon with at least two parties a night. On the last day of the navy visit we were invited on board the *Ark Royal*. We were exhausted with the effort of partying and all we really wanted to do was to sit on a beach, sleep and swim, but it seemed very rude to refuse.

We decided to compromise. Mark skippered the hotel boat and we threw aboard our snorkels, fins, masks and a huge picnic. Then we sped off to the *Ark Royal* moored out at sea, circled her several times, waving our goodbyes to the boys on board.

It took our small power boat several minutes to circumnavigate the monster that was the *Ark Royal*. Viewed close up the gigantic ship was overwhelmingly awesome. The steep grey sides towered high over our heads and the waving sailors leaning out from above were mere specks. The tails of the planes strapped to the deck jutted over the edge. The whole effect was one of a very powerful and threatening war machine.

Then we sped off towards Virgin Gorda heading for little Mosquito Island. Our pirate friend and wreck expert Bert Kilbride insisted the island was named after the Miskito Indians and not those pesky biting insects that plagued our lives. We anchored off deserted Honeymoon Cove and collapsed on the warm and welcoming sand and for the next few hours we just soaked up some sun and lazed and chatted and ate our picnic.

It was a blissful day and much more relaxing than the last occasion when my husband and I went snorkeling together. We had driven across to Long Bay on Beef Island for the afternoon. Being remote from the main island of Tortola it was always deserted and we knew we would have it to ourselves. This was our favourite beach for some 'alone' time.

We were quietly snorkeling out to sea some distance from the beach, idly swimming along looking for bleached sand dollars and sea mice. As usual I flip-flapped along on the surface gazing down and around but for some reason I happened to glance up and ahead.

A barracuda was hanging motionless in the water just a few yards ahead of me, staring fixedly at me, studying me intently and opening and closing its mouth in a most alarming way. Viewed through my mask it was scarily massive, about 6 ft. long, and thick and silver and had very sharp teeth, and it was looking straight into my eyes.

I comforted myself with the thought that my mask was probably magnifying his size, but suddenly I felt very vulnerable. Was he just being inquisitive? Or was he sizing me up for lunch? Had my wedding ring flashed in the sunlight and caught his eye? I remembered barracuda were attracted to glitter, they believed it was a tasty fish.

The big barracuda was between me and the beach, barring the way with his menacing torpedo body. My husband was a few feet over to my left and seemed not to have noticed. Snorkelers wanting to attract the attention of other snorkelers 'hoot' through their tube. I hooted as loudly as I could. My husband turned at the sound, saw the barracuda and in one quick flip he was beside me. The hoot, however, did nothing to disturb the silver torpedo. He remained silently suspended directly in front of us, just observing.

My husband always carried a knife, sheathed in a holster tied to his leg, probably an ineffective weapon against a determined attack from a barracuda, but comforting to him under the circumstances. He pulled it out and took my hand.

207

There is a belief that to frighten a fish you have to appear as a predator, larger than it and totally unafraid. Side by side we were one very big fish and slowly, very slowly, we started to glide towards the barracuda. This, we hoped, would show we were large, unafraid, not necessarily threatening but just merely curious. But the barracuda just hung there, motionless, open-mouthed and showing those terrifyingly sharp teeth. He refused to be intimidated and as the distance between us narrowed, he refused to budge.

We stopped and hesitated still holding hands. Suddenly, in a silver flash so fast we simply didn't see it happen, the barracuda moved. He appeared to have vanished, until we saw he had simply repositioned himself. He was on our right, further away this time and no longer cutting us off from the beach but still watching us intently. We didn't pause. We took off like a rocket for the shore, not slowing down until we hit sand. And as we pulled ourselves on to the beach and looked back we saw a large silver shaped torpedo suspended in the water a few feet away. The barracuda had followed us to shore.

When we relayed the incident to our friends they were alarmed. Other stories surfaced of an enormous barracuda who patrolled Beef Island beach scaring swimmers.

My husband was using his new SCUBA qualification to go out with any of the dive team who needed a 'buddy' and he had some exciting and interesting trips.

George was commissioned by the owners of the new Peter Island Club to take a promotional underwater film, and he needed two divers as 'actors' to add dimension and interest. My husband needed no persuasion to volunteer and went along with Mark. George set about filming them diving around Peter Island and neighbouring Dead Chest.

Peter Island had some beautiful dive sites and one of our favourites was Great Harbour on the north side. At the centre of the bay lay a shallow coral reef which started in about 7 ft. of water and sloped gently to approximately 20 ft. before a vertical drop off. This was a perfect spot for protected snorkeling with a wonderful assortment of colourful corals, 'feather dusters', tube worms, sponges, tunicates.

The fish loved the area and surrounded the diver in a thick undulating tapestry of rainbow colour. But George himself preferred an area off Dead Chest which he called *'painted walls'*. Visibility could be as good as 100 ft. and with interesting coral formations and fantastic colour it was an ideal place to film.

The mail steamship *RMS Rhone* must have been sheltering somewhere near here in 1867 when she sank in the hurricane, for the wreck was not far from this site.

The filming went well and just before they were planning to complete, almost as if on cue, a huge Spotted Eagle Ray came sliding into view. It took absolutely no notice of the divers who were so excited they were (they confessed afterwards) in danger of hyperventilating. George raced off in pursuit of the ray, film spinning, and says it was the biggest he had ever seen. Attempts to express its immense size included statements like *"easily fifteen feet across"* from my engineer husband, *"mammoth"* from Mark, and *"as large as a Texas ball-park"* from George. Even allowing for the standard diver exaggeration and mask magnification it was obviously a very impressive Spotted Eagle Ray.

Shortly after my husband's debut as a movie star we were invited by Mal and Dick to join them for a day sail on board Philippa and Henry's boat. Dick had decided to charter the yacht and wanted us to come along.

My husband often accompanied Dick as his diving 'buddy' and they intended to take their SCUBA tanks and explore the coast around Norman Island while Mal and I planned to sit on deck sunbathing and chatting while Philippa and Henry plied us with drinks and attended to our every need!

It was a delicious delight to see Philippa speechless with surprise when we stepped on board. Dick had been purposefully vague about the identity of his two guests. I must confess it gave me a certain sadistic pleasure to watch Philippa and Henry running backwards and forwards on deck, satisfying our demands, as we sailed across the Sir Francis Drake Channel to Norman Island.

When we reached Norman Island and had anchored offshore, my husband and Dick put on their SCUBA gear and slipped overboard to explore the sloping reef off the western point of Norman Island. Mal and I lounged on deck, gently rocking up and down and soaking up a suntan, while Philippa and Henry slaved away in the galley preparing our lunch.

When the two men finally returned and climbed aboard, they spent at least half an hour enthusing about the spectacular beauty of their dive, and so we four decided to snorkel offshore so that Mal and I could see for ourselves the rocky ridges, narrow canyons, and shoals of angelfish they had been describing so lyrically. We returned with two conchs we had found walking across the sandy seabed close to shore.

Philippa was delighted with our find. She pronounced our conch a *'gastronomic delicacy'* and immediately wanted to change the menu. We hastily but politely refused, using the excuse that Mal was allergic to seafood. Mal had admitted to me privately that she couldn't bear to see the animal inside the shell killed. The shell of a conch is very pretty with its smooth creamy whorls outside and soft pink interior, and although Mal did not really want to kill the occupant, she did want to keep the shell as a souvenir and ornament. She was in a dilemma.

But Philippa had no such scruples and was not to be deterred. She immediately set about trying to extract the poor conch from its shelly home. She was ruthless and determined and a horrified Mal scuttled to the other side of the boat in dismay.

I could have shown Philippa how the local fishermen managed to release the conch meat quickly and easily, but she was so adamant that she knew what she was doing I walked away in disgust and comforted the distressed Mal instead.

A local fishermen would have tapped a small hole in one of the end whorls, expertly slipped a small sharp knife inside to loosen the cemented tongue (which quickly killed the conch at the same time) and then gently and easily pulled the conch from its shell. If he was eating it raw, the conch had to be freshly caught and prepared immediately or it would be too tough. A little squeezed lime juice helped to tenderize the meat and added flavour.

I have to admit conch was really delicious when made into fritters. Minced very small and mixed with flour, baking powder, tomato and herbs, all glued together with a little water, then dropped into hot fat for a few minutes and served with a tangy sauce, they were a gourmet's delight.

Philippa worked like a woman possessed. She tried every way she could think of to extract the conch from its shell, but the conch stubbornly refused to release itself. Believing it to be similar to lobster Philippa dropped the poor creature, shell and all, into a pan of boiling water, letting it enjoy a rolling boil for five minutes before draining it. Using a fork, Philippa managed to spear part of the conch meat just inside the shell. Henry was called to assist and with his help the conch was tugged, pulled and wrenched free from its home.

It was a macabre dance the two performed as they struggled for several minutes to free the meat, but they persevered and finally triumphed, waving aloft a tongue of thick pink meat.

By this time Mal was visibly distraught and in danger of being sick, but nothing we could say would dissuade the insensitive Philippa. She was on a mission. She informed us if *we* wouldn't eat it for lunch she was going to thinly slice it and use it in her salad supper. We fervently wished that once in her stomach the dead conch would find a way to retaliate, with a good dose of diarrhea perhaps.

I could sympathize with Mal's quandary. Wanting the shell but not wishing to hurt the conch, an impossible choice of course. I walked past a fisherman down by the jetty recently. He had caught a turtle, a large and beautiful turtle, and he asked me if I wanted to buy the shell. I looked at the poor sighing turtle, on its back, feet tied together with string, water welling like huge tears in its eyes, and I felt incredibly sad. The turtle would lie like that for a couple of days, slowly dying.

But the fisherman carefully explained to me that this was the traditional way of treating turtles, and that turtle meat was not only delicious but was also very nutritious and would feed his whole family. By selling the shell to a passing tourist he would earn plenty of money. I completely understood, but I didn't buy the turtle shell.

CHAPTER 37

PEEBLES AND PRINCESS MARGARET

Those of us invited to Government House for the visit of Princess Margaret received official invitations. Embossed with a gold crest it requested the honour of our company *'on the occasion of the visit of Her Royal Highness The Princess Margaret Countess of Snowden'*.

The visit was organized by the Governor's wife with meticulous attention to detail and with military efficiency. Cuddles was in her element. Princess Margaret would be taken on a tour of the hospital during her brief visit and was to have the dubious pleasure of *'Receiving'* (note the capital 'R') some of us humble Red Cross volunteers.

We were summoned to Government House and Cuddles drilled us in the art of *'Being Received'*. Stifling our giggles we were shown how to shake the Royal hand and the proper way to curtsey. It was not, Cuddles assured us, as simple as it looked and practice was essential to maintain elegant poise throughout the manoeuvre. She was a hard taskmaster and made us practice until we had perfection.

Cuddles insisted we all wore gloves *'No, not rubber ladies!'* and a hat *'tasteful not tacky'* for the Reception.

In anticipation of the Royal visit the Public Works Department filled in some of the potholes along the East End road to the airport. They said it was to make the journey more comfortable for Princess Margaret as they didn't want her vehicle snaking and bouncing along in the usual bone-shaking manner.

They also planted a handful of coconut palms along the route but sadly no-one thought to water them and they quickly began to wilt. Someone seriously suggested the fronds should be sprayed with green paint in an attempt to make them look *'verdant'* and to disguise their obvious sickly ill-health.

One of our friends, whose husband worked for Cable and Wireless, was approached by Cuddles and asked *'to make herself available'* in case Princess Margaret needed to be *'coiffured'*. There were no hairdressers in the BVI and we relied on each other to cut, trim or perm. As a result anyone with some experience in the field who arrived on the island was pounced upon. Our friend Margaret had worked as a hairdresser before she married and had her children. Cuddles discovered this fact quite by accident and as a result Margaret found herself drafted in as the *'official hairdresser'* to Government House.

She was, understandably, a little nervous about *'doing'* such an important personage as Princess Margaret and was terrified she might spill something toxic over the royal locks in her anxiety to please. We joked that when she returned to the UK she could claim to be a hairdresser *By Royal Appointment*.

We Red Cross volunteers were still trying to paint the hospital but were having difficulty finding anyone prepared to help. It was down to Ulrike and me, and this severely limited progress. Two inexperienced young women painters who spent most of their time gossiping together as they worked didn't get much done.

But also we preferred to spend our time at the hospital in the children's ward where little Patsy lived. The children's ward was usually empty and Patsy was alone much of the time. We liked to visit her and play with her. We would lift her out of the cot and 'walk' her down the corridor and she loved the attention.

Last time we visited she was lying on her back in her cot waving her legs in the air, and Ulrike leant over and tickled her feet for fun. Immediately Patsy looked up and lifted her leg expectantly. She had not forgotten the exercises taught to her by the physiotherapist those many months ago, and when Ulrike had absentmindedly tickled her foot she responded at once.

The new diagnosis on Patsy, recently received from Jamaica, was Cerebral Palsy and not Muscular Dystrophy as had been thought. It was probably caused during the mother's pregnancy or perhaps by a lack of oxygen at birth. She was not deaf, as everyone had supposed, her response to hearing was simply delayed, and with the proper help a great deal could be done for her.

Ulrike and I decided to paint the Sluice Room on our last visit to the hospital. Before we came along and attacked the walls they were a dreary and depressing dark green, soiled by years of neglect. We deliberately chose to paint the Sluice Room because it was so small we thought the two of us might manage to finish the job fairly quickly.

All went well until Ulrike, wielding her paint brush above the sinks, found a clear plastic bag on the draining board, which bulged with something dark red and squidgy. She was curious and leaned closer to inspect the contents. She called me over to look. We peered at the messy red blob in the bag and puzzled over what it might be. Then a nurse breezed in, laughed at our curiosity, and told us it was afterbirth. Somehow we couldn't seem to find the enthusiasm to carry on. So we called it a day and went off to visit Patsy again.

For one reason or another I seemed to be spending quite a lot of my time at Peebles hospital. One of our friends gave birth recently to a very premature baby, at only seven months, and I went up see her. She was looking fine, having produced a tiny baby boy who was struggling heroically in the hospital's only incubator. While I was sitting with her the nurse came in to say that they had at last successfully managed to weigh her baby. He had, she explained, been weighed on both the *'big'* scales and also on the *'little'* scales. On the big scales he weighed 2lb 12 oz. but on the little scales he weighed a grand 3lb 2oz. So if anyone asked the baby's weight, we told them that according to the little scales he was a bouncing, robust, hefty, 3lb 2oz.

CHAPTER 38

THE BIGELOWS AND GUANA ISLAND

Well, the Royal visit passed successfully. After all those weeks of planning it was a rather rapid affair, but of course very Royal. A number of 'snowbird' expatriates had delayed their summer migration back home in order to graciously accept the Government House Reception invitation. Herbie Showering was one such and he thoroughly enjoyed the event.

Her Royal Highness Princess Margaret arrived in the evening, was whisked round the hospital the following morning, had a selection of personages presented to her in the afternoon, including the Red Cross volunteers who, I am proud to say, shook and curtseyed flawlessly. She smiled royally for two hours through the Reception in the evening, and then disappeared the following day.

My husband and I had our own VIP's to entertain and saw little of Her Royal Highness. It just so happened that the plane bringing Princess Margaret from London to Antigua also had on board my own mum and dad, coming out to the BVI to join us for a six week holiday of a lifetime.

Dad had just retired and mum, whose cancer had returned after several years in remission, was determined to make the most of the short time she had left. It was a brave decision they made, coming out to stay with us, but mum was adamant nothing would stand in her way. Regardless of her cancer diagnosis, regardless of the angina she suffered since her heart attack when I was fifteen, regardless of her diabetes, she was resolute. And dad meekly followed where mum led.

It was a wonderful six weeks. My parents were totally spoilt by our friends who arranged boat trips, dinner parties and picnics for them. My enduring image of my mum is of her on the beach at Josiah's Bay, wearing a trendy swimming costume (cleverly designed to disguise her mastectomy), bobbing about in the surf with an inflatable rubber ring round her middle and a huge grin on her face. I see my Dad celebrating his birthday with a night out at Long Bay Hotel, sipping a rum punch cocktail as if it was lemonade, while the restaurant speciality meringue dessert was brought to our table to the accompaniment of Swan Lake.

It was all too brief a visit. When we took them back to Antigua to catch their flight home they told us they had enjoyed a really fantastic time, a truly memorable holiday.

Our own lives returned to normal and Ulrike and I launched into planning our first Red Cross Ball to coincide with the Queen's Birthday Garden Party celebrations in June.

Cuddles had set up her 'team', a small committee of six appointed to organize the Ball. Ulrike and I were nominated the two 'active service' Committee members reporting to the other four at a weekly meeting.

In accordance with Cuddles' instructions all the proceeds were to go towards setting up a school for handicapped children. We were aiming to eventually raise $162,000 which when invested was calculated to give a return of $10,000 a year. Sufficient, we hoped, to cover the school running costs.

The school would initially open as a centre of activity with volunteer help, but we trusted that once we had started the ball rolling qualified help would be forthcoming. We wanted the school to be up and running within three months, hopefully by September, and had already got six children between the ages of two and nine on the register. We decided to hold a 'name the school' competition and to organize more volunteer paint-ins to make the hall we had chosen for the school respectable. Liz, Maggie, Ulrike and I were by now quite experienced painters, or so we liked to think.

The Ball was to be held at the Treasure Isle Hotel. Ulrike and I found ourselves dashing around putting together band, prizes, food, tickets, posters etc. But it was not all graft. We arranged the weekly meetings to take place over a liquid lunch so we could bring our fellow committee members up-to-date in relaxed and convivial surroundings.

But Ulrike and I decided we needed a respite from the painting and panic, so when her husband Bill suggested we should all go over to Guana Island for a peaceful weekend of rest and relaxation we jumped at the chance.

Bill's family guarded their privacy and their island home of Guana zealously and it was hugely flattering to be invited to join them for the weekend. It was the first of many visits to this little piece of paradise where we became regular weekend guests.

The beaches on Guana were considered to be some of the best in the Caribbean, the clean soft sand so white it dazzled. And the sea so clear, warm and shallow, gently kissing the palm fringed bay. Fish, so varied and prolific, and so unused to humans they refused to part ranks for curious snorkelers.

Guana Island operated as a very select private Club. It was bought by Bill's parents Louis and Beth Bigelow in the early Thirties. Louis told us they had travelled the world searching for their own island paradise before they found Guana. It was now officially owned by Bill and his brother, although the family had recently been thinking of selling. Bill's parents still lived on Guana and ran the Club but they were ready to retire and wanted to return to mainland USA.

Under the Club system organized by Louis Bigelow guests purchased 'shares' in varying amounts which were used to build the small stone cottages alongside the sturdy original Quaker Greathouse. The shares entitled the Club members to enjoy holidays on Guana. On our first visit to Guana the four other guests were a couple from Chicago and another couple from Boston.

The only electricity was produced by a throbbing generator which was ritualistically started up at sunset by Louis. The Chicago wife, unfamiliar with the limitations of the system, inadvertently caused a 'brown-out' on our first evening when she tried to use her hairdryer. The lights dimmed and for one awful moment we thought the generator was going to overload. Louis was livid and the poor guest received a very blunt reprimand.

The sunset pre-dinner cocktails on the terrace at six was a pleasant tradition that over time had become a delightful ritual. As the red circle of sun slipped below the horizon we were all instructed to watch for the romantic 'green flash', an optical illusion supposed to be visible just at the moment the crimson orb slides under. Three of our group insisted they saw it whilst others, like myself, must have blinked at the critical second and remained unconvinced.

The two old cannon and shot on Guana seemed totally out of place. Guana was so peaceful and tranquil. One of the cannon had been hauled up the hill and set beside a frangipani tree overlooking the bay below, and the other remained beside the beach, apparently in its original position. They bore witness to some past breaches of the island's tranquility. Since Guana was originally owned by pacifist Quakers, we wondered if the cannon had ever actually been fired.

The first recorded Quaker owner of *'Guanah Island'* was James Parke who lived there from 1743-1759, initially with his first wife Bytha and later, after Bytha's death, James married the widow Mary Vanterpool who lived on *'the Island Camanders'*, presumably the neighbouring island of Camanoe.

Because Guana had been left entirely natural the birds were abundant and unafraid. The humming birds in particular were a joy to watch as they hovered and darted between the red hibiscus petals, their long curling beaks drawing the nectar from the flowers as their beautiful iridescent dark green and black feathers flashed in the sunlight. The yellow and black bananaquits were as cheeky as our British sparrows and deftly knocked the lid off the sugar bowl in their attempts to raid the sweet store.

Evening dinner on Guana was a very formal family affair with visitors treated as honored house guests. All were seated at the same large table outside on the stone terrace with Bill's father Louis at the head. Courses were brought through from the kitchen at the tinkle of a crystal bell and the food was absolutely delicious. All provisions were brought over from Tortola by boat and stockpiled in the original large stone pantry. Given the circumstances the quality and variety of the food was a wonderful surprise, and artichoke in hollandaise sauce was an unexpected gourmet delight.

We spent the weekend playing tennis on the courts beside the beach, swimming, fishing, and exploring the tiny island and generally delighting in a luxurious lifestyle quite unfamiliar to us with our modest background.

We played chess and enjoyed convivial conversation in the evening, exploring local matters like island politics, and larger issues like Vietnam. We discussed topics as diverse as American politics and the British monarchy. Bill believed that President Nixon's policy on Vietnam was the right one and that history would prove it to be so. As an American citizen Bill was called up for service, but was declared medically unfit after showing that he had broken an arm as a youngster. This proved sufficient reason, under the rules of the Vietnam Crisis, to avoid being drafted, but if it ever escalated and was officially declared a war, then I understand different rules would apply and Bill could well be drafted.

The kitchen on Guana was hung with small plastic effigies, placed there by the local girls to keep away the Jumbies. They might have protected against Jumbies but they didn't help to keep harmony between the workers! On our last morning the two kitchen girls employed on Guana had a disagreement over who was to do which chores. They began arguing, loudly and angrily, and then started to fight. One of the men employed on the estate stepped forward to try and separate the hostile females, and was walloped over the head with a large and heavy frying pan for interfering. He was so incensed he set off to his quarters to find his rifle, threatening to shoot the girl who had banged him over the head.

Fortunately Louis arrived at this point and took control. He found the gun first and confiscated it, separated the girls, sacked one on the spot and shipped her straight back to Tortola. All this and breakfast was only five minutes late!

When we four left Guana later that morning Bill decided not to take the usual route to Tortola, the safe and recommended way round the end of Beef Island tying up opposite Marina Cay. To save time Bill wanted to take the riskier route, driving the little boat over and through the reef between Tortola and Beef Island. Bill assured us he had taken this gap through the reef several times before, admittedly with an experienced East End boatman at the helm, but he was certain he could manage it.

As we approached the long, apparently unbroken, line of reef where the surf smashed in great foaming waves, we were not so sure. Bill confidently stated that all we had to do was to keep the hill of Beef Island behind the stern of the boat, and the second hill of Tortola directly ahead. This, he explained, would lead us through a very narrow passage in the reef. It sounded simple enough. Ulrike and I cowered together in the bottom of the boat while Bill and my husband leaned over the side calling out approximate depths to each other as we got closer and closer to the angry reef.

"Four feet!", "Three feet!", "Two foot six!"

Then suddenly we were no longer rolling and bouncing in the swell but we had been lifted and carried high, charging through the spume thrown up by the waves.

"One foot six Bill!" Yelled my husband, grabbing the side of the little boat for support. And then, just as suddenly, we were through the small gap and on the still and sheltered side of the reef with Tortola to our right and Beef Island to our left.

We whooped with relief as the adrenaline rush subsided. But I was still a bit wobbly on my legs as I attempted to climb out of the boat when we tied up beside Queen Elizabeth Bridge a few minutes later.

CHAPTER 39

PETER ISLAND AND THE INFAMOUS YACHT RACE

We returned home after our wonderful Guana weekend feeling refreshed and ready for almost anything. But we had no sooner unpacked our overnight bags than the phone rang. It was the first of many calls from friends bursting to tell us about the scandal involving Philippa and Henry. The island was positively buzzing with the gossip.

While we were on Guana with Bill and Ulrike enjoying our lovely weekend of rest and relaxation there was a two-day yacht race taking place around Tortola. The yacht race was one of the reasons we felt we could slip away unnoticed for a quiet weekend, all attention was on the race. It was an extremely prestigious affair with yachts from St. Thomas and Puerto Rico. The event concluded with the presentation of trophies and an impressive buffet dinner organized by Peter Island Club for the participants.

Philippa and Henry had been looking forward to the race. Their yacht was the largest, fastest and according to Philippa the best entered and Henry had set his heart on winning. A few weeks ago they had decided to sell their beloved yacht and a prospective purchaser in Puerto Rico needed to be convinced that she was capable of winning races before he would commit himself, and Philippa and Henry saw this race as the perfect opportunity to impress.

They were quite confident of success but just to make sure they hired two of Tortola's most experienced sailors as additional crew and Henry was heard to boast that the two-day event was *'going to be a walkover!'*

But things went badly wrong from the very beginning. They somehow managed to split the spinnaker, and then Philippa concussed herself when a ladder fell on her head. As a result she spent the two days of the race not mentally altogether, and nursing a large bump on her skull. So, sadly for their reputation, the sale of the yacht, and their bruised ego, they only managed to limp in at third place. The final indignity came when the engine broke down and they had to beg a tow from a passing houseboat to get to Peter Island for the big buffet supper celebration.

Peter Island Club was becoming a very exclusive, very expensive, very upmarket resort, with a wealthy, distinguished and discerning clientele similar to those who enjoyed the pampered luxurious peace of Rockefeller's Little Dix Bay Resort on Virgin Gorda. The gourmet cuisine and attentive silver service of the waiters was renowned.

On this special occasion the Chef had prepared a stunningly impressive centre-piece to the yacht race celebration, a table lavishly decorated and laden with a sumptuous harvest of fruit and an impressive display of fine and expensive wines from the cellar.

Henry must have thought it a *'jolly wheeze'* when he sneaked one of the bottles from the Chef's magnificent display. According to eye-witnesses who regaled us with the details, he was giggling and laughing as he tried to hide it under his table, crouching down to uncork it before pouring liberal glasses for Philippa and the crew. A waiter happened to notice and went to check that they had actually purchased the bottle. When he discovered they had not, he added the cost to their bill. The price of the bottle being US$38.

Henry should have done the gentlemanly thing and paid up and shut up. But instead he began arguing with the waiter and finally refused to pay. The Manager was called and Henry was politely but firmly escorted to the Manager's office. Henry asked to be excused for a moment and as the Manager waited for him to return, he heard the outboard motor of a dinghy start up. Henry had absconded.

The Manager rushed out to the marina just in time to see Henry and Philippa pulling away from the jetty towards their moored yacht. By this time the Manager, a mellow person, normally a quiet, controlled and extremely proper Norwegian gentleman, was apoplectic with rage. This simply was not the sort of behaviour one expected from diners at a resort with the reputation of the Peter Island Club.

The Manager shouted after them that they were now banned from Peter Island and added that the ban also included the two Tortolian crew members. He felt they could, and should, have used their influence to control Henry.

Philippa and Henry showed no remorse. They were not at all embarrassed or ashamed and once safely back on board their yacht, a grinning Philippa posed for Henry to take a photograph of her holding the empty and expensive bottle in one hand and waving the unpaid bill in the other.

The other diners on Peter Island that night who witnessed Henry's behaviour were all influential yachtsmen from around the islands, and the story swept through Tortola like a bush fire.

Philippa and Henry were disdainfully labelled *'professional bums'* and instantly excluded from Tortola society. They had earned the dubious distinction of being the first people to be prohibited from landing on Peter Island. The Puerto Rican gentleman let it be known he no longer wished to purchase their yacht.

When their plans for selling the yacht fell through Philippa and Henry informed us they now intended to sail their boat across the Pacific. But sailing friends told us this was a big mistake. They had already left it too late and they would be well advised to wait until October before attempting the crossing. In any case they could not do it alone and would need to find an experienced crew, which would mean going down to Antigua first.

I decided it was time for me to learn how to SCUBA. I was fed up with snorkeling or sitting on the sand while my husband went off exploring the depths of the ocean without me. George was planning another series of lessons and asked if I would like to join, so my husband took me through the qualifying tests in the Treasure Isle pool to see whether I was physically fit enough.

Mick and Mark stood on the edge of the pool shouting encouragement and supervising, and just to make sure I didn't cheat. I learned how to put on the regulator and clear it and then my husband strapped a tank onto my back and under I went. It was a lovely feeling. The hiss and bubble of the gas was very comforting and reassuring, just the in and out of my own breath and everything else silent. I sat on the bottom of the pool quite happily, just studying the tiles and bubbling away to *'get the feel of it!'*

Then my husband decided it was time for me to 'buddy breathe' using his regulator. To applause from the poolside, I successfully managed to blow the water in my mouth and the water in the regulator out before sucking in a lungful of air, tricky but essential. I decided to swim around until the air ran out so that I could feel what it was like to switch to the reserve tank. I swam and swam and swam but the tank refused to empty, so we practised mask clearing and other incidentals instead. I sat cross-legged on the bottom of the pool and took off my mask. All the little bubbles whizzing past my face were very disconcerting and I couldn't manage to clear it at all, I just blinked through the sloshing water trapped in my mask and got all confused.

Having miserably failed that test (to the disappointment of all the hotel staff who were lined up peering through the water watching my antics) I tried to tread water using only my feet and not flippers, fingers held above the surface of the pool, for three minutes. Everyone was encouraging me, but after only one minute I sank gracefully under the water. My audience shook their heads. Yet another very public failure.

I seemed to be the only person on island with 'negative buoyancy'. My husband, Mick and Mark needed several heavy weights strapped around their waists in order to balance the tank, but I did not need any at all. So when it came to test number three, floating on the surface for fifteen minutes, I again failed in spectacular fashion by dropping like a stone to the bottom, however I did brilliantly when asked to swim underwater for one and a half lengths on one lungful of air.

CHAPTER 40

CAPITAL PUNISHMENT

Our time in the BVI was flying by and suddenly we had only two months left on our contract. My life was proving hectic. I was still working in the office during the mornings and my afternoons and evenings were packed with social commitments. Monday night was a SCUBA lesson, Tuesday night a ladies darts match at the Pub, Wednesday night was my weekly Judo lesson with Mark and Thursday night the Red Cross. Friday night was usually a dinner invitation, or (much more desirable) a weekend on Guana with Bill and Ulrike.

More and more Cuddles was treating me like her personal assistant. She contacted me several times a day by phone. If she couldn't find me when she needed me she got very agitated and accused me of being 'leave happy'. I explained I was just incredibly busy, but she suspected me of deliberately avoiding her and there may have been a grain of truth in that.

Cuddles was very unsettled and worried. We were facing another island crisis and as Governor's wife she took it very personally.

The crisis surrounded a young man in prison who was waiting to be hung. Capital punishment was the mandatory sentence for a murder conviction in the Territory and the tensions this caused created very strong emotions splitting the community in half. Everyone had an opinion and most talked of nothing else.

Cuddles herself was horrified that a prisoner should face a hanging sentence, but it was the law. The young man in question was accused of killing his girlfriend. In his defence they said she had apparently attacked him but was fatally injured in the struggle which followed. He was found guilty of murder but appealed. The appeal had been rejected, which meant he was due to hang, unless the Queen interceded. It was an extremely delicate situation for the Governor who was trying to steer the Legislative Council towards sensible government without appearing to interfere.

The majority opinion, made up of both expatriates and Tortolians, wanted the young man to hang. They argued it would be a moral warning to others. Indeed there were a few who advocated that the poor boy should not only hang, but that it should be done publicly.

The Minister of St. George's Church started a petition for clemency asking the Governor to use his authority, and he managed to collect over five hundred signatures and the petition was passed to the Queen. This angered some people and they demanded that the Minister be deported for meddling in things which did not concern him. And some renewed their demands for a public hanging.

There were two other prisoners accused of murder waiting for their cases to come to trial. If they were found guilty then they would suffer the same fate as this poor young boy.

The young man in question was about twenty. As I sat in my office on Main Street I could hear them building his gallows. The hammering sound travelled across the street from the police station. The gallows had been designed, I was told, by the Public Works Department. They said the cell floor would be dug up and the boy executed, buried there, and the floor replaced.

By law the Attorney General and the Chief Medical Officer had to be present as witnesses to the hanging, and it was no surprise to learn that both these officials had been 'called away' from the island on 'urgent business', so deputies were found.

The petition for clemency failed. On the morning of the execution my husband and I closed up the office and stayed away from town. As we drove past the prison a small knot of people had gathered and were chatting outside the big wooden gates. St. George's church bell was tolling mournfully and someone (the Minister himself was suspected) had written across the whitewashed outside wall 'ask not for whom the bell tolls, it tolls for thee'.

226

Ulrike and I went up to Government House to be with Cuddles while the execution took place. She had received a phone call the previous evening saying that if the boy was hung, she would find a bomb under her bed. She was so pleased to see us she became very emotional. She felt somehow responsible for the hanging and nothing we could say would ease her feelings of guilt.

Even the weather seemed to be in sympathy with the mood of the island. The first hurricane of the season, Hurricane Agnes, swept through to our north devastating the Dominican Republic and then headed with reckless speed for the United States. But instead of high winds and heavy rain, which would at least have replenished our water reserves and cooled us all down, we experienced very sticky, muggy and hot weather and we missed the fresh breeze which normally passed across us.

We were also facing a water shortage, which could be disastrous as we were only just beginning the 'dry season'. It did not take long before the wells ran saline and since the island had no fresh water except the rainwater we collected, we tried to be very careful with our precious cistern supplies.

This did not help tempers and the atmosphere on Tortola turned tense and electric. People who came to the island for the winter were leaving. Some intended to stay for the Queen's Birthday Garden Party before slipping away, but Herbie Showering left early, cutting short his visit. He was a sick man and was carried off in a wheelchair and we were worried about him, not sure whether he would ever return to Tortola.

CHAPTER 41

QUEEN'S BIRTHDAY GARDEN PARTY AND RED CROSS BALL

The Queen's Birthday Garden Party in June was the colonial social event of the year. We arranged our fund-raising Red Cross Ball to coincide so that distinguished guests could parade through Government House in the afternoon, take a quick nap, and arrive at the Treasure Isle Hotel early evening in time for a reggae knees-up and BBQ chicken supper.

But fate intervened when a member of the Royal family died two days before the Garden Party and as a consequence His Excellency the Governor and Cuddles were plunged into official mourning for a week and were unable to attend any social functions.

For a few ghastly hours we thought we might have to cancel the Red Cross Ball in deference to the Royal passing, but the Governor managed to get special permission from the Foreign Office to go ahead, on the strict understanding that he and Cuddles did not attend. All the flags were dropped to half-mast and to her dismay Cuddles was obliged to wear either black or white during the official mourning period.

HMS Berwick, one of the Royal Navy ships, arrived the night before the Queen's Birthday Garden Party and Cuddles was flapping around trying to persuade suitable couples to adopt an officer for the evening since she herself had been forbidden to entertain.

Ulrike and I ended up with the ship's doctor and three young lads who looked as if they hadn't yet begun to shave. My husband and I piled them into the back of the landrover and bounced and bumped our way up Joe's Hill to have drinks and nibbles with

Ulrike and Bill. The sailors were obviously on best behaviour and so polite and stiff that we began to feel they were suffering an endurance test rather than a jolly night off the ship. So we piled them all back into the truck and bounced and bumped back down the hill to the Sir Francis Drake pub. Much more their scene, and at last they began to look as if they might be having fun.

That was just before the fight broke out. We learned later that one of our little lads had been receiving some grief from his superior officer on board. When they came face to face in the pub it was more than our boy could endure, and primed with alcohol he let fly with his fists, thumping his officer to the ground and knocking him unconscious. It was dark and gloomy in the pub and Ulrike and I were the only two who witnessed the attack. When the M.P.s raced in to sort things out, our lad had fled.

"No" We both said firmly *"We haven't seen a thing!"*

There were five fights in the pub that evening, and in the darkness of the night three young officers enjoyed the intimate company of three expatriate wives. By the following morning the gossip was rife and by mid-day we all knew the names of the imprudent women and as a direct result three marriages ended. It was a memorable evening.

A handful of specially selected senior officers were invited to the Government House Garden Party the following day, and the ship's bugler was invited along to play down the Union Jack as it was ceremoniously lowered at sunset.

Being the Queen's Birthday Garden Party it was a hat, gloves and 'short frock' occasion with lounge suits or uniform for the men. Father Valentine turned up dressed as he had threatened, in his short sleeved blue shirt, open at the neck, with his wide black leather belt holding up his baggy black trousers, polished pink face fringed with silver hair. Father Valentine hated all the pomp and ceremony and deliberately tried to deflate the occasion by saying the most outrageous things. His views, opinions and understanding of life together with his fascinating tit-bits of information did much to broaden my education. His experiences of San Francisco and the drug rehabilitation centre in Puerto Rico had given him a fund of spicy anecdotes guaranteed to make my eyes pop.

As we waited beneath the bougainvillea, shuffling forward in the official Receiving Line, burning under the afternoon sun, overdressed and already weary, Father Valentine kept up a running commentary of derogatory remarks about colonial pomp and ceremony. By the time he had reached the Governor, who was formally resplendent in his white suit and feathered pith helmet, Father Valentine had completely lost his self-control. He grabbed the limp hand cordially extended to him and pumped it powerfully, slapped H.E. on the back and demanded to know where the drinks were.

We quickly grabbed him and steered him hurriedly away across the tennis courts, out of ear-shot of the other guests, and gave him a cigarette and a double rum. The little Girl Guides rushed towards us carrying plates heavy with tiny triangular sandwiches already curling dryly with the sun. It was not a big gathering and we soon sorted ourselves into small gossipy cliques.

Father Valentine wanted to know if any of us had attended the morning parade on the recreation ground. We had and we nodded.

"Tell me" He demanded in his soft Irish brogue *"What was the name of the tune the police band was playing as they unfurled the flag?"*

We had all listened intently but although it seemed vaguely familiar no-one in our group had been able to place it, it certainly bore no resemblance to the National Anthem. Father Valentine knew what it was. We gave a stab at a suggestion, but each time Father Valentine shook his head and laughed. We gave up guessing and demanded the answer.

"It was" he told us triumphantly *"The Red Flag played very slowly!"* We were quite sure he was wrong but we convulsed with laughter all the same.

The police band was not made up of musicians, it was an assortment of constables who practiced together once a week primarily in an attempt to master 'God Save the Queen'. The weekly open air practice on the Green could be heard by most of the Road Town residents. The trumpeter always ran ahead of the others and they would scramble to catch up, losing control of their instruments and producing a cacophony of unrelated notes. The bandmaster would despair, stop them all and then start again, and again, and again. The drummer had a tendency to slip into pan rhythm, catchy and attractive but not really appropriate.

I once heard the National Anthem being played by a Fungi band from the back of a truck as it wound its way past Government House on Christmas Day. It was fabulous. Washboard, gourd and hub caps playing *'God Save The Queen'*, it was an inspiration!

The trumpeter was the most experienced member of the band and had the important job of playing down the Union Jack on ceremonial occasions when there was no navy volunteer. Our trumpeter had been practising for weeks. He would wait until dark and go out onto the very end of Wickhams Cay, as far away from town as he could, and for one or two hours he struggled bravely to master the notes. Unfortunately for us the prevailing wind brought the distressing sound straight across the flat empty cay and funneled it into our lounge.

At the Garden Party the navy bugler selected to accompany the Union Jack was into his fifth rum and was deep in convivial conversation with Father Valentine when we all became aware of activity on the tennis court.

The police trumpeter, flanked by six fellow policemen with rifles on their shoulders, was marching stiffly towards the flagpole. On cue the Governor David Cudmore and Cuddles moved forward to separate themselves from the rabble of guests, and stood solemnly a few feet in front of the Union Jack, which was fluttering at half-mast in respect for the dead Duke. We all stopped talking and turned patriotically to face the front and the flag.

The navy bugler who had been chatting to Father Valentine, wondered under his breath whether he would face disciplinary action for forgetting to be 'at post' when required. He raised his glass in salute to the police trumpeter and wished him luck.

As the constable brought the trumpet to his lips the only thing moving on the tennis court was the Governor's labrador Bruno, who was busy charging from group to group, tail lashing in greeting as he nosed old friends and new. At the first mournful note of the trumpet Bruno stopped, transfixed. He span round, saw the trumpeter, heard the next note and hurtled towards the constable, almost knocking the Governor off his feet as he sped past. Placing himself firmly beside the trumpeter, Bruno lifted his head to the sky, took a huge doggie breath, and began to howl in a piercing, powerful accompaniment.

All credit must go to the trumpeter who was magnificent. He played valiantly on as Bruno howled louder, and during this extraordinary duet the flag was ceremoniously lowered.

Cuddles and the Governor were just in front of our group and I could see her shoulders shaking with laughter. We were all trying to control our hysterics, but an oblivious Bruno howled on. The trumpeter finished with a flourish, grinned down at Bruno and together, in perfect unison, dog and man marched off the court and a spontaneous roar of applause went up from the audience, led of course by Father Valentine who thoroughly approved of Bruno's irreverent behaviour.

I am pleased to say that the Red Cross Ball at the Treasure Isle Hotel later that evening was a resounding success. Everyone came. The navy, the expatriate community, belongers and non-belongers all crowded into the Hotel and it throbbed and swayed until 3.00 a.m. However Ulrike and I were absolutely exhausted, both physically and emotionally, and vowed we would never get ourselves involved in anything similar ever again.

The police were supposed to arrive to deter any unsuitable gate-crashers but they never turned up. Fortunately no fights broke out, as far as we were aware anyway, and most people behaved fairly respectably. We were not the least bit surprised to discover several bodies bobbing around in the pool, rather drunk but at least fully clothed, during the early hours of the morning. And it took us a week to sort out who had won what in the raffle and to deliver the prizes to the rightful winners.

The BBQ chicken legs began the evening at 75c each but mysteriously rose to $1 by the end, the law of supply and demand I supposed, or more likely a lack of available change. The bar was packed to capacity and ran out of beer after an hour, much to the navy's dismay. It was not the dignified fund-raising dance Ulrike and I had anticipated, and it was perhaps just as well the Governor and Cuddles were not able to attend, but everyone agreed it was the best night out the island had seen for years. And we did make a great deal of money for the new school, which was the aim of the evening.

CHAPTER 42

CARNIVAL

Our August Festival was always very popular, a local spectacular. Not perhaps as visually stunning as the Trinidad Jump-up or New Orleans Mardi Gras but hugely enjoyed by our little community who entered into the spirit of the two day carnival with real enthusiasm.

The very first celebration was held over a century ago as a spontaneous reaction to the freeing of the island's slaves, and now it had become a much loved annual event. Anyone could enter into the spirit of the Festival by joining a group and dressing up. The main aim was to produce a day full of colour, music, dance and above all fun, beginning with the *'Rise and Shine Tramp'* at 5.00 a.m. passing through the Grand Parade late morning and culminating in a night of music, drinking and eating. The Festival didn't officially end until Jim Smith's traditional horse races had been held at Sea Cow Bay.

Everyone joined in, from tiny toddlers dressed as angels or villains, to grandmas and grandads swaying along to West Indian rhythms behind the various 'bands'. Cuddles wanted Ulrike and me to enter a Red Cross float in the procession as it wound its noisy way through Road Town on Carnival Day. But we were so debilitated by the Red Cross Ball we just couldn't muster the energy, no matter how persuasive Cuddles tried to be.

First things first though, we had to warm up to the Grand Procession by selecting a Carnival Queen who would supervise the celebrations from her beautiful float. And then we had to choose a Carnival Princess and hold the Calypso King

Competition. All of these events took place in the week before the big day and there was a terrific amount of rivalry.

Carnival Day proved to be a real holiday. Miles of bunting were stretched through Road Town and along the parade route. We were determined to have fun. Everyone joined in and we partied non-stop for almost twenty four hours, throbbing to calypso, reggae and steel pan music.

As usual the Grand Parade started late, two hours late this year, but of course no-one minded in the least. Very few people could tell you what the time was anyway, clocks ceased to have any significance during the two days of the August Festival.

The hot sun was high overhead as the gyrating, pulsating, colourful parade began to wind its slow way through town. Most revellers were on foot, doing a personal jump-up to the nearest music. Quite often the whole procession stopped for several minutes as revelers further ahead found themselves in a log-jam of bodies.

But the dancing and the music never stopped, we just kept on jumping. Some groups had borrowed a lorry from PWD and spent several days decorating it extravagantly.

There was only one steel band but it could be heard up and down the line belting out popular songs like my personal favorite *PP99* and of course everyone's favourite *Bang Bang Lulu*. The Police band joined in too, and our trumpeting constable was in his element as he and his fellow constables let themselves go and simply played, quite independently of each other, whatever took their fancy. No *God Save the Queen* in slow uncertain seriousness today.

Only one solitary sergeant seemed to be actually on duty and he was noticeable by his white pith helmet as he strolled, hands behind his back, in and out of the crowds, chatting and cheering, enjoying the fun as much as anyone.

Cans of beer helped to lubricate the musicians and each one had a supply somewhere within easy reach. The beer must have been warm and frothy but it was swilled down with gay abandon, often quickly followed by swigs of rum direct from a handy bottle.

The Fungi Band rode on a slow moving truck and had plenty of time to call out to friends milling in and around the procession.

One friend sat at the back of the truck mixing lethal cocktails of beer, rum, whisky, and handing them over to the parched participants. An old man with a leathered walnut face was working the gourd, blissfully happy as he scratched the surface backwards and forwards with a steel comb, a huge fat cigar in his mouth and on his head a pink woollen baby bonnet. His tipsy mates playing with him wore an assortment of colourful woollen hats that looked suspiciously like tea-cosies. And the sun scorched down.

It seemed that every island resident had descended on Road Town determined to have as much fun as possible. Rosalind, her tight tangled black plaits firmly controlled under a black chiffon scarf which she had tethered to her head with a large steel clip, was swaying her hips in concentrated effort. When she saw us a huge grin spread across her face and in salute she raised high above her head the half empty bottle of rum she was gripping in her hand. She looked as if she had been going strong for several hours and was primed and ready to keep going for several more. Sweat was pouring down her face and arms, she was having a fantastic time.

Fortunately there was a fairly stiff breeze blowing which helped to cool us down just a little, but it was physically very demanding keeping up all that action in the hottest part of the day. We kept sliding away to have a long cool drink in the shade before rejoining another part of the heaving, moving snake.

The Carnival Queen, the beautiful *Miss BVI*, sat in state on the open back of PC Sylvester's white Cadillac. A pretty girl with an attractive smile she managed to retain a certain regal proudness with her crimson robe trimmed with white fur cascading over the rear of the car. She was probably aching to get down into the street to join her friends in a real jump-up, but she suffered in style and we were very proud of her.

Several very large ladies dressed in pink, lemon and pastel blue baby-doll pyjamas, lurched and wobbled on top of a colourfully decorated truck that was supposed to simulate a bedroom. Presumably it was a slumber party.

Red Indians in headdress jumped and stamped their way up Main Street. Horses had been garlanded with ribbons and flowers and slowly plodded behind an elaborate float on which Fishy and

Margaret were pretending to be prehistoric cave dwellers. In her enthusiasm Margaret wielded her enormous paper-mache club rather too vigorously and walloped Fishy so hard he stumbled, slipped and slid gracefully off the float onto the street.

A boy from St. John was dressed as a Moko Jumbie in dress, black wig and hat, riding an extraordinary bike which he had welded into a personalized machine. The wheels looked more or less normal but the seat and handlebars rose several feet into the air and the boy perched precariously on top some eight feet above the ground. Next year, he told us, he was coming on 12 ft. high stilts.

It must have taken two hours before we finally arrived at the Parade Ground and the entertainment began in earnest. It was very much a family affair and we all gathered together and gossiped, circulated and chewed on chicken legs, drank beer and rum and generally had a thoroughly good time.

Just as well Carnival only happened once a year, it took that long to recover and prepare for the next.

CHAPTER 43

FAREWELL TO THE BVI

As the time of our departure drew closer we started to plan ahead. We made the most of the few weekends left to us by joining Mark in the Treasure Isle boat and speeding off to various uninhabited little Virgin Islands for swimming, sun, sand and the occasional dive.

We picnicked with Bill and Ulrike on Bill's own little island of Sandy Spit. A tiny blot of delicious white sand between Tortola and Jost Van Dyke. We explored The Indians, went to The Dogs, called into Necker Island, popped over to Camanoe and dived off Anegada. We crammed as much as possible into those precious last weeks.

Our dive off Anegada turned out to be, quite literally, a nauseating experience. It was a long boat ride to this flat outpost of the BVI with its miles of beautiful white sand beaches. Fifteen miles north of Virgin Gorda it proved to be quite an expedition for the little Treasure Isle boat.

Hundreds of shipwrecks lie off Anegada, some very old some more modern. Our intention was to dive over the *MS Rocus*, more familiarly known as the 'Bone Ship'. Wrecked in 1929 it was carrying cattle bones from Trinidad to Baltimore for a fertilizer factory. The Rocus was a steel ship and the wreck was mostly broken up but it lay in no more than 35 ft. of water and was considered a good dive. The weather had looked good when we set off from Tortola but then slowly deteriorated.

By the time we anchored over the wreck of the Rocus the undulating, gyrating motion of the boat was making us all feel slightly queasy. The advice was to get into the water as quickly as

238

possible. My husband improved immediately but soon returned to the boat. He said he didn't really enjoy the sight of all those bones scattered over the sea bed and he found it rather eerie. But the sight of the massive anchor and stacks of chains was interesting.

We had fallen in love with Tortola and knew it was going to be very hard to say farewell to the island, to her people and our friends, and return to a completely different life in England.

I hate goodbyes and we wanted to wind down gently and leave with as little fuss as possible, slip away unobtrusively if we could. But we seemed to be attending a dinner party every night, people either wanting to say goodbye to us or inviting us along to say goodbye to them. Several friends were also leaving around the same time as their contracts ended. There seemed to be a natural change-over of people taking place.

In the end we succumbed to pressure and organised a farewell party at our place. Having crated up all our bits and pieces and dragged them off to go on board the next Booker boat to England, we crammed as many friends as we could invite to one last big wonderful bash.

At a rough estimate there must have been over a hundred people. They were hanging off the balcony, squeezing into bedrooms and bursting out of the front door. It was amazing, magnificent and very memorable, and only finished because I fell asleep on the kitchen worktop at 5.00 a.m.

I had even managed to provide a buffet feast for all our lovely friends. I'd come a long, long way since that first frightening week when Porky expected me to hostess his dinner party.

We had deliberately booked ourselves on the early 8.00 a.m. flight so that we could avoid the tear-jerking scenes that accompanied most farewells at Beef Island. No-one ever managed to get up in time for the *'earlybird red-eye'* so we were fairly confident that all goodbyes would be said the night before and not on the tarmac. It would, we decided, be too heart-wrenching to peer out of the window of the plane as it raced down the runway and see a host of friends madly waving goodbye.

Our last night was spent with friends and everyone got very tearful and rather drunk.

"It's the only way to go!" said our friends.

Liz and Terry volunteered to drive us to Beef Island and we checked our baggage and our body weight. Well-proportioned travelers sometimes have their cases thrown off to follow on the next flight, but two skinnies like us are popular with the pilot, we pay for passage but allow him extra poundage for freight.

It was quiet, just three other passengers booked on this early morning flight out of Tortola. We wandered onto the tarmac to wait for the incoming DC3 that would take us away from our beloved Tortola. We didn't expect to see any other friends but Graham from Cable and Wireless had been on early shift up at the Receiving Station on the Ridge and decided to come down for a final wave. Big cuddly Graham was off himself soon, to a new contract in Bahrain.

Our DC3 thundered into Beef Island and lumbered along the runway. We joked that it looked like a relic from World War Two. It sat perched like a giant grey grasshopper on the tarmac with its incongruous huge wheels at the front and one little one at the rear. There was a final tearful hug for Liz and Terry and a big cuddle for Graham. My husband had bought me a trendy pair of sunglasses so that I could weep in private behind their tinted lenses.

It seemed odd to board the plane and climb the steep sloping gangway towards our seats, it was certainly hard work struggling uphill. The plane door closed with a bang and I peered myopically through the thick glass of my tiny round porthole. I could see our three friends standing on the tarmac, quietly chatting.

We taxied slowly to the end of the runway. The sky was so blue, and the sea which lapped the rocks tumbling away at the edge of the runway were so clear and fresh and bright. The hillside behind us was as green as I had ever seen it, and through my tears I looked at the deserted beach beside the airfield, serene in the morning sunshine. A beach I knew so well. The famous beach patrolled by the inquisitive barracuda.

The engines revved and roared deafeningly, and a shudder passed through the plane. One sudden jerk and we were off, racing down the runway, past the little shed which said *'Welcome to Beef Island'* and up and away.

Liz, Terry and Graham were waving frantically, and we waved back through the round little porthole of a window. Off to San Juan, Puerto Rico, and a short holiday in Mexico and the United States before finally reaching England.

West Indians have a saying. They believe that once you have visited the Caribbean and felt the magic of the sand between your toes, you will always come back. As the plane lifted into the sky I squeezed my husband's hand and I knew with absolute certainty we would return.

The end

.... And five years later we did return, with a baby and a toddler, and we lived on Tortola as a family for three years ...... but that's another story!

ABOUT THE AUTHOR

Born and bred in Yorkshire, England, **Lally Brown** embraced the Swinging Sixties with naïve enthusiasm. As a teenager in search of adventure she trekked overland to war-torn Israel, working on a small kibbutz driving a tractor and picking oranges to earn her keep. She managed to hitch-hike around the country staying in Haifa, Jerusalem and Acre. This amazing, and occasionally dangerous experience, was the spark that ignited her lifelong love of adventure and travel.

Lally has lost count of the number of homes she has had over the years but says her most memorable are those on remote St. Helena Island where ex-Emperor Napoleon Bonaparte was imprisoned and where he died, Montserrat in the Caribbean, Turks and Caicos Islands and the British Virgin Islands.

Now, in her twilight years, Lally is writing about her adventurous life using the journals she kept at the time. Her books prove that truth can indeed be far stranger than fiction, with erupting volcanoes, hurricanes, earthquakes, evacuations, abduction, drug smugglers, people smugglers, armed robbery, hangings, stowaways, bribery, corruption, political intrigues, riots, and much, much, more.

ALSO BY LALLY BROWN

THE VOLCANO, MONTSERRAT AND ME

'An enchanting slice of Paradise' is how the travel brochures described the tiny Caribbean island of Montserrat in 1995. Advertised as *'a piece of heaven on earth'* it was a romantic tourist destination with beautiful tropical scenery and a laid-back lifestyle. Then on the morning of Tuesday 18th July 1995 everything changed. After 350 years of dormancy the volcano in the Soufrière Hills above the capital of Plymouth stirred awake.

The Volcano, Montserrat and Me is a powerful and graphic eyewitness account of the realities of living with an unpredictable and extremely dangerous volcano, with the added hazard of several hurricanes. There is tension, tragedy, stress and fear, but there is also much laughter and love.

'A moving and detailed story of a courageous people with insights only an eyewitness can give'
Terry Waite, CBE

THE COUNTESS, NAPOLEON AND ST HELENA

A fascinating true story about Countess Françoise Elisabeth 'Fanny' Bertrand who, with her husband and children, accompanied ex-Emperor Napoleon Bonaparte into exile to the remote island of St Helena after the Battle of Waterloo in 1815.

Fanny remained on St. Helena with Napoleon for almost six years and was at his bedside when he died on 5th May 1821.
Written in the form of a diary it is the story of Fanny's trials and tribulations with Napoleon on an island she hated.

Researched from unpublished primary source documents written on St. Helena at the time.

'I congratulate you on your research efforts and dedicated work' Ben Weider, founder of The Napoleonic Society

Made in the USA
Middletown, DE
27 June 2023